CLOSE ENCOUNTERS: ENGLISH CATHEDRALS AND SOCIETY SINCE 1540

Studies in Local and Regional History No. 3

Edited by

DAVID MARCOMBE

and

C. S. KNIGHTON

University of Nottingham
Department of Adult Education
1991

ISBN 1 85041 038 0

Printed by THE SHERWOOD PRESS (NOTTINGHAM) LTD.

TABLE OF CONTENTS

EDITORIAL NOTE

Throughout this collection quotations have been modernised and new style dating has been employed. Mrs. Linnell has asked that it be known that she is opposed to the series policy of modernisation of spellings. The introduction was written by David Marcombe and the index compiled by C. S. Knighton.

The idea for a collection of essays on English Cathedrals was first raised at the Reformation Studies Colloquium at Southampton in 1980 and it was finalised at the same event at Bangor in 1990.

Reformation Studies Colloquium,
University College of North
Wales.
April 1990.

David Marcombe
C. S. Knighton

NOTES ON CONTRIBUTORS

Dr. Dorothy M. Owen is an Emeritus Fellow of Wolfson College, Cambridge. She is Archivist to the Bishop and Dean and Chapter of Ely and was the University of Cambridge Archivist between 1978 and 1987. She is author of numerous papers on ecclesiastical administration and canon law, as well as major books and catalogues such as *Church and Society in Medieval Lincolnshire* (1971) and *Records of the Established Church* (1970). She is now living in active retirement in Lincolnshire.

Dr. C. S. Knighton has written on the history of Westminster Abbey and Rochester Cathedral. He has contributed to the Catalogue of the Pepys Library at Magdalene College, Cambridge, and has prepared a *Calendar of State Papers, Domestic, Edward VI* for the Public Record Office.

Dr. David Marcombe is Director of the Centre for Local History, Department of Adult Education, University of Nottingham. His Ph.D. thesis was on Durham Cathedral during the Elizabethan period (1973) and since then he has written papers on the ecclesiastical history of the sixteenth and seventeenth centuries: he is editor of *The Last Principality: politics, religion and society in the Bishopric of Durham, 1494–1660* (1987).

Professor Claire Cross is Professor of History at the University of York where she has taught since 1965. Previous to that she was the County Archivist of Cambridgeshire and Research Fellow at Reading University. She is a leading authority on the English Reformation and has written national surveys such as *Church and People, 1450–1660* and *The Royal Supremacy in the Elizabethan Church.* Local and regional research has included *The Puritan Earl: the life of Henry Hastings third Earl of Huntingdon, 1536–1595* and a major contribution to Aylmer and Cant's *History of York Minster.*

Naomi Linnell was Librarian of Lincoln Cathedral (1974–79) and Keeper of Printed Books at Canterbury Cathedral (1979–88). She has written and lectured extensively on library history. She is co-author with Oliver Postgate of *Becket* — an illumination of the life and death of Thomas Becket — and is currently working on a similar project on Christopher Columbus. With A. J. Welland she is writing a crime novel set in an English Cathedral.

Patrick Mussett is Senior Assistant Keeper of Archives and Special Collections at the University of Durham: amongst the records in his care is the extensive archive of the Medieval Prior and Convent of Durham and later the Dean and Chapter. He is particularly interested in New Foundation Cathedrals and has written on the eighteenth century for the forthcoming history of Rochester Cathedral. With P. G. Woodward he gave the 1988 Durham Cathedral Lecture on 'Estates and Money at Durham Cathedral, 1660–1985'.

The Revd. Philip Barrett is Rector of Compton and Otterbourne, near Winchester. Between 1976 and 1986 he was Vicar Choral of Hereford Cathedral. He has written several articles on Cathedral history, including contributions to the *Journal of Ecclesiastical History* and *The Portsmouth Papers.*

The Revd. Arthur E. Bridge is Priest Director of the Hunter Life Education Centre, Newcastle, N.S.W., Australia, and editor of *Drug Watch,* a national Australian journal for drug and alcohol preventative education. In 1989 he received the Order of Australia for services to youth. While at University College, Oxford, he completed an M.Litt. thesis on Walter Kerr Hamilton.

The Revd. J. H. Churchill taught at King's College, London, and the University of Sheffield. After a spell as Director of Clergy Training in Suffolk he became Dean of Carlisle in 1973 which post he held until his retirement in 1987: in 1980 he was Secretary to the Deans and Provosts Conference. He has written books on spiritual life and worship. Jack Churchill died as this volume was going to press in 1990.

The Revd. Dr. Alan Webster began his career as a parish priest, before becoming Warden of Lincoln Theological College in 1959. He was

Dean of Norwich (1970–78) and of St. Paul's (1978–87), when he retired. He is author of *Joshua Watson* (1954) and was created a K.C.V.O. in 1988.

INTRODUCTION

A study of English Cathedrals after the Reformation is rather like looking at a whale in an aquarium – it should never really be there in the first place, but given the unlikely event of its presence both keepers and onlookers might be understandably perplexed as to what to do with it. The fact that secular Cathedrals survived the Reformation – and, indeed, that their number was enhanced by it – brought home to churchmen of all complexions the difficulties of reconciling individual patterns of belief with the needs and requirements of the new order. Protestantism might logically be expected to find no place for institutions the *raison d'être* for which was bound up with the Catholic past, yet right up to the twentieth century justifications continued to be sought to allow Cathedrals to live on unmolested. And at times these points were indeed hard to argue. Case studies of Norwich in the late seventeenth century and Winchester in the early nineteenth show these churches to have been beset by mediocrity, their estates abused and their clergy displaying less than a zealous concern for their vocations. All this seemed the more reprehensible, of course, in view of the extensive lands and tithes owned by all Cathedral Chapters, a propensity for wealth which stood starkly juxtaposed against the poverty of many parochial clergymen. Not surprisingly a chorus of protest emerged as disillusioned Protestants called for the expropriation or reform of Cathedral churches: John Field in the sixteenth century, William Cobbett, in the nineteenth – and in our own age the recently retired Dean of Lincoln, Oliver Fiennes.

Although the Cromwellian era was the only period in which Cathedrals vanished – institutionally, if not visually – government on other occasions did attempt reforming initiatives with varying degrees of enthusiasm and success. The first was Henry VIII's creation of the

New Foundation Chapters between 1538 and 1542, an event which attempted to give the new Cathedrals created after the dissolution of the monasteries a greater sense of communal responsibility and evangelical bite: this was particularly so in the sphere of education, perhaps, where Cathedral grammar schools and University exhibitions were endowed, the whole policy being pursued with 'care and vigour' and at least coming close to success at Ely. Despite the fact that the Old Foundations began to be remodelled along similar lines, the seventeenth century high churchmen saw Cathedral reform in another light – as an embodiment of Archbishop Laud's 'beauty of holiness' – and as a result the years before 1640 saw a breakdown of any consensus which might have existed, especially in cities such as York where powerful puritan oligarchs came into sharp conflict with Arminian Chapters. For them the Act which abolished Cathedrals in 1649 must have seemed a long awaited fulfilment of God's just design.

The problem of the eighteenth century was one of lethargy and inertia rather than the dangerous enthusiasms of earlier days, and during the Victorian era evangelicals and high churchmen alike sought to mobilise Parliament in an attempt to initiate fundamental reforms – to prune and galvanise the old Chapters and to create new ones for the benefit of church and society at large. Of the many schemes of 'Cathedral reform' which were devised at this time one of the most remarkable was that of Walter Kerr Hamilton, precentor (and later Bishop) of Salisbury, but today even Hamilton's far sighted and selfless vision is regarded as old-fashioned by clergy in search of greater 'outreach', seeking to make these institutions relevant to a modern and rapidly changing world. Indeed, the relationship between Cathedral and society is a constantly recurring theme in this collection – the partnership between the 'matrix ecclesia' and the people who make up the community of the diocese at large, and, indeed, beyond that. This is seen to be manifest in many contrasting ways – in Cathedrals as centres of worship and pilgrimage; as principal providers of social services such as education and charitable relief; and as landlords whose estates embraced extensive properties both in towns and the countryside . People were often thrust into relationships with Cathedral Chapters whether their beliefs led them in that direction or not, and this, like the contemporary tourist market, might be a major doorway to the power of faith: a subtle pathway from the secular world to the world of the spirit.

If the constant desire for reform and development in the relationship between Cathedral and society is one of the themes of this book, another must surely be the impact of great individuals who from time to time transcended the institutional tendency towards inertia and conservatism. Hamilton was one such man whose ideas eventually permeated far beyond Salisbury. Another was Humphrey Prideaux, Dean of Norwich, who made it his task to reform the Chapter he took over in 1702. Characterised as 'forceful, frank and persevering' Prideaux forms a total contrast to his near contemporary Michael Honywood, Dean of Lincoln, described by Pepys as 'weak' but nevertheless a remarkable man in his own way. Honywood underlines the contribution our Cathedrals have made to scholarship and the arts, because it was he who accumulated a magnificent private collection of books, donated it to his Cathedral and commissioned Sir Christopher Wren to construct a library to house it in. Neither of these men was a great theologian or divine, but Prideaux was a hard-nosed administrator and Honywood a great collector, and in their own ways these were skills that were necessary to enhance the totality of the Cathedral experience, multi-faceted as it always has been.

The nine case studies in this book aim to examine some aspects of Cathedral Chapters within the changing context of the Church of England after 1540. Within their specific terms of reference important questions are answered, but many more are raised. What role did seventeenth century prebendaries play in the religious life of their dioceses? Was the mid-eighteenth century really such an arid period for English Cathedrals as is popularly supposed? What was the impact of the new and 'reformed' Chapters of the nineteenth century which spanned the country from Newcastle to Truro? And – as many contemporary churchmen will ask – what is the way ahead for Cathedrals in the twenty-first century? If a collection such as this can play its part in generating new research, as well as providing a forum for work already done, its aims will have been achieved. If a fairly average English Cathedral (Winchester) has powers of regeneration sufficient to achieve 'a tradition of sound scholarship, civilised life and religious earnestness', then the prospects for the future look bright and Henry VIII is at least to be congratulated on taking his catch alive when he might have used a harpoon.

From Monastic House to Cathedral Chapter: the experiences at Ely, Norwich, and Peterborough

Dorothy M. Owen

With the perception that one can always look for in his work, Hamilton Thompson reviewed the statutes of the Cathedral Churches of the New Foundation which emerged after the dissolution of the monasteries including the 'old' monastic chapters such as Durham, Ely and Norwich, which were now 'refounded'.[1] It is clear from what he wrote that he had found little evidence about the mechanics of the change, important though it plainly was in many parts of the country, and it seemed useful therefore to put together what can be found for at least one part of the country, in the hope of eventually presenting a coherent picture.

There are two aspects of the problem presented by the New Foundations: on the one hand, how were the new Cathedrals constituted, through what mechanics, and on the other hand, what role did the new ecclesiastical authorities contemplate for the Cathedrals in the contemporary diocesan structure? The Medieval secular Cathedrals had some clearly defined functions within the diocese. The bishops had a seat in the Cathedral Chapters, the archdeacons were leading prebendaries, and often residentiaries. Other members of the Chapter served as officials of diocesan courts and as counsellors of the bishop: members of the Chapter had usually played an important part in diocesan life and continued to do so after the Reformation.

The monastic chapters of Ely and Norwich rarely had any perceptible role in their dioceses. The territorial interests of Ely stretched far into Norfolk and Suffolk, thus ensuring that its monks were drawn from a wide area and had fewer and weaker links with the diocese in which it lay. Only one Ely monk (Hugh of Balsham) became bishop of the diocese. Norwich, with less scattered estates, had four monk bishops from the Cathedral Priory: William Turbe, Simon of

Elmham, Roger of Skerning and Alexander Tottington, and was perhaps better 'integrated' into its diocese. In Ely, moreover, there was a single Archdeacon whose responsibility extended only to the portion of the 'old' county of Cambridge which lay within the diocese: the North Eastern deanery of Fordham, to the East of Devil's Dike, which had been the boundary of the kingdom of East Anglia, and continued to be that of the diocese of Norwich, lay with Norwich. The Isle of Ely was the direct responsibility of the bishop, acting through his commissary; an old claim of the sacrist to this jurisidiction terminated with a *laudum* of Archbishop Thomas Arundel of 1401.[2]

It is true that the sacrist had acquired some diocesan importance as president of the diocesan synod, an office he sometimes shared with the Abbot of Barnwell: the surviving obedientiary rolls of the sacrists have a regular item among forinsec expenses[3] –

> in expensis sacriste et sociorum suorum apud sinodum tentum apud Barnwelle crastino sancti Luce..ivs.

The sacrist was occasionally deputed by the bishops in the fourteenth and fifteenth centuries to receive the purgation of clerks, to induct masters of St. John's hospital at Ely, to hear confessions of the Ely laity, to act as a penitentiary in the deanery of Ely, and even on one occasion to become Vicar General of the diocese. During the fifteenth century the Prior emerged as an episcopal commissary for audience court hearings and as the leading name in the commission of the peace for the Isle.[4]

It is not easy to discover on what occasions the bishops of Ely used their Cathedral Church, apart from the ceremony of enthronement and their visitations of the monastery. It was only one of several churches where ordinations were regularly celebrated. Purgations of accused clerks were staged in it, Bishop Fordham once at least, in 1404, consecrated chrism for the diocese in it, and on several occasions during the fourteenth century hearings of the bishop's audience court were held there. There is even less evidence of resort by lay people to the Cathedral Church, apart from regular pilgrimages to the shrine of St. Etheldreda on her festival (July 17), and the occcasional flight by a sanctuary seeker. Pentecostal visitations by parochial processions, headed by banners, and bringing the regular Pentecostal dues, had evidently taken place at one time but had ceased long before 1377. All told there is little to suggest that, apart from the shrine, the cathedral played any significant part in the devotional life of the diocese.

It may well be that the insignificant size and relative poverty of the

Cathedral city, which after the thirteenth century was not a commercial centre of any importance, helps to explain the lack of interest. Norwich was almost equally cut off from diocesan life, although as in Ely, the priors were playing some parts as vicars general in the fourteenth century, and while the former Norwich monk Adam Easton was active in Rome, the community had some part in general ecclesiastical politics. The archdeacons, of course, had no part to play in the Chapter, and the only hint of popular interest in Cathedral affairs is the custom of preaching from the cross in the Green Yard, which is said to have continued after the dissolution. It is true that in the last century before the dissolution the gilds and fraternities of the city (a wealthy and prosperous community) were closely allied with the Cathedral. Dr. Norman Tanner has recently shown how much this was utilised as an instrument of devotional life, when 'regular pilgrimages' to the Cathedral (by which I assume he means annual processions) were a marked feature, and when bishops' chantries had in more than one case an arrangement for the cantarist to preach to the people of the diocese during Lent and Advent. Dr. Tanner also reports that after about 1360 the Norwich monks preached regularly to the people, inspired thereto by Adam Easton.[5]

Peterborough, of course, had never functioned as a diocesan centre. It lay within the cumbrous, impersonal diocese of Lincoln, but its chief diocesan link was through episcopal visitation. There had been occasion when during the twelfth century the archidiaconal synod for Northamptonshire had met in the Abbey Church, but there is no other evidence that the monastic church and community served in any way as a subsidiary Cathedral. On occasion later Medieval bishops of Lincoln used the monastery as a convenient staging post close to the Great North Road, and between the two episcopal palaces of Liddington in Rutland and Buckden in Huntingdonshire. On the occasions of such stays the bishops occasionally heard causes brought to their audience, but this was entirely unofficial.

The two monastic Cathedral Chapters might have been expected to have some part to play when the diocese was vacant.[6] In Norwich, it is true, the Cathedral Chapter succeeded, after an appeal to the Pope, in asserting some claim to the exercise and profit of jurisdiction *sede vacante*. At Ely there was no composition during vacancy, for the Archbishop retained all jurisidiction and the monastic chapter had no part to play. In one regard, of course, all three houses played significant, though not explicit parts in the economy and social structure of their local communities, so that their successors were in some degree prepared for the secular side of their administrative functions. Ely and Peterborough, in particular, had important secular functions, and because of these, and of their temporal endowments, were in a way prepared to play a leading role in their communities.

The time for this came, of course, with the dissolution of the monasteries and the declared intention of Henry VIII to found and endow from the proceeds of the dissolution several new Cathedrals –

> that God's work might the better be set forth, children brought up in learning, clerks nourished in the university, old servants decayed to have livings, almshouses for poor clerks to be sustained in, readers of Greek, Hebrew and Latin to have good stipends, daily alms to be ministered, mending of highways and exhibition of ministers to the church.[7]

How this was achieved, if it was achieved, is not always easy to discover. Peterborough, at least, can be examined in some detail from a series of accounts, lists and letters which the late Mr. Mellows put together and published. The last occasions when monks of Peterborough were ordained was at the parish church of the town, on September 18 1535, and three months later at All Saints, Northampton, when the same seven monks were deaconed and priested: Thomas Ketteryng, William Exeter, William Wisbech, John Lezingham, Geoffrey Lynne, John Crowland, and Stephen Harlesden, all of whom were to sign the deed of surrender. As late as October 26 1540 Bishop Longland named a new episcopal commissary in the archdeaconry of Northampton, and the last entry of a Northamptonshire institution occurs on October 26 1541, when an institution by the dowager Lady Grey of Mr. John Style, to the mediety of Woodford is followed by the Registrar's note –

> this institution had no effect by reason of the erection of the bishopric of Peterborough: the fee has been restored to Style's proctor.[8]

Peterborough had already experienced some changes by this time. In common with other monasteries and Cathedral Chapters the Abbot, Prior and 39 monks had acknowledged the Royal Supremacy over the church on July 27 1534. Quite soon after this date royal visitors, under the direction of Thomas Cromwell, came to Peterborough to value the endowments and dispose of papal documents, at which time some papal bulls copied into the Abbey's cartularies were struck through. There appears to be no detailed record of this visitation but it seems very certain that once it had been decided, in February 1536, to dissolve the smaller houses, with annual values of less than £200, Abbot

Chambers began to arrange for the security of his own house. It has
been suggested that he had already opened negotiations with the King,
through the royal visitors and probably, Cromwell. Several
circumstances assisted him in this negotiation. The King's divorced
wife Katherine of Aragon had died at Kimbolton, where she had been
in captivity, on January 7 1536, and the King decided that she should
be buried in the Abbey Church at Peterborough. The elaborate
ceremonial of the burial on January 29 was well described by the
Spanish ambassador, who was present, and no doubt Abbot Chambers
was able to seek advice and comfort from the Bishops of Lincoln, Ely
and Rochester, and his fellow Abbots of Ramsey, Crowland and
Thorney, all of whom took part in the ceremonial of burial.[9]

Quite soon after this a serious threat was presented to Peterborough
by the outbreak of the Lincolnshire rebellion in September 1536: the
supposed ringleader of the revolt was Lord Hussey of Sleaford, who
was High Bailiff of the Abbey and obviously one of the local gentry
on whose support Abbot Chambers might well have relied in face of
the threat of suppression. He now set out to rid himself of any charge
of complicity in the revolt, which would have resulted in instant
suppression. He kept the townsmen of Peterborough out of the
fighting, he intercepted treasonous correspondence, and made constant
assurances to the visitors, especially to Cromwell himself, and Sir John
Russell and Thomas Heneage, who were actively engaged in putting
down the revolt. There is no doubt that from this time onwards, and
perhaps before this, Chambers was in active correspondence with a
number of men who might influence his own fate and that of the
Abbey, and although the letters have not survived there is evidence that
Chambers' opponents in the neighbourhood were suspicious of his
'plotting'. Far more influential in the long run, however, was the new
royal policy, initiated it is thought by Cromwell in 1537, by which some
at least of the greater monasteries were to be taken over to endow
Cathedrals in new dioceses, or re-established as collegiate churches.
The new Cathedrals named in a list which is attributed to Bishops
Gardiner, Tunstall, and Sampson, included Westminster, Bristol,
Gloucester, Oxford, Peterborough and Chester, and it is thought that
Chambers negotiated with the former royal visitor, Sir John Russell,
the inclusion in it of his own house.

The 'erection' of the new bishoprics was authorised in the course of
an Act of Parliament of 1539 which vested in the Crown all monastic
possessions surrendered or to be surrendered, and it was no doubt the

knowledge of this which finally moved the Peterborough monks to make a voluntary surrender on November 29 1539.[10] By the terms of this surrender the visitors were empowered to make an inventory of the Abbey's plate and to take away what was suitable for the King, while also surveying all the possessions of the house, and certifying how much of them would not be needed for the erection of the bishopric and Cathedral. All members of the foundation were immediately to relinquish their monastic habits; those to whom pensions, or other positions would be assigned were to remain in the house until the King's pleasure was known. The list of these persons is headed by the name of John Chambers, the late Abbot, who is appointed guardian, with a stipend of £266 13s. 4d. Four of the former monks John Cheyne (Prior), William Judde, Robert Pierson and Richard Whyte were named as prebendaries and eight others were named as minor canons, while twenty others were dismissed with pensions, but re-appear for the most part as incumbents within the new diocese.[11] Chambers' accounts for the following year (1540-41)[12] have survived, and reveal the sort of limbo in which members of the new body must have found themselves until the royal letters patent of September 4 1541, by which the bishopric was endowed with an annual stipend of £368 11s. 6d. and the Cathedral endowment was fixed at £835 8s. 1d. At some unknown date the King issued statutes for the new body, which survive, as at Ely, only in an Elizabethan version. Hamilton Thompson suggests that the Peterborough statutes were issued during June and July 1544 and demonstrates satisfactorily that there was a common body of text in all the statutes issued. By this the Dean, whose nomination belonged to the Bishop, was the only dignitary, the prebendaries, who had rights only as a Chapter and not as individuals, were nominated by the Crown, and the Bishop's right of visitation was no more than his ordinary right over the whole diocese. Much emphasis is placed on the functions of the minor canons, who while not a corporation, with freehold, were nevertheless given control of the services. This emerges with great clarity from Chapter 23 (Of the Precentor and his Office) –

> from the minor canons one riper in age and more distinguished in conduct and in knowledge be elected as precentor by the Dean and Chapter...to lead the singing of the psalms...that no discord may arise...He shall cause the books appointed for the choir to be well kept and cared for...

The whole foundation, with one exception, consisted of former monks, all except the Dean formerly professed at Peterborough. We know very little about the details of the assignment of dwellings, and the organisation of the new common life for the foundation.[13]

Norwich's refoundation was simpler, and relatively direct: in a charter of May 2 1538 Henry VIII assented to the transformation of the Prior and Convent of Holy Trinity, Norwich, into a Dean and Chapter, giving them full liberty to make statutes, allot stipends and recruit the whole establishment except the deanery, which he retained as a royal gift. Nowhere else was continuity of this sort permitted, and in Ely, at least, even the dedication of the Cathedral was altered. No statutes seem to have been issued for Norwich at this period.[14]

At Ely, where the surrender was made on November 18 1539, a new 'college' was established by the King in 1541.[15] The Prior, Robert Steward, was named as Dean and a number of monks were 'appointed to remain in the said monastery' to form a nucleus for the new foundation. Here, as at Peterborough, the foundation provided from the start (September 10 1541) for a Dean (the late Prior), eight prebendaries (three of them former monks), eight minor canons (all former monks of the house), a gospeller and epistoler, four students in divinity (one a former monk), eight singing men, eight choristers, and a master for them, two sextons, 24 schoolboys, with a master and usher, six almsmen, two porters, a butler, two cooks and a caterer, all with appropriate stipends. Matthew Parker, who was himself assigned to the second prebendal stall, was evidently responsible for dividing the former monastic buildings among the members of the new foundation, and although there is no proof that his arrangements, as recorded in a paper preserved in Corpus Christi College, Cambridge, were adopted in their entirety, they resemble sufficiently closely the state of things found in 1649, at the beginning of the Interregnum, to make it probable that they were carried out.[16] The document begins thus –

> *The Dean's lodging:* all the edifices and ground from the great hall to the gallery wall Westward, and from the old hall with the kitchen called the Prior's kitchen, with the chapel and gallery Southward...The great hall to be for the petty canons with all the other ministers and officers to dine and sup in, with the vaults underneath the same...
>
> *Doctor Cox:* the cellarer's lodging from the infirmary Northward, with all the edifices both beneath and above so far as the building goeth Southward.
>
> *Dean of Stoke:* the painted chamber, from the infirmary of the South to the outermost part of the building Northward, and from the churchyard Westward...

A common table was to be provided for minor canons, lay clerks, choristers, grammar school masters and boys, and all were to wear common livery.

There was little in the statutes to suggest what, if any, part was to be played by the new foundation in the diocese, but in the event it seems likely that the four university studentships (later to be replaced by the opportunities afforded for boys from the diocese at Jesus College, Cambridge), and even more, the development of the grammar school, were the Cathedral's major contribution to the diocese.[17]

There is little to say about the ways in which the new policies were implemented in the rest of Henry VIII's reign and in that of Edward VI. From Peterborough we know of building maintenance and dismantling, whereas at Ely and Norwich we have only inference to work on. Peterborough seems to have retained a semblance of the old worship twisted to new purposes. Wax and torches, singing bread, bells, and banners were all purchased in 1548/9, and though King Henry was now hailed as the founder of the house a *dirige* was celebrated for him, with candles, bells and a feast and the maundy *in cena domini* was celebrated with bread and drink for thirteen poor children. These all suggest old habits, but at the same time the Dean was conforming to the new by purchases of Erasmus' *Paraphrases*, psalters, and service books.[18]

At Ely the changes were clearly orchestrated by Parker and Coxe, but apart from the appearance of Parker as Bishop Goodrich's agent in accomplishing the destruction of altars and superaltars throughout the diocese, there is little direct evidence.[19] The Chapter's estate records continue during the period, as do its leiger books of leases and presentations, but there is no central Chapter account before 1587 and no systematic registration of Chapter Acts or orders before 1550, when leases and appointments were spasmodically recorded. The only indication of method in the new administration is provided by a chance survival among the Parker manuscripts dated November 25 1551, by which the distribution of patronage among the members of the Chapter was determined –

> First that the Dean and every prebendary in his course nominate and present the petty canons, priests, clerks, grammar children, choristers, bailiffs, benefices so often as any of them shall hereafter be void.[20]

A similar system had evolved at Peterborough before 1567, when it was recorded.[21] Statute four of the Ely foundation required the Dean to 'safeguard the charters, muniments, court rolls and writings without waste' and statute 32 ordered the provision of a common treasury with two rooms, the outermost of which was to contain the chests and pigeon-holes for writings. The monastic muniments thus passed in their entirety and with their old presses to the new foundation, but Dean Steward interpreted his responsibilities somewhat liberally. It is clear that he thought of muniments and library books as his own personal property, to which he applied his armorial bearings. A number of these books passed to his heirs at his death and have come to light in Lambeth Palace Library and the British Library as well as in Corpus Christi College, Cambridge.[22]

The Marian reaction is equally dark. The first lease register at Peterborough, which began in 1551, continues to record leases and appointments, and appears to be the only systematic administrative record maintained at the time: its only hint of change is a note of Cardinal Pole's constitution concerning confessors. John Boxall succeeded James Curthoope as Dean in 1557 and was himself deprived in the next year. At Norwich three Deans followed each other very rapidly in Mary's reign (Christopherson, Boxall and Harpsfield) but in 1559 the displaced Edwardian Dean Salisbury returned. The general confusion of Chapter administration in Norwich is exemplified by a complaint made to the Chapter in 1567 against Dr. Tedman, who had been a prebendary since 1540, that he had in his own possession, and would show to no other member of the Chapter, accounts and quittances, including some of Queen Mary's time. At Ely Andrew Perne, who succeeded Steward as Dean in 1557, retained his place until his death in 1589, but Richard Coxe and Matthew Parker, Richard Wilkes and Robert Hammond, were all deprived in the period 1553 to 1557 and did not return.

The death of Queen Mary and the initiation of the Elizabethan settlement at last cleared the way for a clear definition of the role to be assumed by the new Cathedrals in the diocese and in local society. The 'hard line' Marian clergy were deprived fairly promptly. Bishop Poole went from Peterborough, Bishop Thirlby from Ely, Dean Harpsfield went from Norwich, Dean Boxall from Peterborough; one prebendary (Harcourt) went from Norwich, three (Byckerdyke, Peacock and Boxall) from Ely.[23] The way was now clear for the new bishops, who were in each of these three Eastern Cathedrals visitors of the foundation, to prepare to mould the Chapters to their own purposes. Were they to find alternative functions for the Cathedrals and their staffs, as preachers and teachers in the Cathedral towns, and in the Cathedral itself, and as patrons of Cathedral schools which would train the future clergymen? The statutes of Peterborough and Ely name the diocesan as visitor and prescribed certain standards for the foundation. It remained to see to what extent they would be supported in their efforts by metropolitical authority. Parker had initiated a visitation of all the Cathedral and collegiate churches of his province on May 19 1560. The articles of visitation were directed very closely to the observance of residence, the conduct of divine service, and the doctrine and preaching of members of the foundations. Article six is explicit on these points –

> you shall inquire of the doctrine and judgement of all and singular head and members of this your church as your Dean, Archdeacons, prebendaries, readers of divinity, school masters, vicars, petty canons, deacons, conducts, singingmen, choristers, scholars in grammar schools, and all other officers and ministers as well within your church as without, whether any of them do either privily or openly preach or teach any unwholesome, erronious or seditious doctrine or discourage any man soberly for his edifying from the reading of the holy scriptures or in any other point do persuade or move any not to conform themselves to the order of religion reformed and restored and revived by public authority in this church of England.[24]

Parker's *Advertisements* of 1566 make clear what he saw as the ideal of worship in a Cathedral Church –

> Item, that in Cathedral Churches and colleges the Holy Communion be ministered upon the first or second Sunday of every month at least...the principal minister shall use a cope with Gospeller and Epistoler agreeably.

When Parker came to visit the foundation at Ely in 1563, he turned to the perennial problems of lax administration, the listing of plate, and proper control of the profits from sales of plate.[25]

Dr. Ralph Houlbrooke has demonstrated the difficulties created in Norwich for the diocesan visitor (Parkhurst) by his insecure hold on nominations to the Chapter, since his predecessors had granted away some of such rights to their Archdeacons and the Crown, and also by the longevity of some members of the foundation. There is no doubt that Parkhurst made consistent and prolonged attempts to promote some 'new' clergy to the Chapter, to divert some power away from the Dean, George Gardiner, who was a protégé and nominee of the Earl of Leicester, to the rest of the Chapter, but his success was only partial.[26] Gardiner's replies to the Archbishop's strictures in the metropolitical visitation of 1567/8 show to what extent control still lay in the Dean's hands.[27]

Meanwhile at Peterborough in August 1559 three royal commissioners had exhibited to the Dean and Chapter a series of injunctions aimed at the observance in the Cathedral and in its appropriated churches both the Royal Injunctions and the Cathedral's own statutes. These latter were designed to provide daily morning service for the grammar scholars and the artificers of the town, a daily exposition of the gospel, and a weekly lecture in divinity as well as regular courses of sermons by the dignitaries and prebendaries. Those ministers of the church who had not yet proceeded Bachelors in Divinity were to provide themselves with, and to study, the Bible in Latin and in English and the *Paraphrases* of Erasmus, on which the Bishop and his Chancellor were to examine them. Most significantly of all, boys likely to be apt ministers in the church were to be sought out and preferred to places in the grammar school.

This was followed up by Bishop Edmund Scambler (1561-85) who at his primary visitation, after administering the articles of visitation, prescribed a series of injunctions which were to be observed not only in the Cathedral but throughout the diocese. He required regular sermons to be preached in the Cathedral by the Dean and prebendaries and the reading in their other churches by the prebendaries of the confession of faith, that is, the articles. A further series of injunctions came from the Bishop in July 1567, repeating earlier provisions about residence, regular sermons in their courses, and attendance by all at the divinity lecture. There were a number of specific orders about the moral behaviour of all members of the foundation, and about regular study by the petty canons of Erasmus' *Paraphrases*. Finally, the Archbishop's strictures at Ely about sales of plate were repeated here: accounts were to be made up of what plate, vestments and copes had been sold, and of the application of the resultant funds. [28]

This is all rather thin information and tells us very little about the way in which the New Foundations conducted their affairs, still less about the contribution they made to the equipping of a new generation of ministers. This is particularly true of Peterborough, where the history of the school remains rather obscure, and the diocesan sources are somewhat thin. Despite Dr. Sheils' admirable study of Puritanism in the diocese, there seems to be no evidence to reveal whether the plain liturgical exemplar presented by Bishop Scambler had any impact in the diocese.

In Norwich the inherent difficulty of an awkward and meddling personality (Dean Gardiner) and an absence of statutes to which appeal could be made against him, is very clearly revealed. It is clear from the Archbishop's case against him what damage he could and did do within Norwich, and how he was able to undermine the reformed church. On the whole Ely makes a better impression than either of the others. Some of its Deans and prebendaries, notably Perne, Whitgift, Matthew Hutton, Humphrey Tindall and William Fuller, were leading churchmen by any standard. The prebendaries included notable Archdeacons such as John Parker, Daniel Wigmore and Robert Tinley, as well as a distinguished episcopal official and canonist, Thomas Ithell. Roger Andrewes and John Bois, prebendaries and beneficed clerks in the diocese, played a leading part in the translation of the 'King James' Bible. Thomas and Andrew Willett were distinguished theologians and preachers. There was, in fact, much two-way traffic between Ely and the University of Cambridge. The proximity of Cambridge undoubtedly stimulated the school and raised its standards in the first sixty years of its life, and contributed to the service of the diocese. If there had been no long vacancy after the death of Richard Coxe in 1581 it is possible to suggest that Ely might well have been the most distinguished and successful of the Cathedrals of the New Foundation.

NOTES

1. *The Statutes of the Cathedral Church of Durham,* ed. A. H. Thompson, Surtees Society, 143 (1929).
2. *Vetus Liber Archidiaconi Eliensis,* ed. C. L. Feltoe and E. M. Minns, Cambridge Antiquarian Society Octavo Series, 48 (1917), pp. xxiii-xxiv, 180-96.
3. D. M. Owen, 'Synods in the diocese of Ely', *Studies in Church History,* 3 (1966), pp. 217-22; *Sacrist Rolls of Ely,* 2 Vols, ed. F. R. Chapman (1907), 2, p. 71.
4. University Library, Cambridge (ULC), Ely Diocesan Records (EDR), G/l/1, ff. 17, 22v; G/l/2, ff. 1, 5v, 13, 20, 22, 23v, 44, 81; G/l/3, ff. 2, 12, 189; G/l/4, ff. 12, 23; G/l/5, ff. 17, 49, 52, 117, 130v, 188; G/l/6, ff. 12, 79, 80, 208.
5. N. P. Tanner, *The Church in late Medieval Norwich, 1370-1532* (1984), pp. 11, 81-2.
6. I. J. Churchill, *Canterbury Administration,* 2 Vols (1934), 1, pp. 194-207, 2, pp. 61-79.
7. 31 Henry VIII, c. 9, cited in *The Foundation of Peterborough Cathedral,* ed. W. T. Mellows, Northamptonshire Record Society (NRS), 13 (1941), pp. xvii-xviii.
8. Lincolnshire Archives Office, Episcopal Register 28 (Longland).
9. *The Last Days of Peterborough Monastery,* ed. W. T. Mellows, NRS, 12 (1947), pp. lxxii-lxxiii.
10. *Ibid.,* pp. lxxxvi-lxxxvii.
11. *Ibid.,* pp. 50-1
12. *Ibid.,* pp. 33-48, 114-28.
13. NRS, 13, pp. 1-7, 75-103.
14. *The Statutes of the Cathedral Church of Durham,* Introduction; *Extracts from the earliest minute books of the Dean and Chapter of Norwich, 1566-1649,* ed. J. F. Williams and B. Cozens-Hardy, Norfolk Record Society, 24 (1954), pp. 5-8.
15. *Letters and Papers of Henry VIII,* 14 (2), p. 542; ULC, Ely Dean and Chapter (EDC), 1/E/2c and 1/E/14 (confirmation by Elizabeth I of Henry VIII's grant).
16. Corpus Christi College (CCC) Ms. 120, ff. 319-20, and EDC 6/2/13 (Parliamentary survey).
17. *The King's School, Ely,* ed. D. M. Owen and D. Thurley, Cambridge Antiquarian Record Society, 5 (1982), prints a number of the documents discussed above and surveys the contribution of the school.
18. NRS, 12, pp. 33-48, 93-113.
19. EDR, G/l/8, f. 18.
20. CCC, Ms. 120, f. 288v.
21. NRS, 13, p. 73.
22. D. M. Owen, *The Library and Muniments of Ely Cathedral* (1973), pp. 12-13. Steward's arms appear in or on Lambeth Ms. 448, Bodleian Laudian Misc. 647, EDR, G/2/4, CCC Ms. 287, 355; Gonville and Caius Ms. 485.

23. H. Gee, *The Elizabethan Clergy and the Settlement of Religion, 1558 – 1564* (1898), pp. 252-70; Harcourt of Norwich is otherwise untraced.
24. *Registrum Matthei Parker,* 3 Vols. ed. E. H. Thompson and W. H. Frere, Canterbury and York Society, 35, 36, 39 (1928-33), 2, pp. 621-3.
25. *Visitation Articles and Injunctions,* 3 Vols, ed. W. H. Frere, Alcuin Club, 14, 15, 16 (1910), 14, pp. 171-80.
26. *Ibid.,* pp. 143-4.
27. *The Letter Book of John Parkhurst,* ed. R. A. Houlbrooke, Norfolk Record Society, 43 (1974-5); *Registrum Parker,* 3, pp. 763-6.
28. ULC, Peterborough Ms. 30, articles 12 and 13.

The Provision of Education in the New Cathedral Foundations of Henry VIII

C. S. Knighton

The diocesan and Cathedral foundations of Henry VIII have been recognised as among the few positive results of the dissolution of the monasteries.[1] Some of the sixteen dioceses of Medieval England were overlarge and cumbersome to administer. At a time when the Crown was increasingly reliant on the episcopate for implementing its ecclesiastical policy there was a clear need for more bishops with smaller areas of jurisdiction. Despite the reservations of so influential a figure as Archbishop Cranmer and the unwavering hostility of more radical reformers, the new dioceses were equipped with Cathedral bodies of deans, canons and other attendant clergy and ministers. While the Cathedrals also had educational and charitable purposes, they had no cure of souls. Their principal purpose was in essence the same as that of the monasteries which they replaced – the offering of the daily round of worship. This was, of course, quite at odds with Protestant notions of liturgy: Cathedral clergy and choristers continued to be as offensive to extremists as were the bishops. That the Cathedral system not only survived the Reformation but was augmented in its process (to the extent of 128 new deaneries and canonries) is one of the paradoxes of English ecclesiastical history.

Projects for diocesan and Cathedral reform had been aired for many years. Cardinal Wolsey had considered a scheme for creating thirteen new bishoprics; but in this as in much else he took no action.[2] Between 1537 and 1539 twelve suffragan bishops were consecrated. But it was not until the dissolution of the greater monasteries, which included the Cathedral Priories of Canterbury, Durham, Winchester, Worcester, Norwich, Ely, Rochester and Carlisle, that measures were necessary to preserve these churches as Cathedrals by providing them with secular Chapters. At the same time six former Abbeys were made into

Cathedrals for the newly created dioceses of Westminster, Chester, Peterborough, Bristol, Gloucester and Oseney. There was considerable continuity of personnel in these arrangements – abbots, priors and monks emerging as deans, canons, or other members of the new collegiate bodies. The first such transformation took place at Norwich in 1538 where the new Dean and Chapter was permitted to organise its own constitution. This resulted in a somewhat atypical scheme; but in 1547 the Dean and Chapter was obliged to surrender to the Crown and the Cathedral was reconstituted in a fashion more in accordance with the other new foundations which had by then been set up in a generally common form.[3] Less than a year after the first foundation at Norwich the bill for dissolving the greater monasteries provoked further discussion of the need for diocesan reform and the use of monastic riches for educational and charitable ends. It was probably in response to this feeling that in May 1539 Thomas Cromwell, the Vicar General, introduced into the House of Lords a bill enabling the King to create any number of new bishoprics and Cathedrals, to endow them and to make statutes for the Cathedral bodies.[4] The King personally drafted the preamble to this quickly enacted legislation which expressed the intention of making the new Cathedrals not only houses of prayer but also centres of a wide range of social usefulness from the education of the young and the care of the old to the maintenance of the highways.[5] This preamble has been derided as 'the most extraordinary collection of largely irrelevant jargon'[6] – but all the purposes it mentioned were at least attempted.

The orderly conversion from monastic to secular community at Norwich had established a precedent which could be followed elsewhere. The remaining twelve New Foundations were treated almost identically, the letters patent and subsequent statutes being issued in common form. There was a necessary distinction between the arrangements for the existing Cathedrals and those for churches in which bishoprics and chapters were newly erected. In the latter cases a single grant established both diocese and Cathedral, whereafter separate grants of endowment were made to the bishopric and to the Dean and Chapter.[7] For a time, therefore, prelates whose Cathedrals had been monastic were without chapters, though the churches remained Cathedrals. At Rochester the monastic chapter survived – perhaps was intentionally allowed to – just long enough to elect Nicholas Heath as Bishop and so avoid the constitutional awkwardness of a diocese simultaneously devoid of Bishop and

Chapter.[8]

In most cases there was an interval of over a year between the surrender of the monastery (whether Cathedral Priory or Abbey) and the foundation of the new Cathedral body. But this was not a period of vacuum: what evidence survives from various institutions makes it clear that the liturgical, educational and other functions of the churches were maintained. Although the deeds by which the houses designated for refoundation surrendered differed in no way from those of places which were to be wholly extinguished, the commonly expressed purpose of placing the house into the King's hands 'for a better purpose' had more justification. The commissioners appointed to take surrender were directed to explain to the assembled inmates and townspeople the King's reasons in altering the house 'from an unchristian life to a trade of virtuous and honest living to the honour of God and the profit of the commonwealth of the realm'. They were required to make inventories and to select from among the former monks such as were worthy of appointments in the new foundation; those for whom no such place was found received the customary pensions. If suitable the former Abbot or Prior was to be placed as warden or guardian of the house until the formal constitution of the Dean and Chapter.[9] This had the effect of creating a collegiate church, but the warden and his colleagues did not automatically become the Cathedral Chapter; this status was only conferred by the letters patent of foundation. The further patent of endowment was needed before the new Dean and Chapter was fully in control of its finances. In most instances endowment followed within a few days or weeks of foundation; Westminster, singularly, underwent an interval of over a year and a half between foundation in December 1540 and endowment in August 1542, and during this time the payment of all stipends and expenses remained the responsibility of the Court of Augmentations.

Several draft schemes have survived which show that the eventual foundations (with which should be included short-lived collegiate churches at Burton-upon-Trent and Thornton, Lincolnshire) were made only after the rejection of more ambitious plans to provide a diocese coterminous with every English county.[10] All lists envisaged the survival of the Cathedral priories save for Coventry and Bath, whose bishops also had secular Chapters at Lichfield and Wells respectively; despite a request by Bishop Lee that his Cathedral at Coventry should be remodelled as a secular college, this was to be the only ancient English Cathedral to be destroyed as a result of the

Reformation.[11] Of the six Abbey churches selected for erection as Cathedrals Oseney survived only until 1547 when the see was transferred to Oxford and the erstwhile Cardinal College, latterly King Henry VIII's College, was made into the unique hybrid of Cathedral and University college which is Christ Church. Westminster lasted until 1550 as Cathedral of its own diocese; after short periods as a second Cathedral for London and then as a restored Benedictine Abbey it was finally refounded in 1560 as a collegiate church, on much the same lines as the Henrician Cathedral. By the common nature of their foundation and organisation these creations of Henry VIII are distinguished from the nine Cathedrals – York, London, Lincoln, Salisbury, Hereford, Wells, Chichester, Exeter and Lichfield – which had secular Chapters before the Reformation (the 'Old Foundations') and whose constitutions were not much affected by it. These existing secular Cathedrals had long been important centres of education; their chancellors had oversight of all schools within the Cathedral cities and in some cases in the dioceses at large.[12] The degree of association between the Old Foundation Cathedrals and their Cathedral schools varied; the most recent foundation, that of St Paul's by Dean Colet, was deliberately placed outside the control of the Dean and Chapter, reducing the existing Cathedral grammar school to an institution for the choristers alone.[13] If St Paul's thus symbolised and expressed the declericalisation of education inspired by Erasmus and his disciples, then the New Foundations of Henry VIII seem to suggest a reversal of this trend; the grammar schools set up in almost all the new Cathedrals were integral parts of those new collegiate bodies, and subject in all areas to the rule of the respective Cathedral Chapters. But of course ultimate authority in the church now lay with the Crown; the New Foundations and their schools were Erastian rather than Erasmian.

The education of the young was placed second only to the teaching of God's word in the Enabling Act for the New Foundations and in the letters patent by which they were severally established.[14] There was ample precedent for this in the history of the Old Foundations, as there also was for using the proceeds of monastic dissolution for educational benefit. The suppression of the alien priories had provided some of the endowments of Eton and King's College, Cambridge. In the early years of the sixteenth century Jesus and St. John's Colleges had risen on the sites of defunct religious houses in Cambridge. Cardinal Wolsey's foundation at Oxford followed this pattern.[15] There was consequently much expectation that the comprehensive dissolution of religious, collegiate and chantry foundations begun by Henry VIII would provide considerable resources for social and educational advancement. Disappointment followed in view of the limited extent of the provisions actually made, and cynicism continued to be directed towards Henry VIII's pose of educational patronage.[16] At least within the New Foundation Cathedrals the cause of education was promoted with care and vigour, in the Cathedral schools themselves and by their links with the Universities. Grammar schools were incorporated in almost all the New Foundations, former Cathedral priories and former abbeys alike. The largest school was at Canterbury, where places were made for 50 scholars. Westminster and Worcester each had 40; numbers elsewhere varied in proportion to the overall size of the collegiate body: in the smallest of these – Carlisle, Bristol and Gloucester – no numbers were specified.[17] For obvious reasons no Cathedral grammar school was needed at Winchester, though there is a suggestion in the Edwardine statutes for Christ Church, Oxford, that Winchester College was subsumed into the new system of royally established Cathedral schools (preference being allowed to potential Christ Church scholars 'ex scholis nostris Cantuariensi Cestrensi Westmonasteriensi Roffensi Wintoniensi').[18] The earlier and 'non standard' foundation at Norwich did not include a school. In much the same way as in the Cathedrals, grammar schools were attached to the later collegiate foundations of Christ Church and Trinity College, Cambridge. The Trinity school is known to have opened and the names of its first pupils are recorded; there is less evidence for Christ Church. But both these schools disappeared as a result of the 1549 commissions which prohibited the teaching of grammar within the Universities.[19]

The claim of the New Foundation Cathedral schools to be wholly new is disputable; some of the 'King's Schools' now prefer to date their foundation before the establishment of the English monarchy (Canterbury 600, Rochester 604) or the Conquest (Ely 970).[20] These schools see themselves in lineal descent from those attached to the Benedictine monasteries – institutions about which much debate was possible because of the sparsity of information which exists about them. The principal historian of Westminster School (which chooses to regard Elizabeth I as fundatrix) wrote of the monastic school there –

> If it was, as some have thought, a school of novices, it was no place of education in any worthy sense of the word.[21]

John Sargeaunt was a Victorian and so could be confident about what sort of education was worthy and what was not. In our more cautious age a less severe judgement is perhaps needed. It seems fair to make distinction between a school which serves only the needs of the monastery by which it is maintained and one which, in however limited a way, is open to those not destined to remain in the cloister. The schools of the greater monasteries may properly be placed in the second category. Westminster Abbey's school is first recorded in the middle and its schoolmaster at the end of the fourteenth century. By the end of the fifteenth century this school was clearly distinguished from the claustral school where the novices were trained and also from the choir school under the control of the sub-almoner and (from 1479) its own master.[22] There was undoubtedly a measure of personal and institutional continuity between the schools of the dissolved Cathedral priories and abbeys and those of the secular Cathedrals which replaced them. Just as monks were transmuted at the wave of the sceptre into secular clergy, so monastic schoolmasters were retained to serve in the 'new' schools. This occurred at Canterbury, Ely and Durham (where the master of the former Cardinal Langley's School became head of the new royally founded school and the master of the old almonry school was appointed his deputy); probably also at Westminster – while at Peterborough the usher or second master of the new school was a former monk of Peterborough Abbey.[23] The boys, too, seem in many cases to have passed from monastic to collegiate school. At Ely sixteen or perhaps nineteen of the 24 scholars named in the 'erection book' of 1541 setting out in full the new Cathedral establishment had appeared in a list made shortly after the surrender of the Priory two years earlier, and so may be presumed to have attended the monastic school.[24] The monastic school of Westminster was probably not much smaller than that of 40 scholars established by Henry VIII; 39 boys were named in the earliest list of the new foundation, drawn up before the formal creation of the Cathedral in December 1540; eighteen of these were still at school in March 1541.[25] But some indication of the increased importance of the school is shown by a grant to the Dean and Chapter from the Court of Augmentations of £200 for expenses after the dissolution of the Abbey which included the building of a school house;[26] later the school would take over part of the old monastic dormitory, the other part becoming the Chapter library – so providing a neat architectural metaphor for the changed priorities of the new order. Westminster, along with the other New Foundation schools, was assigned an under master as well as the (head) master, whereas none of the monastic schools is known to have had more than one master.

The appointment of the masters was to be in the gift of the Deans and Chapters; but at Worcester (where the school does seem to have been an innovation) the first master was appointed directly by the Crown on the advice of the King's chaplains at a time when the church was as yet unprovided with a Dean and Chapter.[27]

Lack of evidence makes it impossible to judge if the New Foundation schools served the same functions – in respect of catchment areas, the social backgrounds of the pupils and the actual instruction they received – as the schools previously under monastic auspices. The *curricula* for the new schools laid down in the statutes cannot be compared with anything which went before. It is likely that the monastic grammar schools were attended predominantly by local boys; in this they would have been similar to the schools maintained by the Old Foundation secular Cathedrals. There is no reference in the New Foundation statutes to the geographical origins of the scholars; they were, however, supposed to be *pauperes et amicorum destituti*.[28] The Elizabethan statutes for Westminster were more specific, prohibiting the election to scholarships of boys who were or would be heirs to estates worth more than £10 a year.[29] This was never a realistic stipulation in a school already becoming popular with those who lacked neither money nor friends. There was a pertinent debate at Canterbury in 1539 between Cranmer and the commissioners appointed to organise the new Cathedral and school. The commissioners would have preferred scholarships to have been restricted to the sons of gentlemen, on the grounds that they alone had need of instruction in the affairs of government and the commonwealth. Cranmer argued to the contrary –

> Poor men's children are many times endowed with more singular gifts of nature which are also the gifts of God...and also more given to apply their study than is the gentleman's son delicately educated.[30]

Cranmer (himself of gentle parentage) won the point, and his views are echoed in the terms of the statutes issued in 1544 in common form to most of the new Cathedrals. These required the boys to be chosen by the Dean and Chapter; they were to have some knowledge of grammar before admission, and to be able to read and write – their skills to be examined by the Dean or Vice Dean and the master of the school. Choristers on the foundation were to be given preference, but were not to be elected scholars until they were at least ten years of age or if they had reached sixteen (though an ex-chorister already in the school might continue there after his sixteenth birthday). The boys would spend four or at the most five years as scholars, learning to perfect their reading and speaking of Latin. They occupied a common table, and were bidden to prayer twice daily. The master and under master were likewise appointed by the Dean and Chapter – the former had to be learned in Latin and Greek, the latter requiring Latin only; the masters were not required to be graduates. Should any boy be found notably dull, stupid or disinclined to study, he was to be expelled, *ne ueluti fucus apum mella deuoret* ('lest like a drone he consume the honey of the bees') – a phrase which recalls a familiar humanist image.[31]

In practice the admission of the scholars, as with other appointments in the gift of Deans and Chapters, was often shared out among the members of the capitular body. At Westminster in 1547 the Dean was allowed to make nominations for four of the scholars' places and the twelve canons had three such nominations each. Places at Westminster were particularly keenly sought as the school's reputation grew, a result of its location and also the influence of Alexander Nowell as Head Master from 1543 to 1555. In 1552 the Chapter found it necessary to order that if any of their number received payment for nominating a scholar the offending party would lose such right of nomination in future.[32] Similar distribution of scholarship nominations is found at Ely and Worcester.[33] Candidates so nominated still had to be examined before they were admitted.

The establishment of the New Foundation schools has proved to be an enduring achievement of the Henrician Reformation. By contrast the original scheme by which the new Cathedrals were also obliged to support students at the Universities lasted no more than a few years. Such an arrangement was made for most of the New Foundations, and the names of the scholars to be maintained (usually known as 'exhibitioners' to distinguish them from the scholars of the Cathedral grammar schools) appear in the 'erection books' and subsequent treasurers' accounts where these survive. The statutes of 1544 gave orders for their election and payment. But in 1545 and 1546 this system was abolished and the Crown resumed lands from the Cathedrals to the value of the students' stipends. This has generally been seen as an indication of the hollowness of Henry VIII's professed concern for the advancement of scholarship. A. F. Leach called the withdrawal of the Cathedral studentships a 'severe blow' and Geoffrey Baskerville criticised the cooling of the King's educational fervour.[34] But the operation of the scheme has never been examined in such modest detail as the surviving evidence allows; nor has it been proved that the scheme's abolition meant a setback to the King's educational policies or to the careers of the individual scholars who had briefly received financial support from the Cathedrals.

The maintenance of scholars at the Universities was mentioned in the Act of 31 Henry VIII for the creation of dioceses and Cathedrals although not in the letters patent by which the new Cathedrals were subsequently founded. As in other departments of the New Foundations there is some variation between the draft schemes and the arrangements eventually put into effect. The number of students provided was, like that of the grammar scholars, proportionate to the size of each collegiate body; at Canterbury, which had the largest school, 24 students were simultaneously maintained.[35] Westminster had twenty, Durham, Worcester and Winchester twelve each, Chester, Ely, Peterborough and Rochester four each.[36] Oxford (Oseney) was naturally a special case, as was the earlier refoundation at Norwich: in neither instance did the Cathedral participate in the scheme. This also appears to have been true of Bristol, Gloucester and Carlisle.[36] In most cases the students were equally distributed between Oxford and Cambridge; Worcester was unusual in having all its students at Oxford.[38] In addition the Dean and Chapter of Westminster was charged with the support of ten readers in divinity, Greek, Hebrew, physic and civil law, one in each discipline at each University.[39]

Where mention of the students is made in the statutes it occurs not, as might have been expected, immediately after the regulations for the grammar scholars, but in the chapter *De Eleemosinis.* Those chosen for studentships were to be 'poor scholars', between the ages of fifteen and twenty, appointed by the Dean and Chapter. Preference was given to boys from the Cathedral grammar school. The Dean was responsible for seeing them boarded at some college or hall and for arranging their payments, which were set down on a scale based on their academic status. At Peterborough this was £5 a year to undergraduates, £6 to Bachelors of Arts and £6 13s. 4d. to those reading for the degree of Bachelor of Divinity.[40] At Winchester the payments at the same levels were £6, £8 and £10.[41] The Westminster students were originally to have received £6 13s. 4d. a year each, but this was raised to £8 6s. 8d. in the final draft of the establishment, and this sum was paid to all the students irrespective of their academic attainments.[42] At Chester and Ely the rate was £6 13s. 4d.[43] The Canterbury students received various sums between £6 and £10, but no correlation can be discovered between these payments and the University careers of the recipients.[44] Durham and Worcester paid their students the seemingly unusual sums of £9 11s. 8d. and £6 7s. 4¼d. each respectively.[45]

In some cases particular properties may have been designated by the Cathedrals to meet these obligations.[46] It is perhaps unfair to accuse the King of merely using the Cathedrals to finance this educational benefaction since its cost was taken into consideration in the endowments which the Cathedrals received. The payments were, nevertheless, an inconvenience to the Cathedrals concerned, and difficulties in transferring the money to the distant scholars may explain why they did not receive their stipends as regularly as did resident members of the foundations: some Westminster students were paid quarterly, some half yearly, some annually; such irregularity also occurred at Chester.[47]

Although often referred to as 'divinity students' they were not exclusively so – indeed the statutes prescribed studies in divinity and the arts; most of those appointed were still undergraduates and so engaged on the arts course. Of seventeen Westminster students whose careers can be traced with some certainty, six were undergraduates on appointment, three were Bachelors and six Masters of Arts, while two graduated B.A. and three M.A. in the course of their time on the foundation.[48] The Canterbury students seem to have belonged to a slightly younger generation: of eighteen who have been identified in the University registers only four were graduates by 1540, but the remainder took their B.A. degrees by 1545, eleven of them in the year 1542/3.[49] Some of the Cathedral students, as the Duke of Somerset was to recall in 1549, had been lawyers – among them John Gunwyne, recommended to Cecil two years later as having been diligent in civil law at both Universities.[50] In all three Westminster students were to proceed to degrees in law, as did three of those on the Canterbury foundation and two on that of Worcester Cathedral. Others became medics; but as was to be expected the majority of them went on to pursue clerical careers.[51] Since the statutes were not delivered to the Cathedrals until 1544 or 1545, just as the studentships were about to be abolished, there is an explanation for the fact that some of those appointed to studentships at the foundation of the Cathedrals were more senior in age or status than the statutes were to require. The students were not supposed to be fellows of colleges according to the statutes, but among the Westminster appointees three or possibly four were so.[52] One case of interest is that of Richard Marshall, on the Westminster foundation at Oxford. Until 1540 he had been a probationary fellow of Corpus Christi College, but did not succeed in advancing to full fellowship; in 1539 he had written to Thomas Cromwell seeking financial assistance to continue his studies, and it was perhaps in response to this appeal that he was found a place on the Westminster list and his academic career was rescued.[53] Another Corpus man, James Brookes, was one of two Winchester students who retained fellowships.[54] Both men were above the age which the statutes were to specify, while two of the Canterbury students, Richard Masters and Peter Lymyter, were about 25 and 27 respectively at the time of their appointments.[55]

The first students also included a number of former monks from the dissolved monasteries – some of whom may already have been at the Universities, others perhaps too junior to be appointed to canonries but too promising to be relegated to lesser posts in the new Cathedral bodies. At Ely one of the four students, Thomas Wilberton, had been a monk of the Cathedral Priory.[56] On the Westminster foundation four former monks were named as students, two of them already in priest's orders. One of those described as a monk of the dissolved house, Henry Thacksted, may not in fact have been a 'true' Westminster monk, but one who had transferred there in the last days before the dissolution after his own house had fallen – his name is not on the deed of the Westminster surrender, which was among the last to take place. One who had been a monk of Glastonbury, John Hilpe, surrendered his pension to take up a studentship on the Westminster foundation. Another Westminster monk, John Lathbury, was originally appointed to a studentship but resigned this in 1541 and instead seems to have enjoyed a succession of benefices in the gift of the Dean and Chapter.[57] The new studentships can be seen as a continuation of the obligation placed on the greater monasteries of sending representatives to the Universities. Westminster had regularly sent its quota of (two) monks to Oxford – and significantly the monks who were given places in the new Chapter were mostly those who had benefited from this experience – and in the early years of the sixteenth century had also developed links with the Benedictine house at Cambridge which became known as Buckingham College.[58] Canterbury Cathedral Priory also had long-standing and formal links with Oxford in its daughter house of Canterbury College, and at the dissolution two of the Cathedral monks, John Cross and Peter Langley, were students there.[59] Eleven monks were proposed as 'scholars' on the new foundation – not King's Scholars but University students, because Cross and Langley are included, and eight of the nine who can be identified from another list were said to be in their twenties and thirties. Of the eleven monks originally chosen, only seven appear in the first list of students paid, and only one survives in the second and third such lists.[60] It was possibly envisaged at an early stage that former monks should participate in the studentships to a greater extent than in fact took place.[61] It has also been suggested that those named as students on the Canterbury foundation were largely members of the pre-Reformation school.[62] Apart from one John Callowe, who was named as a scholar and then as a University student in the account for 1542/3, this seems an improbable assertion in view of the fact that so many of the Canterbury students were of the same academic generation.[63] But there is a strong suggestion that at least some of the Canterbury students were natives of the city or the county of Kent.[64]

Westminster Abbey's ties with the Universities were strengthened in 1504 when Henry VII provided for three graduate monks to serve his chantry foundation and for three others to be maintained on exhibitions of £10 a year at Oxford.[65] An even more important step had been taken in the previous year by the King's mother in endowing the Abbey with estates from which the Lady Margaret praelectorships or readerships in each University, and subsequently the Lady Margaret preachership based at Cambridge, were to be financed.[66] After the dissolution of the Abbey these payments were not transferred to the charge of the new Dean and Chapter, but met directly from the Court of Augmentations, whose treasurer was in two decrees obliged to support the readers and preacher.[67] However, the precedent of the Lady Margaret foundations surely accounts for the burdening of the new Westminster Cathedral in 1540 with the maintenance of the ten (as yet not so called) Regius Professors. The first Henrician scheme had proposed only five such appointments, in Greek and Hebrew at £30 a year, in physic and law at £20 each, and one for humanity and divinity receiving £40.[68] The second proposal would have established a resident divinity reader at Westminster and one reader in divinity, Greek, Hebrew and civil law at each University.[69] The final arrangement dropped the resident Westminster reader and provided for five readers in each Univeristy with stipends of £40.[70] This was seen by F.D. Logan as the second of three phases by which the original Regius chairs of Oxford and Cambridge were brought into being. In 1536 a lectureship had been set up in each University, to be named after and in a subject chosen by the King, but appointed to and funded by the Universities (in exoneration of the payment of first fruits and tenths). Logan assumed that this 1536 post was absorbed into the 'Westminster phase' after 1540.[71] But more recently Dr. G. R. Duncan has shown from examination of Oxford college accounts that payments continued to be made towards the 1536 readership in divinity there – until 1542 to Richard Smith, who also held the 1540 readership on the Westminster foundation, and thereafter to Philip Brode while Smith continued to receive payments from Westminster.[72] It does not necessarily follow that the two chairs also existed briefly side-by-side at Cambridge. Here the 1536 reader was supported not (as at Oxford) by subventions from the colleges, but by diversion of funds from the mathematical lecture, for which permission was given by grace in 1536 and the two following years.[73] But thereafter there are no such graces, and when the proctors' accounts first appear in the Audit Book (1544/5) regular payments to the mathematical lecturer are recorded.[74]

The Westminster readers, unlike those of 1536, were appointed by the Crown. Only five had so been by March 1541: these included Thomas Wakefield, whose placement in the Hebrew chair at Cambridge is mentioned in a letter to the Augmentations official administering the Westminster properties before the endowment of the Dean and Chapter.[75] The Westminster archives (muniments) are the most complete of those of any of the New Foundations, and examination of them has made it possible to amplify our knowledge of the early holders of the Regius chairs.[76] They were, of course, established scholars, and were not associated in any other than a financial way with the collegiate body. Resident lecturers in Greek, Hebrew, divinity, civil law and physic were originally envisaged at Canterbury Cathedral; Cranmer, indeed, hoped that they might take the place of the prebendaries. It was almost certainly his influence which provided the Canterbury foundation with the unique body of Six Preachers, who had salaries of £20 and social equality with the members of the Chapter.[77] Westminster, as has been mentioned, was at one stage to have had a solitary resident reader; when the collegiate church was refounded by Elizabeth I a readership was at last established although only as an additional function for one of the canons.[78]

The University studentships maintained by the Cathedrals lasted for only five years. In 1545 the Bishops of Westminster, Worcester and Chichester along with the Chancellor of the Court of Augmentations were appointed to report on the operation of the scheme.[79] In reply to this commission the Dean and Chapter of Westminster submitted a certificate naming the students on their foundation and stating the times at which they had received their stipends. Their answer concluded with a frank admission that there was not much communication between the Chapter and the students they were supporting –

> And what every of the said scholars do profess the said Dean and Chapter cannot tell.[80]

On March 13 1545 the Dean and Chapter of Westminster sealed a grant of lands to the Crown in exoneration of the maintenance of their twenty students.[81] In the following year further surrenders were made when the ten readerships were removed from the Westminster foundation. On July 4 the manor and rectory of Long Bennington, Lincolnshire was given up – but this was worth only £40, the equivalent of just one of the readers' stipends.[82] Later in the month a much larger surrender was made in the form of an indenture between the King and the Dean and Chapter. No explanation was offered for this transaction, which merely recorded the foundation and endowment of the studentships and readerships and their subsequent removal from the Westminster collegiate body.[83] A list of the lands surrendered at this time shows that the readers' lands were valued at £400, the precise sum of the ten stipends. But for the students lands worth £167 18s. 11½d. were yielded up, whereas the students' stipends had amounted only to £166 13s. 4d.[84] This left the Dean and Chapter short by £1 5s. 7½d. a year, for which they were obliged to petition the Crown; in addition they sought reimbursement of £10 8s. 4d. paid to the students before receipt of letters of discharge from the royal commissioners.[85]

The other Cathedrals maintaining students were required to make similar surrenders to the Crown in 1545; the Durham Chapter complied on March 21, that of Ely on May 20.[86] Westminster was not alone in having to seek redress for unfavourable terms. The Dean and Chapter of Peterborough complained to the commissioners that they had surrendered the manors of Stanwick and Polebrook, valued at £35 16s. 2¼d. but that maintenance of their (four) students had cost them only £26 13s. 4d., whereby they had lost £9 2s. 10¼d. a year, together with the advowson of Stanwick reckoned at £20.[87] There must have been a spate of complaints from Deans and Chapters resulting from these deals, for among instructions to Sir Richard Sackville on his appointment as Chancellor of Augmentations in February 1550 was an order to recompense the Deans of New Foundation Cathedrals so that they might have the value of their original endowments.[88] As a result the Dean and Chapter of Ely was given a rent of 7s. 9½d. on June 2 1551, five years after the surrender of their students' lands.[89] The lands surrendered in these exchanges returned to the administration of the Court of Augmentations. Some former Westminster lands were granted out again almost immediately to Crown officials, particularly those of the Augmentations Office. On March 28 1545, a fortnight after the surrender, Sir Richard Rich paid £100 for the lease of the manor of Newark in Good Easter and other Essex properties which he had formerly held from the Dean and Chapter of Westminster but at a much higher rent.[90] On March 31 Sir William Petre was granted the Gloucestershire manors of Toddenham and Sutton along with other former Westminster property.[91] Shortly afterwards Walter Hendle, Attorney of the Augmentations, was granted the manor of Stokenchurch, Buckinghamshire, which had also been surrendered by the Dean and Chapter of Westminster on March 13.[92] A detailed survey of all the surrendered properties was made by the Court of Augmentations, although only one extract appears to have survived (concerning an almshouse in the precinct of Westminster Abbey which was sold in August 1546 to William Cecil's father Richard, then a Yeoman of the Wardrobe).[93] But other surrendered land would in due course be used in grander and more rational benefaction to the Universities. We cannot know when it entered into the mind of Henry VIII to take upon himself the singular distinction of simultaneously founding colleges at both Universities. But the dismantling of the earlier and clearly unsatisfactory system of Cathedral supported University endowment was a preliminary stage in that achievement. In personnel and to a lesser extent in endowment Trinity College, Cambridge, and Christ Church, Oxford, were heirs and successors to the aborted Cathedral system. Trinity was granted the manor of Perton, Staffordshire, the rectory of Swineshead, Lincolnshire, together with all the former Westminster properties in and around the town of Grimsby.[94] Christ Church received a number of rectories and their advowsons in Worcestershire which had come to Westminster from Evesham Abbey – Hampton, Offenham, Hadsey, Aldington, Wickenford and the Littletons – valued in all at £74 5s. 9½d.[95] From among lands surrendered by the Dean and Chapter of Ely it was destined to receive the manor of Barnham.[96] Christ Church was to incorporate the site of the old Canterbury College: this had been surrendered to the Crown on April 10 1540, six days after the monks of the mother house of Christchurch, Canterbury, received their pensions. The site of the college was among the endowments of the new Dean and Chapter of Canterbury in 1541, and they subsequently leased it to Richard Masters, one of the students on their own foundation. The college was again surrendered by the Cathedral to the Crown in 1545 (when the other Cathedral surrenders were being made) and was in due course to form part of the endowment of Christ Church.[97] It would probably be possible to identify further portions of the endowments of Christ Church and Trinity which had been among properties surrendered by the Cathedrals in 1545 and 1546 – though both University colleges had in all endowments of over £2,000 each (approximately the sum for the whole of the Cathedral based studentships and readerships).[98]

It is of more interest to consider the fate of the individual scholars whose financial support was seemingly terminated by the surrender of the Cathedral lands. It would appear that most of the students of the Westminster foundation at least did not lose royal patronage in consequence of the transactions of 1545. Rather, they were brought into the new University colleges. Of the nine students at Cambridge named by the Dean and Chapter of Westminster in their 1545 certificate to the royal commissioners, six were given places on the foundation of Trinity – five as fellows and one as chaplain. In addition a former Westminster student, Edmund Cosyn, also became a fellow. Information for Oxford is less complete owing to the comparative inadequacy of records there; but at least four of the Westminster students at that University were to become members of Christ Church. Almost all those who did not become attached to one or other of the new colleges can be shown to have continued at their respective Universities.[99] The Westminster students are the best documented, but a telling number of those maintained on other foundations can be traced to Christ Church and Trinity. Paul Boswell and Thomas Francisse, at Oxford on Chester Cathedral's exhibition from 1541 to 1545, became students of Christ Church in 1547.[100] Two of the former Peterborough students went to Trinity: William Doddington as an original fellow, William *alias* Walter Blunt as a pensioner in 1549.[101] Edward Cratford, at All Souls on the Worcester foundation, transferred to Christ Church in 1547.[102] Eight former Canterbury students joined Christ Church or Trinity at or shortly after the colleges were founded, while one of their erstwhile colleagues was made a fellow of Merton by royal command in January 1547.[103] Put the other way around at least 31 of the early members of

Christ Church and Trinity had formerly been Cathedral students. Sparse though this evidence is, its cumulative effect is to suggest the deliberate gathering of these variously supported scholars within the two new royal foundations.

It may still be objected that the dismantling of the original scheme deprived the Cathedral grammar schools of opportunities for sending their distinguished *alumni* to the Universities, by virtue of the preference accorded to such boys in the election of the students. The system operated for so short a time that it is not possible to cite many examples of those who, as envisaged by the statutes, proceeded from the Cathedral grammar schools to the Universities in this way. One instance, from Canterbury, has already been given.[104] Chester furnishes the case of John Hulme, senior King's Scholar in 1541, who went on to become a University student on the Cathedral's foundation in 1545.[105] At Westminster George Harvye was a scholar from 1540 to 1544 in which year he matriculated at Trinity Hall, Cambridge. In 1545 he appeared as one of the Westminster maintained students and in the following year became a scholar fellow of Trinity.[106] After what has been noted of the apparent disinterest of the Dean and Chapter of Westminster in their students it is pleasing to find that when Dean William Benson died in 1549 he left twenty angels to 'his exhibitioner' George Harvye. Harvye took his B.A. in 1552 and went on to become Archdeacon of Cornwall.[107] Another Westminster student who became a founding fellow of Trinity in 1546, Roger Carew, had also probably been at Westminster School along with his brother Matthew.[108] The names of 29 other Westminster students are known, but since most of them were already at University on the inception of the scheme it is not surprising that further links with the school cannot be shown. Of boys in the school between 1540 and 1560 175 names can be found; nine of these certainly went to Oxford and Cambridge, and similar claims for a further 24 can be advanced with varying degrees of probability and possibility. It is of special interest that identification can be made or suggested in eighteen cases with members of Christ Church or Trinity.[109] When the church and school of Westminster was refounded by Elizabeth I in 1560 the bond uniting her father's three foundations at Westminster, Oxford and Cambridge would be formalised, but an association had clearly developed in the preceding twenty years. This should occasion no surprise when it is remembered that the heads of both Christ Church and Trinity sat in the Chapter of the first collegiate church at Westminster: Richard Coxe, who had been a member of the commission which gave the New Foundations their statutes, was made Dean of Christ Church on its creation and became also Dean of Westminster in 1549; John Redman, the last Master of the King's Hall and then the first Master of Trinity, was senior canon of Westminster from 1540 to 1551. Redman's role was particularly prominent; he headed the commission which led to the foundation of Trinity and also appears to have been associated with the origins of Christ Church. At Westminster he was engaged in the negotiations for the surrender of the students' lands which, as has been seen, anticipated the University foundations. In the association of Westminster and Trinity may be seen an echo of an arrangement of two centuries earlier by which choristers of the Chapel Royal had proceeded to the King's Hall, which in itself has been seen as the original linking of school and college, the pattern to be followed by William of Wykeham and Henry VI.[110] The notion of a conveyor belt of educational patronage attracted benefactors for half a millenium. It is a system now seemingly discredited, but which provided innumerable opportunities of academic advancement, and in which the original New Foundation plans of Henry VIII have their modest place.

NOTES

The author is indebted to the owners and custodians of the manuscript sources consulted, in particular to the Dean and Chapter of Westminster and the Keeper of the Muniments of Westminster Abbey.

1. A. G. Dickens, *The English Reformation* (1964), pp. 149-50; M.D. Knowles, *The Religious Orders in England* (1948-59), 3, pp. 390-2; J. J. Scarisbrick, *Henry VIII* (1968), pp. 521-5; J. Youings, *The Dissolution of the Monasteries* (1971), pp. 84-6. For the Medieval Cathedrals see A. H. Thompson, *The Cathedral Churches of England* (1928) and *The English Clergy and their organisation in the later Middle Ages* (1947), and most importantly K. Edwards, *The English Secular Cathedrals in the Middle Ages* (1949. 2nd edn 1967).
2. A. F. Pollard, *Wolsey* (1929. Paperback edn 1965), pp. 183-4.
3. *The Statutes of the Cathedral Church of Durham,* ed. A. H. Thompson, Surtees Society, 143 (1929), pp. xxvi-xxxi. P[ublic] R[ecord] O[ffice], Exchequer, Augmentations Office, Monastic Surrenders, E 322/176. C[alendar of] P[atent] R[olls], 1547-8, pp. 59-61.
4. *Journals of the House of Lords,* 1, pp. 108, 112, L[etters and] P[apers, Henry VIII,]* 14 (1), no. 988 (Marillac to Francis I, May 20 1539). *Statutes of the Realm,* (1810-28), 3, p. 728 (31 Henry VIII c. 97).
5. B[ritish] L[ibrary], Cotton Ms. Cleopatra E 4, f. 366 (*LP*, 14 (1), no. 868 (2)). Printed in H. Cole, *King Henry the Eighth's Scheme of Bishopricks* (1838) pp. 75-6, with facsimile as frontispiece.
6. Youings, *Dissolution of the Monasteries*, p. 85.
7. For the foundations see Thompson, *Durham Statutes;* also *The Foundation of Peterborough Cathedral, A.D. 1541,* ed. W. T. Mellows, Northamptonshire Record Society, 13 (1941 for 1939) and *Documents relating to the Foundation of the Chapter of Winchester,* ed. G. W. Kitchin and F. T. Madge, Hampshire Record Society, 1 (1889). Dates of the various foundations and endowments are set out in C. S. Knighton, 'Collegiate Foundations, 1540 to 1570, with special reference to St Peter in Westminster', (unpub. Ph.D. thesis, Cambridge Univ. 1975), pp. 12, 25.
8. Knighton, thesis, p. 10.
9. PRO, Exchequer, Treasury of Receipt, Miscellaneous Books, E 36/116 (*LP*, 14 (1), nos. 1189, 1190).
10. (1) BL, Cotton Ms. Cleopatra E 4, f. 365 (*LP*, 14 (1), no. 868(3)). Printed in J. Strype, *Ecclesiastical Memorials* (1822), 1 (2), p. 406. (2) PRO, Exchequer, Augmentations Office, Miscellaneous Books, E 315/24, ff. 1-80 (*LP*, 14 (2), no. 429). Printed in Cole, *King Henry the Eighth's Scheme,* pp. 1-73. (3) PRO, E 315/24, f. 80v. (4) BL, Cotton Ms. Cleopatra E 4, f. 363 (*LP*, 14 (1), no. 868(4)). Printed in Strype, *Ecclesiastical Memorials,* 1(2), p. 407. (5) PRO, State Papers, Henry VIII, SP 1/154, ff. 86-93 (*LP*, 14 (2), no. 430). (6) PRO, SP 1/154, f. 94v. (*LP*, 14 (2), no. 430(2)). (7) PRO, SP 1/243, ff. 49-55 (*LP*, Add, 1457). These various drafts are discussed and

compared in Knighton, thesis, pp. 6-8.

11. BL, Cotton Ms. Cleopatra E 4, f. 311 (*LP*, 14 (1), no. 34).

12. Edwards, *English Secular Cathedrals,* pp. 176-205.

13. *A History of St Paul's Cathedral and the men associated with it,* ed. W. R. Matthews and W. M. Atkins (1957), pp. 115-16.

14. 31 Henry VIII c. 9.

15. M. Morgan, 'The Suppression of the Alien Priories', *History,* New Series, 16 (1941), pp. 204-12; Knowles, *Religious Orders,* 2, pp. 163-5; J. Simon, *Education and Society in Tudor England* (1966), pp. 82, 137-8; Youings, *Dissolution of the Monasteries,* pp. 26-9; Pollard, *Wolsey,* pp. 183-4.

16. G. R. Elton, *Reform and Renewal* (1973), pp. 28-34, 139-40; Simon, *Education and Society,* pp. 179-86; Knowles, *Religious Orders,* 3, p. 359; Dickens, *English Reformation,* 149-50; Scarisbrick, *Henry VIII,* pp. 516-20.

17. Thompson, *Durham Statutes,* p. xlix; Simon, *Education and Society,* pp. 186-7; N. Orme, *English Schools in the Middle Ages* (1973), pp. 263-7.

18. Christ Church, Oxford, Ms. D.P.vi.b.i., ff. 120v-121.

19. Trinity College, Cambridge, Senior Bursar's Muniments, Box 29, C.II.a, ff. 2-2v. See W. W. Rouse Ball, *Cambridge Papers* (1918), pp. 13-14. PRO, State Papers, Domestic Series, Edward VI, SP 10/7, no. 10 (mentioning surrender of Trinity school). The Christ Church school's existence is presumed only because of a subsequent reference to a former schoolhouse in *Remarks and Collections of Thomas Hearne,* 10, ed. H. E. Salter, Oxford Historical Society, 67 (1915), p. 30.

20. *Whitaker's Almanack* (1983), p. 536.

21. J. Sargeaunt, *Annals of Westminster School* (1898), p. 2.

22. A. F. Leach, *Educational Charters and Documents, 598-1909* (1911), pp. 2-3 and 'The Origin of Westminster School', *Journal of Education,* New Series, 27 (1905), pp. 78-81; L. E. Tanner, *Westminster School: its buildings and their associations* (1924), pp. 1-2 and *Westminster School* (1934), pp. 2-3; E. Pine, *The Westminster Abbey Singers* (1953), pp. 19-36. For the more ancient school at Canterbury see C. E. Woodruff and H. J. Cape, *Schola Regia Cantuariensis: a History of Canterbury School, commonly called the King's School* (1908) and D. L. Edwards, *A History of the King's School, Canterbury* (1957).

23. Simon, *Education and Society,* p. 186; *Durham School Register,* ed. T. H. Burbidge (1940), pp. 6-7; Knighton, thesis, p. 263; W. D. Larrett, *A History of the King's School, Peterborough* (1966), p. 14.

24. Corpus Christi College, Cambridge, Ms. 120, pp. 295-6; PRO, Exchequer, Ancient Miscellanea, E 314/13/1; E 315/245, f. 61 (*LP*, 14 (2), no. 542).

25. Leach, *Journal of Education,* New Series, 27, pp. 78-81; Tanner, *Westminster School* (1934), p. 2; BL, Additional Ms. 40061, f. 2v; W[estminster] A[bbey] M[uniments], 6478, f. 2v; PRO, E 315/24, ff. 81v-82.

26. PRO, E 315/104, ff. 77v-78; Special Collections, Ministers' Accounts, SC 6/Hen VIII/2421, m. 5.

27. *Documents illustrating early education in Worcestershire, 685 to 1700,* ed. A. F. Leach, Worcestershire Historical Society, 31 (1913), pp. lvi-lxi; PRO, SP 1/168, f. 101 (*LP*, 16, no. 1421, printed in Leach, *Documents,* pp. 120-1).

28. Mellows, *Foundation of Peterborough Cathedral*, p. 91. This edition is cited as it provides the only available edition of the standard form of new foundation statutes.
29. Printed in the appendix to the *First Report of Her Majesty's Commissioners appointed to inquire into the state of the Cathedral Churches of England and Wales* (1854), p. 88. Cited hereafter as *Westminster Statutes*. No copies of the Henrician statutes for Westminster have survived, but it is evident from entries in the treasurers' accounts that statutes were received there in 1544, the year in which they were delivered elsewhere (Knighton, thesis, pp. 69-74).
30. BL, Harleian Ms. 419, ff. 115-16. Printed in *Miscellaneous Writings and Letters of Thomas Cranmer, Archbishop of Canterbury, Martyr*, ed. J. E. Cox, Parker Society (1846), pp. 398-9.
31. Mellows, *Foundation of Peterborough Cathedral*, pp. 91-2, 94, 103. Bishop Richard Fox described his foundation, Corpus Christi College, Oxford, as a 'bee hive' (*Statutes made for Corpus Christi College, Oxford* (1911), p. 6).
32. WAM, Chapter Act Book I, ff. 36v-37, 72v.
33. Corpus Christi College, Cambridge, Ms. 120, pp. 288-9; Leach, *Documents*, pp. 169-71.
34. Leach, *Documents*, p. lxiii; G. Baskerville, 'The Dispossessed Religious of Gloucestershire', *Transactions of the Bristol and Gloucester Archaeological Society*, 49 (1927), p. 72. Not all accounts of the scheme have been quite correct: Knowles (*Religious Orders*, 3, p. 389) supposed it only to have been tried at Canterbury and Winchester; Simon (*Education and Society*, p. 184) mentions five readers only at Westminster instead of ten.
35. Canterbury Cathedral Library, Chapter Archives, Domestic Economy, DE 164 (ii) [list for ? 1541] and Volumes of Miscellaneous Accounts, VMA 40, f. 3 [payments for 1542/3]. These lists were printed by B. K. J[effery] and W. Urry in *The Cantuarian*, 26 (1) (December 1956), p. 42 and 23 (3) (July 1949), pp. 249-50 respectively. The later list is also given, but less accurately, in Woodruff and Cape, *Schola Regia Cantuariensis*, pp. 62-3. An early draft of the Canterbury foundation allowed for only 20 students [BL, Cottonian Ms. Cleopatra E 4, ff. 359-359v].
36. WAM, 6478, ff. 3-3v; *LP*, 20 (1), no 400; Leach, *Documents*, p. 160; Kitchin and Madge, *Foundation of the Chapter of Winchester*, p. 55; R. V. H. Burne, *Chester Cathedral, from its founding by Henry VIII to the accesssion of Queen Victoria* (1958), p. 11; Corpus Christi College, Cambridge, Ms. 120, p. 194; Mellows, *Foundation of Peterborough Cathedral*, p. 72; Kent County Archives Office, Records of the Dean and Chapter of Rochester, DRc/Asl, pp. 33-5. No mention of students is made in a draft of the Rochester establishment appearing in PRO, SP 1/58, ff. 79-82v (*LP*, 15, no. 379).
37. Thompson, *Durham Statutes*, p. 172 n. 9 observes that students are mentioned in the statutes of Canterbury, Chester, Rochester, Winchester and Worcester only. The Durham statutes he prints are Marian and so naturally have no mention of the students. The Ms. printed in *The Statutes of the Cathedral Church of Carlisle*, ed. J. E. Prescott (1903) is a

later copy of the Henrician statutes. I have been unable to locate the versions for Bristol and Gloucester cited by Thompson (pp. xviii-xix) and he was unaware that statutes, now lost, were delivered to Westminster (see n. 29 above).

38. Leach, *Documents,* p. 160, which prints receiver's account for 1543/4; but the statutes (*ibid.,* p. 143) were to prescribe six students at each University.
39. WAM, 6478, f. 2.
40. Mellows, *Foundation of Peterborough Cathedral,* pp. 100-1.
41. Kitchin and Madge, *Founding of the Chapter of Winchester,* p. 141.
42. BL, Add. Ms. 40061, f. 3; WAM, 6478, f. 3.
43. Burne, *Chester Cathedral,* p. 11; Corpus Christi College, Cambridge, Ms. 120, p. 294.
44. Canterbury Cathedral Library, VMA 40, f. 3.
45. *LP,* 20 (1), no. 400; Leach, *Documents,* pp. 150, 160.
46. Mellows, *Foundation of Peterborough Cathedral,* pp. 54 n. 1, 62, 100 n. 3.
47. WAM, 37043, ff. 11v-12, 37044, ff. 4v-5, 37064, f. 4. Burne, *Chester Cathedral,* p. 11.
48. Biographical information about the Westminster students is collected in Knighton, thesis, pp. 408-10.
49. For sources of the Canterbury names see n. 35 above. I have checked these against entries in *Alumni Cantabrigienses,* 1, ed. J. Venn (1922-7) and *A Biographical Register of the University of Oxford, A.D. 1501-1540,* ed. A. B. Emden (1974).
50. PRO, SP 10/7, no. 30; SP 10/7, no. 23.
51. Westminster students' details in Knighton, thesis, pp. 408-10. For Canterbury see n. 49 above. Worcester names from Leach, *Documents,* p. 160 checked against Emden, *Biographical Register 1501-40.*
52. Mellows, *Foundation of Peterborough Cathedral,* p. 100. Westminster students included Richard Caldwell, Senior Bursar of Brasenose, John Gowe or Gore, Fellow of Oriel, John Hilpe *alias* Markes, Fellow of Lincoln and John Sadler, perhaps, Fellow of King's. [Details and sources in Knighton, thesis, pp. 408-10].
53. Emden, *Biographical Register 1501-40,* pp. 380-1.
54. The other was John Estwyke, Fellow of Merton (Emden, *Biographical Register 1501-40,* p. 194). Both were named in the 'book of portions' of 1541 (Kitchin and Madge, *Founding of the Chapter of Winchester,* p. 55).
55. Emden, *Biographical Register 1501-40,* pp. 390 (Master), 368-9 (Lymiter).
56. PRO, E 314/13/1. Corpus Christi College, Cambridge, Ms. 120, p. 294.
57. BL, Add. Ms. 40061, f. 3; WAM, 6478, ff. 3-3v. The four ex-monks were Robert Barnard, John Ambrose *alias* Ambrale, Simon Underwood and Henry Thacksted *alias* Chackster; the two former were ordained priest in 1536/7 (E. H. Pearce, *The Monks of Westminster* (1916), pp. 190-2). The Westminster surrender deed is PRO, E 322/260 (*LP,* 15, no. 69). For Hilpe see Knighton, thesis, p. 307 n. 2.
58. H. F. Westlake, *Westminster Abbey* (1923), 1, pp 175-7, 2, pp. 447-9; Pearce, *Monks of Westminster,* p. 29. The Abbey's University links are now fully described in B. F. Harvey, 'The Monks of Westminster and the University

of Oxford', *The Reign of Richard II,* ed. F. R. H. Du Boulay and C. M. Barron (1971), pp. 108-30.

59. W. A. Pantin, *Canterbury College, Oxford,* 3, Oxford Historical Society, New Series, 8 (1950 for 1943-4), p. 153. From PRO, SP 1/116, ff. 44-6 (*LP,* 12(i), no 437), which Pantin dates after February 8 1538 and which may well have been drawn up closer to the dissolution in 1540.

60. PRO, E 315/245, ff. 78-9 (*LP,* 15, no. 452(2); Canterbury Cathedral Library, Receiver's Account, New Foundation 1 (1541/2); DE 164 (ii).

61. For fuller details of the Canterbury students see C. S. Knighton, 'Canterbury Cathedral's University Studentships under Henry VIII', *The Cantuarian,* 49(2) (April 1985), pp. 110-13.

62. W. Urry, in printing the names from the 1542/3 list in *The Cantuarian,* 23 (3), p. 249, said they 'undoubtedly include those of boys who attended the old pre-Reformation school'. In Emden, *Biographical Register 1501-40* the Canterbury students are all assumed to have been members of the King's School or its pre-Reformation predecessor.

63. Canterbury Cathedral Library, VMA 40, f. 3. Cf. above n. 49.

64. Two of the Canterbury students Richard Masters and Peter Lymyter, bore names which suggest connexion with Canterbury citizens: Richard Maister and Thomas Lymyter received the freedom of the city in 1518 and 1544 respectively (*The Roll of the Freeman of the City of Canterbury from A.D. 1392 to 1800,* ed. J. M. Cowper (1903), pp. 286, 284).

65. *Calendar of Close Rolls,* 1500-9, no. 389, pp. 139-42; Harvey, 'Monks of Westminster', pp. 126-8.

66. C. H. Cooper, *Annals of Cambridge* (1842-1908), 1, pp. 271-2; G. Dyer, *The Privileges of the University of Cambridge* (1824), 1, pp. 103, 104. The original regulations dealt only with the readers.

67. C[ambridge] U[niversity] L[ibrary], University Archives, Collectio Admin. 9, pp. 8-9, 10-12.

68. PRO, E 315/24, f. 5 (*LP,* 14 (2), no. 429).

69. PRO, E 315/24, f. 37; BL, Add. MSS 40061, f. 2.

70. WAM, 6478, f. 2.

71. F. D. Logan, 'The Origins of the so-called Regius Professorships: an aspect of the Renaissance in Oxford and Cambridge', *Renaissance and Renewal in Christian History,* ed. D. Baker (1977), pp. 271-8.

72. *The History of the University of Oxford, 3, The Collegiate University,* ed. J. K. McConica (1986), pp. 343-7, 353.

73. *Grace Book [Gamma],* ed. W. G. Searle (1908), pp. 310, 315, 327.

74. CUL, Univ. Archives, U.Ac.2(1), pp. 3, 4, 5, 12, 13 (*bis*), 24, 35, 36, 49, 50 (*bis*), 61, 63 (*ter*), 75 (*ter*), *et seq.*

75. PRO, SP 1/164, f. 77 (*LP,* 16, no. 365).

76. Knighton, thesis p. 309.

77. BL, Cotton Ms. Cleopatra E. 4, ff. 359-359v, printed in Cox, *Writings and Letters of Cranmer,* pp. 398-9; *cf.* also *ibid.,* pp. 396-7. See also Simon, *Education and Society,* pp. 183-4 and D. I. Hill, *The Six Preachers of Canterbury Cathedral, 1541-1982* (1982), pp. 5-7.

78. *Westminster Statutes,* pp. 86-7; WAM, 33617, f. 9 and subsequent

treasurers' accounts.

79. This commission has not been traced.
80. WAM, 43048.
81. *Ibid.,* Chapter Act Book 1 f. 25.
82. *Ibid.,* 18400.
83. *Ibid.,* Register Book 3, ff. 76v-77v.
84. *Ibid.,* 12960.
85. *Ibid.,* 6481, 6482, 6483, 43933; Chapter Act Book 1, ff. 26, 36.
86. *LP,* 20 (1), no. 400; *CPR,* 1550-3, p. 173.
87. Northamptonshire Record Office, Records of the Dean and Chapter of Peterborough, PDC MD/62.
88. PRO, Chancery, Patent Rolls, C 66/827, mm. 9d-10d (*CPR,* 1549-50, pp. 241-6); SP 10/4, no. 48 (mis-dated in *Calendar of State Papers, Domestic,* 1547-80, p. 10).
89. *CPR,* 1550-3, p. 173.
90. *LP,* 21 (1), no. 1383 (18 no. 9), p. 681. Rented there at £6 0s. 3d. *per annum* but at £66 6s. 8d. in the Chapter lease of February 12 1543 (WAM, Register Book 3, ff. 1-1v).
91. *LP,* 20 (1), no. 465(100), p. 227.
92. *Ibid.,* no. 1335(53), p 670.
93. PRO, SP 1/223, f. 85 (*LP,* 21 (1), no. 1442).
94. *LP,* 21 (2), no. 648(51), pp. 342-5.
95. *Ibid.,* no. 648(25), pp. 335-8.
96. PRO, Exchequer, King's Remembrancer, Various Accounts, E 101/348/39. No such manor appears, however, in the endowment (*LP* 21 (2), no. 648 (25), pp. 333-8).
97. Pantin, *Canterbury College,* pp. 155-7.
98. *LP,* 21(2), no. 648(25), pp. 333-8 (Christ Church); *Ibid.,* no. 648(51), pp. 342-4 (Trinity).
99. WAM, 43048; Trinity College, Cambridge, Senior Bursar's Muniments, Box 29, C.II.a; *LP,* 21 (2), no. 648(43), p. 340. Fellows were Richard Barnard, Roger Carew, George Harvye, Robert Kynsey and the chaplain Henry Thacksted *alias* Man. For the others see Knighton, thesis, pp. 408-10. For Christ Church: PRO, State Papers, Domestic Series, Elizabeth I, SP 12/31, no. 40; Bodleian Library, Oxford, Ms. Top. Oxon. c. 22, ff. 63-63v, c. 23, ff. 39-42v; *Register of the University of Oxford,* ed. C. W. Boase, 1, Oxford Historical Society, 1 (1885). James Bycton, Richard Caldewall, Nicholas Chamber and Richard Marshall are named in WAM 43048 and subsequently appear as Students of Christ Church. In addition John Bornam may perhaps be identified as John Barnes of Christ Church.
100. Burne, *Chester Cathedral,* p. 11; *Alumni Oxonienses,* 1500-1714, ed. J. Foster (1891-4), pp. 153, 531.
101. Mellows, *Foundation of Peterborough Cathedral,* p. 72; *Admissions to Trinity College, Cambridge,* ed. W. W. Rouse Ball and J. A. Venn, 2 (1913), pp. 7, 15.
102. Leach, *Documents,* p. 160; Emden, *Biographical Register 1501-40,* p. 148.
103. Peter Lymyter, Richard Masters, Thomas Randall (Christ Church);

Nicholas Morton, Stephen Nevynson, John Stokes, Henry Wylshawe and George Harres (Trinity); Edward Markwest (Merton). See n. 35 and n. 49 above.

104. See n. 63 above.
105. Burne, *Chester Cathedral,* p. 11.
106. BL, Add. Ms. 40061, f. 2v; WAM, 37044, f. 74, 43048; Trinity College, Cambridge, Senior Bursar's Muniments, Box 29, C.II.a, f. 1v; Ball and Venn *Admissions to Trinity,* 2, p. 7; *The Record of Old Westminsters,* ed. G. F. R. Barker *et. al.* (1928-63), 1, p. 434.
107. PRO, Prerogative Court of Canterbury, Registered Wills, PROB 11/32, f. 290v. Knighton, thesis, p. 409, from various sources.
108. WAM, 43048; Trinity College, Cambridge, Senior Bursar's Muniments, Box 29, C.II.a., f. 1v; Barker *et. al., Records of Old Westminsters,* 1, p. 162 (*s.a.* Carew, Matthew).
109. Knighton, thesis, pp. 318-19, 411-13, based on WAM, Chapter Act Book 1, WAM, 37044, 37045, 37713, 54001; Bodleian Library, Brasenose College Ms. 31; Barker *et. al., Records of Old Westminsters, passim.*
110. A. B. Cobban, *The King's Hall within the University of Cambridge in the later Middle Ages* (1969). The boys sent from Court to the King's Hall may not actually have been former choristers (I.D. Bent, 'The Early History of the English Chapel Royal, *ca* 1066-1327', unpub. Ph.D. thesis, Cambridge Univ. 1968, pp. 227-8). ·

Cathedrals and Protestantism: The search for a new identity, 1540 — 1660

David Marcombe

> On Tuesday the 12 of December, 1642, about twelve of the clock...[the rebels] sat down before the city of Winchester...and entered the city that afternoon between two and three: being masters of the city, they instantly fell upon the close...they seize the prebends horses, and demand their persons with many threatening words: that night, they break into some of the prebends houses;...on Thursday morning between nine, and ten of the clock...they violently break open the Cathedral Church, and...pollute his temple...they enter the church with colours flying, their drums beating, their matches fired...until they came to the altar...and burnt the Book of Common Prayer, and all the singing books belonging to the choir.[1]

And this was not an isolated case. Lichfield and Peterborough Cathedrals were similarly sacked by Parliamentarian troops, and following the victory at Dunbar Cromwell ordered 3,000 Scottish prisoners to be detained at Durham – not only did they destroy the monuments and burn the woodwork, they also deposited a prodigious amount of urine which unhappily was to re-emerge when the new central heating was installed some 300 years later in the 1960s. But this sort of vandalism was not universal. York Minster, for example, was spared from pillage and decay because in 1645 it was taken over by the corporation for use as a centre for the godly exposition of the gospel with four comparatively well paid puritan ministers permanently based there.[2] But whether the short term answer was pillage and dereliction or conversion to puritanical purposes, the government of the Commonwealth soon decided that the English Cathedrals should never again exist in their old form. Accordingly, on April 30 1649, only twelve weeks after the execution of the King, Parliament passed 'An Act for abolishing of Deans, Deans and Chapters, Canons, Prebends and other offices and titles of or belonging to any Cathedral or Collegiate Church or Chapel within England and Wales'. Interestingly, the Act did not begin with a tirade against the evils of Cathedral Chapters; the preamble merely stated that 'the Commons of England in Parliament assembled...are necessitated to sell the lands of Deans and Chapters for the paying of public debts and for raising of £300,000 for the present supply of the present necessities of this Commonwealth', but it is difficult to believe that the members of the purged Long Parliament who passed this Act did not feel some measure of satisfaction at the demise of a set of institutions which many of them would have considered godless in the extreme.[3] In fact, for those who knew their history, their actions represented a culmination of 100 years of protest directed against Cathedrals in England by militant forces both within the Church and outside it.

The word 'puritan' is perhaps misleading in this context because of the wide spectrum of opinion it was used to describe in contemporary parlance. Archbishop Toby Matthew of York was described as a 'puritan' in much the same way as Oliver Cromwell, but clearly a huge doctrinal gulf separated them. The difference was between those, like Matthew, who wanted to reform the Church from within – and in the context of that rethink the role of the Cathedral – and those, like Cromwell, who wished to purge the Church of England 'root and branch' and lop off the Cathedral Chapters as one of the infected members. The radical approach went back long before the Civil War, and certainly during the reign of Elizabeth there were those who regarded Cathedrals as Popish dinosaurs polluting a world that looked forward to the rule of the Saints. In the famous polemical work *A View of Popish Abuses,* probably written by John Field in about 1572, the author sets out his objections in the following vitriolic fashion –

> We should be too long to tell your honours of Cathedral Churches, the dens aforesaid of all loitering lubbers, where master Dean, master Vice Dean, master canons or prebendaries the greater, master petty canons or canons the lesser, master chancellor of the church, master treasurer, otherwise called Judas the pursebearer, the chief chanter, singingmen, special favourers of religion, squeaking choristers, organ players, gospellers, pistellers, pensioners, readers, vergers, etc., live in great idleness and have their abiding. If you would know whence all these came, we can easily answer you, that they came from the pope, as out of the Trojan horse's belly, to the destruction of God's kingdom. The church of God never knew them, neither doth any reformed church in the world know them.[4]

The same theme was taken up again in 1587 by the anonymous author of the *Petition to Parliament for the Succession and Restoring of Christ to his full Regiment –*

>These are indeed very dens of thieves, where the time and place of God's service, preaching and prayer, is most filthily abused in piping of organs, in singing, ringing, and trouling of the psalms from one side of the choir to another, with squeaking of chanting choristers, disguised, (as are all the rest) in white surplices, others in cornered caps and filthy copes, in pistelling and gospelling with such vain mockeries, contrary to the commandment of God and true worshipping of God, imitating the manners and fashions of antichrist, the pope, that man of sin and child of perdition, with his other rabble of miscreants and shavelings...These unprofitable members, for the most part dumb dogs, unskilful sacrificing priests, destroying drones, or rather caterpillars of the word, they consume yearly, some £2,500, some £3,000, some more, some less, whereof no profit, but rather great hurt cometh to the church of God and this commonwealth. They are dens of lazy, loitering lubbards, the very harbourers of all deceitful and time-serving hypocrites.[5]

He went on to call for a complete overthrow of Cathedrals and the re-direction of their resources towards the provision of godly and learned preachers. Beneath the rhetoric the theme of both complaints was the same. Firstly, that Cathedrals were overstaffed with idle and non-productive clergy who consumed valuable resources which could have been better spent elsewhere. Secondly, that they were centres of crypto-Catholic devotional practice which did little or nothing to further the word of God by means of preaching.

Whatever the accuracy of these allegations, more moderate churchmen also added their voices to the growing chorus of protest. No less a person than Archbishop Cranmer criticised Henry VIII's constitution of the New Foundations in the 1540s and especially the financial remuneration allocated to the new Canterbury prebendaries – 'they spend their time in much idleness and their substance in superfluous belly cheer'. He wanted to see the title of prebendary abolished and resources spent on the provision of University scholarships instead.[6] Twenty years later Archbishop Grindal condemned the pluralistic incumbent who 'longed for a prebend also, there to spend at ease the milk and the fleece of the flocks he had never fed'.[7] Non-residence and superfluous wealth were indeed amongst the most common and recurring criticisms, and though there were great contrasts in the incomes enjoyed by Deans and prebendaries, the wealthier ones were certainly comfortably provided for by any standard. In 1578/9, for example, Dean Hutton's income from York Minster was about £450, and in the 1590s Dean Matthew of Durham could expect somewhere in the region of £1,000 from the Cathedral and his rectory of Bishop Wearmouth. A fairly typical York prebendary, William Goodwin, drew about £125 from the Minster in 1593/4, and at Durham Leonard Pilkington's income in the 1590s was around £800.[8] Although there were many canons who were much poorer than these figures might imply, it was the richer brethren who were invariably quoted for the purposes of propaganda. And similarly with non-residence. Despite variations – and especially the rather better standard of residence in the New Foundation Chapters – the usual pattern was perhaps the four or so canons who resided at Lincoln and York during the reign of Elizabeth: four out of 54 and four out of 30 respectively.[9]

All over the country Bishops in their visitation articles thundered against vicars choral and minor canons who were often considered to be quarrelsome and inattentive to their duties. In contrast to the prebendaries the disorders amongst the minor corporations were believed to be the result of *poor* pay, and the stipends of £10 and £8 *per annum* enjoyed respectively by vicars choral and singingmen at York in the early seventeenth century were fairly typical.[10] Like the senior clergy the incomes of the ordained men might be improved somewhat by the possession of benefices, but since these were generally the poorer urban parishes – the service of which would not have hindered their Cathedral duties – their prospects were not that greatly improved. Examples of drunkenness and immorality are to be found at Chichester, York, Canterbury, Carlisle and Lincoln, and in 1628 the Durham organist, Richard Hutchinson, distinguished himself by hitting a lay clerk across the head with a candlestick in an ale house and seriously wounding him.[11]. John Earle, later to become Bishop of Worcester and Salisbury, summed up the situation in his *Micro-cosmographie* of 1628 –

> Common singingmen in Cathedral Churches...are a bad society, and yet a company of good fellows, that roar deep in the choir, deeper in the tavern...Their pastime or recreation is prayers, their exercise drinking, yet herein so religiously addicted that they serve God oftest when they are drunk...Upon work days they behave themselves at prayers as at their pots, for they swallow them down in an instant. Their gowns are laced commonly with streamings of ale, the superfluities of cups or throat above measure.[12]

Like all stereotypes Earle's picture is to be treated with caution, but the undoubted turbulence of some of the minor corporations may well be connected with the contentiousness of the canons themselves, because there was a common belief that many prebendaries spent much of their time arguing and set a bad example to others. Kathleen Edwards highlighted this problem for the Middle Ages, but it was equally true in the sixteenth and seventeenth centuries.[13] Durham was rocked by serious internal disturbances in the 1570s and 1620s which caused some of the prebendaries to have grave doubts about the way in which they were regarded by society at large. In one of these conflicts it was suggested that two prebendaries had conspired together to rob the Treasury of almost £163 and a few years later the Chapter stated with disarming honesty –

> It hath been cast often in our teeth that we teach others but amend not ourselves, that we speak of charity but live in hatred, talk of concord but sow discord. We are ashamed to hear it, but the accusation is true in some part we cannot deny it...And thus being complained upon abroad we are also misliked at home as men that deserve not the place and credit committed to us.[14]

But the most sensational case, perhaps, came from Exeter. In 1632 the Star Chamber heard an extraordinary tale in which three members of the Exeter Chapter, including the precentor, William Cotton, and the Archdeacon of Totnes, Edward Cotton, falsely accused the Dean, Robert Peterson, of fathering an illegitimate child by his kitchen maid. Samuel Travers, a prebendary and the main architect of the rumour, was said to have stated that 'they would besplatter him (i.e. the Dean) as would bring him into disgrace with his best friends, and hinder his preferment for ever'. This 'foul conspiracy', as Laud termed it, evoked outraged comment from the Privy Councillors who tried it. Sir Thomas Richardson, Chief Justice of Common Pleas, said:– 'This scandal extends not only to Mr. Dean but to the Church and to religion: it extends to his Majesty'. The Earl of Arundel was similarly aware of the potential risks:– 'That these men being divines should thus scandalise an eminent person of their own coat, this is dangerous'.[15] Problems like these stemmed directly from the hothouse politics of the Cathedral close where highly intelligent men with administrative and financial ambitions were often carelessly thrown into close proximity with one another. In these circumstances controversy was perhaps more likely than concord.

But it was not just the clergy, with their wealth, misbehaviour and contentiousness, that came in for adverse criticism. In many ways the most public indictment of the Elizabethan or Jacobean Cathedral was what it had physically become. The nave of St. Paul's Cathedral, for example, Paul's Walk as it was known to contemporary Londoners, was a well known scandal which went back to the Middle Ages and

was condemned by successive Bishops of London without much hope
of amendment. Preaching after the burning of St. Paul's in 1561, Bishop
Pilkington of Durham suggested the disaster was a judgement from
God brought about, in part, by the 'walking, jangling, brawling,
fighting, bargaining, etc. namely in sermons and service time'. He went
on to explain how business was actually done there – 'the South alley
for usury and Popery, the North for simony, and the horse fair in the
midst for all kinds of bargains...and the font for ordinary payments of
money'.[16] Indeed, so far had St. Paul's become a commercial centre for
the city of London that a countryman apprehended for urinating
against a pillar in 1632 said in his defence 'he knew it not to be a
church'. And this situation was not peculiar to St. Paul's. The naves of
Norwich, Durham and York were fashionable promenades and covered
markets where the noise of hand carts and children at play sometimes
drowned the sound of the services in the choir.[17] Although the
Laudians did something to curb the worst of these excesses the
problem lingered on and undoubtedly did much to colour the popular
conception of the Cathedral.

So the complaints about English Cathedrals were many and varied,
and the complainants voiced very different solutions to the common
problems. To Field and his friends the answer was expropriation, but
to the majority – to Cranmer, Grindal and Whitgift, for example, – the
solution was to purge the Cathedrals of their worst abuses and try
somehow to incorporate them into the reformed Church of England.
After centuries of inertia the period between 1540 and 1600 stands out
as an era of Cathedral reform, an era which has often passed unnoticed because of its gradual and *ad hoc* implementation. But that was
in the nature of the institutions themselves. Not only were Cathedrals
very different in size, wealth and constitution, they were also
corporations in their own right, acutely conscious of their wide
privileges and immunities, and because of this the progress of any
administration which flinched from full frontal assault – such as was
imposed upon monasteries in the sixteenth century and the Cathedrals
in the nineteenth – would necessarily be slow. Given the reluctance of
Tudor or Stuart government to initiate a thorough reform of the
Cathedrals, change depended largely on piecemeal governmental
activity or the individualistic efforts of archbishops, bishops and deans
who felt that the problem was worthy of their attention – and, of
course, many did not, and many who *did* found their paths blocked by
reactionary forces in their own dioceses.

When all of the miscellaneous sources are collected together there is, in fact, considerable evidence of new thought being directed towards the Cathedrals during the Reformation period. Undoubtedly the most significant move was the creation of the New Foundations, by Henry VIII in the early 1540s. When the larger monasteries were dissolved in 1539 eight bishops, whose seats had been in monastic churches, were left without Chapters, so these churches were re-endowed as secular Cathedrals (Canterbury, Rochester, Winchester, Norwich, Worcester, Durham, Carlisle and Ely). In addition to this Henry created six new sees all of which required Cathedral Chapters for their bishops (Westminster, Gloucester, Peterborough, Chester, Oxford and Bristol).[18] In this way the fourteen New Foundation Chapters were born, and from the start they differed significantly from their Medieval counterparts. Firstly, they were smaller in terms of personnel, with twelve, six or four prebendaries and a correspondingly smaller number of vicars choral, now termed minor canons. Secondly, in general terms they were not as wealthy as the monasteries they replaced and during the transitional period one or two choice estates invariably stuck in the hands of the King: at Peterborough, for example, the new diocese and Dean and Chapter were funded out of estates previously owned by the Abbey, a classic example of 'two for the price of one'. Thirdly, they were governed by stricter rules of residence, the Dean was given extensive powers of control, and the Bishop was permitted to undertake visitations of the Chapter from time to time. Finally – and very important – a new emphasis was placed on the role of the Cathedral in the community by way of evangelism, the provision of educational services, charitable relief and even the repair of local roads and bridges. Having made these general observations we must at once introduce some qualifications. For example, some of the refounded Chapters were still extremely wealthy – such as Durham where a new diocese did not have to be endowed – and in most places it took the new ideas some considerable time to filter through because the first prebendaries in the new Cathedrals were invariably conservative ex-monks of the old monasteries. But nevertheless the orientation was different, and it is clear that the people who devised the statutes for these churches had both learned from the criticism directed against the old Cathedrals, possibly from having observed the statutes of fifteenth century collegiate foundations, and had also been influenced to a degree by the prevailing beliefs of contemporary Protestantism.[19]

In the Old Foundations reform was more piecemeal. Although York received new statutes in 1541 there was no general policy of revision, and what alterations there were came as a result of the royal visitations undertaken by Edward VI and Elizabeth or the visitation articles of reforming Protestant clerics such as Archbishops Holgate and Grindal at York, or Bishops Taylor and Bullingham at Lincoln. Firstly, as a general rule the Old Foundations lost property. For example, the revenues of the treasurers of York and Lincoln were both siezed by the Crown, as well as the emoluments of five Lincoln prebends and four York ones. Secondly, the size of the minor corporations contracted and stricter rules of residence were enforced for the prebendaries. After 1541 the numbers of residents at York rose from about two a year to about four, and the vicars choral were reduced from their Medieval complement of 36 to five. Moreover, in order to create a stronger bond between prebendaries and the Cathedral, a Pentecostal Chapter was established at Salisbury which even non-residents were obliged to attend, and a similar idea was promulgated at York by Grindal. Finally, evangelical and educational ideas filtered through to the old Chapters largely as a result of the activities of the royal visitors who sought to amend ancient statutes in ways which would bring them into line with more modern modes of thought. At Lincoln, for example, provision was made for regular sermons and divinity lectures as well as improvements in the local grammar school, and, according to Professor Cross, Archbishop Holgate of York 'devised a scheme which...could have turned the Minster into an institution for educating young men for the Protestant ministry'.[20] Of course, it is easy to be over optimistic on the strength of selected evidence, and it would be a mistake to pretend that the Old Foundations were in any sense altered fundamentally. Prebendaries remained in often embarrassingly large numbers, Lincoln having 52, Wells 50 and Salisbury 45. Ancient statutes which permitted wholesale non-residence and sometimes denied the bishop's right to visit remained in force.[21] But the Old Foundations were nevertheless trimmed and adapted, and despite their blemishes were brought closer to the reformed concept of the Cathedral initiated by Henry VIII.

Why was the reform so partial, especially when we bear in mind Cranmer's suspicion of Cathedral Chapters and some of the radical pronouncements being made by the court preachers under Edward VI? In fact, sixteenth century governments rarely took fundamental initiatives if they could be avoided, partly because they were reluctant to break with tradition and outrage conservative opinion, and partly because they did not have the bureaucratic machinery to put their dictates into effect or, indeed, the physical force to impose them if things went wrong. Certainly a radical shake-up of Cathedral Chapters would have fallen foul of the first of these criteria. They epitomised tradition and continuity, and their links with general diocesan administration were so strong as to put the bishops' position in some jeopardy if they changed too drastically in complexion; indeed, even a scheme for a wholesale revision of statutes in 1562 came to nothing because of a general inertia and reluctance to change the *status quo.*[22] Twenty years later a similar scheme at Durham put forward by the reformer Ralph Lever failed largely because of lack of enthusiasm on the part of the majority of the Chapter –

> The alteration of our state is hard to be brought to pass. These exulcerant times considered when the state ecclesiastical is everywhere gainsaid, by some under colour of Reformation, by others of greediness gaping for the fall of Cathedral churches, and by all men for our contentions late among us, it is perilous to put our state in balance.[23]

The truth was that too many people had too strong a vested interest in seeing the old system grind on with minimal alteration, and this was true for clergy and gentry just as it was for the Crown and the bishops. Indeed, if Latimer is to be believed it was selfish considerations of this sort which hindered the whole progress of the Reformation in England, and Cathedrals are just one example of this general lost initiative.

The Crown had little desire to dismantle the network of Cathedrals for several reasons. They formed important administrative centres in the secular, as well as the ecclesiastical field, and their deaneries and prebends were still an important source of patronage. Sir John Mason, the diplomat, spent many years as Dean of Winchester, and Thomas Wilson, Elizabeth's Secretary of State, spent his last years as Dean of Durham to the great and general detriment of the Cathedral.[24] Lay prebendaries turn up in most of the Old Foundation Chapters providing comfortable annuities for lawyers or diplomats in the service of a bishop or of the state. Even that stalwart old puritan Sir Francis Walsingham was prepared to come to terms with his conscience in using Cathedral patronage as a means of diverting embarrassing obligations from the state to the Church. In 1585 he championed the cause of one Edmund Curtis, vicar of Cuckfield, to be reinstated as a prebendary of Chichester despite the protests of the Dean and Chapter that he was not a preacher and was 'very unquiet and full of imperfections which can neither be hid nor reformed'. Walsingham's main consideration in backing his candidature seems to have been to relieve the Cuckfield poor rate from the need to maintain the vicar's huge and impoverished family, a charitable action doubtlessly designed to heal local feuds, but hardly in the best traditions of capitular reform.[25] With a rudimentary system of administration which did not pay its offficials or provide cushioning for the socially deprived, jobs in the Church were well worth hanging on to.

Secondly the Cathedrals themselves were sometimes highly resistant to reform or interference from outside, a stance which was often impossible to break because of their extensive and ancient privileges. Despite the implementation of Protestantism under Edward VI and Elizabeth many crypto-Catholic clergy were able to avoid deprivation and remain in office by a show of conformity. Although many Cathedrals lost up to half of their personnel as a result of the 1559 visitation, Catholic survivalism remained a real problem in many Chapters into the 1570s. At Lincoln an inner ring of reactionaries headed by Dean Mallet ruled the roost until 1565, and at Durham the last ex-monk of the Priory to serve as a prebendary, George Cliffe, died as late as 1596, having caused consternation for four successive Protestant bishops. Whereas in the parishes these individuals could be looked on as isolated cranks, their presence in the Cathedral was somewhat more pernicious since by concerted action they could block reforms suggested by their Protestant colleagues, Deans and Chapters being corporations in law and therefore required to function in harmony. A test case is provided at Hereford. Here the continued presence of the treasurer, William Lucan, 'a rank papist', blocked all attempts at reform initiated by Dean Ellis and Bishop Scory, the Bishop's position being particularly difficult because he was unable to enforce his right to visit. Eventually it took a royal visitation in 1583 to sweep out the reactionaries and initiate reforms which in many places had been established for over twenty years.[26]

Finally, by 1560 virtually all sections of the influential clergy and laity had financial interests tied up with the continued existence of the Cathedral foundations. During the troubled years between 1530 and 1560 successive Deans and Chapters, be they Protestant or Catholic in complexion, had frequently leased out their best manors and rectories either to the Crown, to influential local magnates or to their own relatives and friends. Grants were invariably for long terms – 60, 70 and 80 years – often with reversions which mortgaged the future well into the seventeenth century. The fact that these lands were let at unrealistic rents in an inflationary period posed Elizabethan and

Jacobean Chapters with a real problem, as is indicated by this example from Peterborough. Here two manors were leased for £5 *per annum* in 1557: in 1638 it was estimated that this property, still in lease, was worth £560 *per annum* over and above the rent paid to the Church.[27] Arminian churchmen might have grumbled at figures such as these, but in a perverse way they helped guarantee the survival of Cathedral churches in the face of their critics. With so many people standing to lose so much by the expropriation of Cathedral estates, it was unlikely that Crown or Parliament would move to alter the balance that already existed. So it was largely non-religious factors which ensured that Cathedrals would remain, at best, merely half reformed. Their administrative contribution, their patronage, their lands and their stubborn inmates both guaranteed protection from above and frightened off over-active reformers.

Despite their blemishes, and the huge obstacles in the path of concerted reform, Cathedrals had begun to come to terms with society by 1620 and were discovering an identity in the reformed Church of England. In line with the new ethos initiated under Henry VIII enlightened Protestant bishops were regarding their Cathedrals as the focal points of their dioceses, centres of preaching and education which had an invaluable role to play in the evangelisation of the hinterland. Durham, which may have been untypical because of its proximity to the Anglo-Scottish borders, was described by an enthusiastic visitor from Oxford in 1583 as 'the light of the North', a role which was also conceived for Hereford on the Welsh Marches though with less hope of success.[28] But it was not just in the border region that the Cathedral had a part to play. Bishop Coxe of Ely had positive ideas about the place of his Cathedral as the mother church of the diocese, and Professor Collinson has highlighted the relationship between Archbishop Grindal and Dean Hutton of York which led to the Minster – for a while, at least – being a focal point of Protestant ambitions –

> In 1571 the prospects for converting the Minster into a powerhouse of reform were good. Matthew Hutton was energetic, the only active, resident Dean of York for a century and a half. Between them Grindal and Hutton would conspire to bring competent theologians and preachers on to the staff as vacancies occurred.[29]

And this picture was far from being an isolated one, even though Professor Collinson is correct to emphasise the need for deans and bishops to work in harmony and to share the same evangelical objectives. With a united clerical establishment – which broadly speaking existed in England before the ascendancy of the Arminians in the 1620s – the Protestant conception of the Cathedral could become a reality.

From the bishop's point of view much depended on his ability to use valuable Cathedral patronage as a way of attracting able clergy to his diocese or of rewarding those already there, the emphasis of policy altering according to the laws of supply and demand as they affected the clergy at large. At York, during the 1570s, Grindal spent most of his energies attempting to attract promising outsiders, while his seventeenth century successors, notably Richard Neile, preferred to promote their own home-grown talent.[30] This policy was well used by Archbishop Sharpe in the later seventeenth century whose attitude to his Cathedral prebendaries was described by his biographer –

> [The Archbishop] made it his unalterable practice always to elect them [i.e. the prebendaries] out of such as lived in his diocese, and had recommended themselves by doing their duties in their respective parochial cures. By which means no Cathedral in England was better attended by clergy, and the service more regularly performed than at York; or the ministers in small livings more encouraged to attend to their charge; because this good bishop would reward their diligence by such compensations, more especially those in York city, on whose conduct the world had a more especial eye; hoping this example would influence his successors to take the like course.[31].

Although Chapters continued to be dominated by close-knit cabals of resident prebendaries associated closely with the Cathedral and its politics, it seems that the 'outer ring' of canons identified increasingly with the parochial structure of the diocese: to some of them a prebend was the high water mark of a long and relatively successful career in the church, to others it was merely a stepping stone to higher preferment.[32] But, however a man regarded his prebend, there is no doubt that it brought him status and additional income, and his contribution must therefore be measured against the sort of economic and doctrinal objections levelled by the puritan critics of the Elizabethan period.

A consideration of the role of Cathedral prebendaries within the diocese really lies at the heart of a serious assessment of their contribution to the reformed church. Much work remains to be done in this area, but it seems clear already that by sheer hard work many prebendaries earned the supplement to their wages which a Cathedral appointment gave them. At York Edmund Bunny used his emoluments to subsidise preaching tours of the North, and at Durham the prebendaries were amongst the principal parochial ministers of the diocese active in preaching and instruction not only in their own parishes but also in the region at large.[33] Indeed, there seems to have been a real attempt to encourage the Cathedrals to revert to their ancient Saxon role as missionary centres and further research may well confirm discoveries already made at York and Durham, sigificantly representative of both 'old' and 'new' Chapters. This Protestant vision of the Cathedral was usefully set down by William Harrison in his *Description of England* in 1577. Deans were 'especially chosen to that vocation for their learning and godliness' and canons were 'not idle and unprofitable persons (as in times past they have been...) but such as by preaching and teaching can and do learnedly set forth the glory of God and further the overthrow of antichrist to the uttermost of their powers'.[34] Harrison, of course, is stating the ideal for which the reformers aimed rather than the reality, but that the ideal was at least partially implemented indicates that Cathedrals had travelled a long way from their Medieval liturgical preoccupation and were beginning to come to terms with a new set of imperatives. At best a Cathedral prebend gave a man a perception of his region beyond the parish pump, a sense of unity with his fellow clergy and contacts with bishops and archdeacons who had the power to formulate strategy. With the right sort of leadership the Cathedral could become a powerful dynamo of reform.

What tolled the death knell of Cathedrals as Harrison and others understood them was the apathy of many bishops, deans and prebendaries and the Arminian revolution which hit the English church in the 1620s. High Church views first began to develop at Cambridge in the 1590s, but owing to the patronage of Buckingham and Prince Charles they became imposed on the church in general as James I lapsed into premature senility. Bishoprics and deaneries, in the direct patronage of the Crown, were amongst the first offices to be taken over, and Cathedral churches, because of their vastness, their antiquity and their impact on the public eye, soon became centres of pseudo-Catholic ritualistic practice. When James I visited Durham in 1617 he 'would have all things done in plain manner without either singing or organ playing': when his son paid a similar visit in 1633 the prebendaries were bedecked in new copes, *Te Deum*s were sung and a pilgrimage was made to the shrine of St. Cuthbert.[35] The physical contrast underlined an important shift in attitude. No longer were Cathedrals regarded principally as centres of evangelism in the 1630s, but rather as great temples to the divine majesty which embodied in their fabric Laud's much quoted Biblical *cliché* 'the beauty of holiness'. Bishop Corbet of Norwich in a sermon in 1634 summed up the Arminian view of the Cathedral very well –

> We admire those things for the most part which are the oldest and the greatest: old monuments, huge buildings do effect us above measure; and what's the reason? For what is ancient comes nearer to God for the antiquity, and what is great comes near his works for their spaciousness and magnitude: so that in honouring these we honour God, whom old and great do seem to imitate.[36]

This new cult of 'Cathedral veneration' perhaps found its most passionate support at Durham where Bishop Neile, Dean Hunt and John Cosin worked in harmony to make the Cathedral an 'exemplary' place, though not without fierce opposition from the traditionalist prebendaries headed by the vitriolic Peter Smart.[37] How did these changes show through in the physical appearance of the Cathedral and the attitude of the Chapter? Firstly, much more emphasis was placed on the *opus dei* – the formal recital of services in the choir – rather than preaching: some amusing stories are told, for example, of the Arminian prebendary Marmaduke Blakiston who bowed so low in his devotions he struck his nose on the ground and made it bleed. Old-fashioned Protestants saw all this as a retrograde step, moving the Cathedral ethos back to pre-Reformation days. 'You think you do service enough to God and the church if you sit now and then in your stall like an idle drone...to hear piping and chanting' said Peter Smart – and in saying so he voiced the views of those who saw the Cathedral as an evangelical unit.[38] Secondly, the appearance of the Cathedral changed drastically with the introduction of altars, copes, candles, images, crucifixes and all the trappings of High Church Anglicanism, much to the annoyance of outraged conservatives. 'I hate them that hold of superstitious vanities, ceremonial fooleries, apish toys and popish trinkets', raged Peter Smart, who went on to describe his capitular colleagues as 'mangy pack of Arminian hell-hounds' and 'spiritual fornicators'.[39] Finally, in line with the policy promulgated by Archbishop Laud at the centre, the new Chapter followed a policy aimed at augmenting its own wealth both at the expense of the local leaseholding gentry and those families of pre-Arminian prebendaries who were already established on the Cathedral estates: the classic example of this is Dean Hunt's seizure of Sir John Fenwick's lease of Bywell rectory to help pay for Cosin's 'repairs' to the Cathedral.[40]

All of this proved to be an explosive mixture, because it threatened cash and conviction in a way which no seventeenth century Englishman could ignore. It divided the clerical establishment, which had hitherto been united, and it separated the Cathedral still further from the society it purported to serve. Laud was astute enough to foresee the dangers implicit in this sort of situation – 'there is no speedier cause of ruin and to make way for men ill affected to break in upon them; when they come to bite one another they are in danger to be devoured.'[41] This prophetic statement, uttered at the height of the Peterson scandal in 1632, sums up the almost totally myopic vision of the Arminian revolutionaries of the 1630s. The Durham case, which was discussed at length in Parliament in 1629, became something of a *cause célèbre,* and it struck at the very heart of the question of how the Cathedral was to be regarded in society. But it was not unique. Indeed controversies such as those dividing Cosin and Smart were all too typical in the Cathedral cities in the 1630s. At York, for example, there were bitter controversies between the Arminian Chapter and the corporation, partly about jurisdiction within the liberty of St. Peter and partly because of physical alterations in the Minster which included a gilded altar screen and 'a most excellent-large-plump-lusty-full speaking organ which cost... a thousand pounds'.[42] At Winchester the Chapter and corporation were similarly at odds with one another over questions of precedence in the Cathedral and a lavish altar screen built by Inigo Jones 'standing upon marble pillars' and incorporating brass statues of James I and Charles I.[43] All of this illustrates the extent to which society was becoming polarised on the eve of the Civil Wars, and in this polarisation the changes wrought in the English Cathedrals by the Arminian clergy in the 1630s played a small, though not insignificant, part.

In this sort of context it is easier to understand the motives of the Parliamentarian soldiers who battered Inigo Jones' choir screen at Winchester and of the Scots who used Cosin's 'temple' as a lavatory. They were reacting not against Cathedral churches as such – York Minster was never more popular amongst the townsmen than it was between 1645 and 1660 – but what these churches had become since the accession of Charles I. In 1620 the rhetoric of the Elizabethan puritans had faded into insignificance because between 1540 and 1620 a unified Protestant church interest had succeeded in moulding a new profile for the Cathedrals which was acceptable to the vast majority of Englishmen, apathetic though they might have been towards matters ecclesiastical. It was only the division of that church interest in the

1630s when prebendary fell upon prebendary, and the widening gulf between the Arminian clergy and the laity, illustrated in the quarrels between the Chapters and the corporations, that caused the Cathedrals to stand vulnerable to attack during the Civil War. The radical puritans of the 1580s, once an isolated minority, were now joined by solid Calvinist churchmen, gentry and city merchants to resist what they regarded as an unacceptable and profligate set of institutions. Few people, it would seem, seriously regretted the demise of the Cathedrals in 1649, except, perhaps, a handful of Anglican exiles such as John Cosin and Michael Honywood – even in the 1590s they seem to have been tolerated rather than loved. Their estates were sold off, sometimes to the individuals who occupied them anyway, and provision was made for evangelism and educational development through other channels. The Commonwealth period proved decisively that England was well able to survive without her Cathedral churches, and when they came back in 1660 it was in a form more acceptable to Cosin than to Grindal. The 'Cathedral reform' movement of the Tudor and Jacobean periods represented a bold attempt to thrust the English church into the future by returning it to its ancient roots, but its success was never more than partial because of the ever present drag-anchors of apathy, self interest and schismatic division. Like other areas of the Church, Cathedrals remained no more than half reformed, an enduring monument to the uneasy compromise which was Anglicanism.

NOTES

1.   F. Bussby, *Winchester Cathedral, 1079-1979* (1979), p. 137.
2.   G. E. Aylmer and R. Cant (eds.), *A History of York Minster* (1977), pp. 214-15.
3.   *Acts and Ordinances of the Interregnum, 1642-60,* 2, pp. 81-104.
4.   C. Cross, 'Dens of Loitering Lubbers: Protestant protest against Cathedral foundations, 1540-1640,' in D. Baker (ed.), *Schism, Heresy and Religious Protest,* Studies in Church History, 10 (1972), p. 231.
5.   *Ibid.,* pp. 231-2.
6.   *Cranmer's Miscellaneous Writings,* ed. J. E. Cox, Parker Society (1846), pp. 396-7; J. Youings, *The Dissolution of the Monasteries* (1971), p. 85.
7.   C. S. Collingwood, *Memoirs of Bernard Gilpin* (1884), p. 106.
8.   Cross, 'Dens of Loitering Lubbers', p. 236; D. Marcombe, 'The Dean and Chapter of Durham, 1558-1603', unpub. Ph.D. thesis, Durham Univ. 1973, p. 39.
9.   R. B. Walker, 'Lincoln Cathedral in the reign of Queen Elizabeth', *Journal of Ecclesiastical History,* 11 (1960), pp. 189-90; Aylmer and Cant, *History of York Minster,* pp. 197-8.
10. C. Webb, 'York Minster, 1625-77: a prosopographical study', unpub. M.A. thesis, York Univ. 1988, p. 102.
11. *Ibid.,* pp. 92, 103; Marcombe, 'The Dean and Chapter of Durham', pp. 45-51. The 1628 incident seems to have been the result of heated tempers during the Peter Smart episode (see below) and does not appear to have been typical of the minor corporation as a whole.
12. P. A. Scholes, *The Puritans and Music in England and New England* (1934), p. 226.
13. K. Edwards, *The English Secular Cathedrals in the Middle Ages* (1967), p. xii.
14. Durham University Department of Palaeography and Diplomatic, D(urham) C(hapter) R(ecords), Prior's Kitchen, York Book, ff. 79-80, 81-3.
15. *Reports of Cases in the Courts of Star Chamber and High Commission,* ed. S. R. Gardiner, Camden Society, New Series, 39 (1886), pp. 153-75.
16. *Documents Illustrating the History of St. Paul's Cathedral,* ed. W. S. S. Simpson, Camden Society, New Series, 26 (1880), pp. xlvii-xlviii, 120-5.
17. *Reports of Cases in... High Commission,* pp. 280-1; *Documents... of St. Pauls Cathedral,* pp. 1-li.
18. D. Knowles, *The Religious Orders in England,* 3 (1959), pp. 389-92; J. J. Scarisbrick, *Henry VIII* (1968) p. 514; Youings, *The Dissolution of the Monasteries,* pp. 84-6.
19. A. H. Thompson, *The Cathedral Churches of England* (1928), pp. 190-2. For a more detailed discussion of the refoundation as it affected Durham, see D. Marcombe, 'The Durham Dean and Chapter: old abbey writ large?' in *Continuity and Change: personnel and administration of the Church in England, 1500-1642,* ed. R. O'Day and F. Heal (1976).
20. Aylmer and Cant, *History of York Minster,* pp. 193-232; Walker, 'Lincoln

Cathedral in the reign of Elizabeth', pp. 186-201; *Chapter Acts of the Cathedral Church of St. Mary of Lincoln, 1547-59,* ed. R. E. G. Cole, Lincoln Record Society, 15 (1920), pp. 12-16.

21. Cross, 'Dens of Loitering Lubbers', p. 234.
22. Walker, 'Lincoln Cathedral in the reign of Elizabeth', p. 197.
23. D. C. R., York Book, f. 43.
24. See *Dictionary of National Biography.* For the dissensions at Durham during Dean Wilson's non-residence, see Marcombe, 'The Dean and Chapter of Durham, 1558-1603', pp. 260-6;
25. *The Acts of the Dean and Chapter of the Cathedral Church of Chichester, 1545-1642,* ed. W. D. Peckham, Sussex Record Society, 58 (1959), pp. 116-17.
26. *Calendar of State Papers, Domestic, 1547-80,* p. 196; *1581-90,* p. 89.
27. *Peterborough Local Administration,* ed. W. T. Mellows, Northamptonshire Record Society, 9 (1939), pp. lxv-lxvi. For the case of Durham, see D. Marcombe, 'A Rude and Heady People: the local community and the Rebellion of the Northern Earls', pp. 124-8, in D. Marcombe (ed.), *The Last Principality: politics, religion and society in the Bishopric of Durham, 1494-1660* (1987).
28. Durham University Library, Mickleton and Spearman Ms. 62. The poem 'Inter Boreale' describes the visit to Durham made by the Oxford scholar Thomas Eades in 1583. Of Hereford Bishop Scory said 'this church which should be the light of all the diocese is very darkness'. *The Camden Miscellany, 9* (1895), sect. 3, pp. 20-1.
29. P. Collinson, *Archbishop Grindal, 1519-1583* (1979) pp. 199-200. For the work of Bishop Coxe at Ely, see above p. 11-15.
30. Webb, 'York Minster', p. 114.
31. T. Newcombe, *Life of John Sharpe D.D.* (1825), pp. 117-19.
32. Webb, 'York Minster', pp. 53, 57; Marcombe, 'The Dean and Chapter of Durham' pp. 271-309.
33. Aylmer and Cant, *History of York Minster,* p. 209; Marcombe, 'The Dean and Chapter of Durham', pp. 306-7;
34. W. Harrison, *The Description of England,* ed. G. Edelen, Folger Shakespeare Libary (1968) pp. 23-4. Some of Harrison's ideas appear to be drawn directly from Jewel's *Apologia.*
35. C. J. Stranks, *This Sumptuous Church: the story of Durham Cathedral* (1973) pp. 53-4; R. Surtees, *History of Durham,* 4 (1840), p. 28.
36. *Documents...of St. Paul's Cathedral,* p. 135.
37. For a full discussion of Arminianism in Durham see M. Tillbrook, 'Arminianism and Society in County Durham, 1617-42', in *The Last Principality,* pp. 202-26.
38. *The Correspondence of John Cosin,* 1, ed. G. Ornsby, Surtees Society, 52 (1869), p. 185.
39. P. Smart, *A Sermon Preached in the Cathedral Church of Durham, July 7 1628,* p. 23.
40. *The Correspondence of John Cosin,* 1, pp. xxii, 167.
41. *Reports of Cases in.... High Commission,* pp. 172-3.

42. Aylmer and Cant, *History of York Minster,* pp. 211-13. See also below, pp. 62-9.
43. Bussby, *Winchester Cathedral,* pp. 127-9.

Conflict and Confrontation: The York Dean and Chapter and the Corporation in the 1630s

Claire Cross

On May 24 1633, a day as Laud noted, of 'extreme wind and rain', Charles I, *en route* to Edinburgh for his coronation as King of Scots, paid a ceremonial visit to York, and the Chapter recorded the momentous event in its Act Book. Having been met by the York sheriffs with a numerous retinue at Tadcaster bridge, the boundary between the West Riding and the Ainsty, Charles progressed to Micklegate bar, the chief entry to the city where he –

> shining forth with royal pomp, and accompanied by many nobles and magnates of the kingdom, was received by the Lord Mayor, Recorder and aldermen, with dutiful salutations and supplications. The whole then formed a procession unto the Cathedral and metropolitan church of St. Peter; whither having arrived, the King alighted from his carriage, and at the Western door he knelt down, and worshipped Almighty God, by whom kings do reign, and princes exercise their power. After this, having advanced somewhat farther into the church, he stopped near the font or baptistery, where the venerable Henry Wickham, Doctor of Divinity, Archdeacon of York, and canon residentiary of this church, congratulated the King on his arrival, in a Latin oration (the King having first sat down on a chair there prepared); which oration being concluded, the King arising proceeded into the choir, the venerable John Scott, D.D., Dean of the said church, – George Stanhope, D.D., precentor, – Phineas Hodgson, chancellor, – the aforementioned Henry Wickham, D.D., the other canons of the said church, bearing over our lord the King a veil or canopy supported by silvered staves, and divine service having been solemnly performed, he withdrew into the nave of the church, and the canopy having been raised as before, he walked to the Chapter House; and, having returned thence, and walked for a little while in the middle aisle, he departed to the Manor or Palace of St. Mary of York.[1]

At the King's Manor, though the Chapter Act Book failed to mention this, Charles honoured the new Archbishop and Laud's great patron,

Richard Neile, by conferring a knighthood on his son. Quite clearly in his grandiloquent description the Minster annalist designed for posterity an edifying account of York clergy and people joining in harmonious co-operation to greet their monarch.[2]

York, however, in 1633 was very far from being a city at unity with itself. Relations between the Minster and the corporation had worsened noticeably over the previous five years, and the royal inspection of the Cathedral served only to exacerbate a difficult situation. The first signs of strain had emerged in 1627 when certain inhabitants of the city, simultaneously tenants of the Dean and Chapter, had complained to the corporation of a summons to attend a sessions of the liberty of St. Peter. The corporation in response had ordered 'that none of them shall appear neither at that time nor any other to do any service at that court, and if they be sued or molested for the same, they shall be defended and saved harmless by this court.' The city had then gone on to take legal advice about the liberties claimed by the Dean and Chapter, but to no avail, with the result that in 1632 the corporation had subjected the charter of St. Peter to a fresh and detailed scrutiny. By this date the city had discovered an additional grievance in that residents of the Minster Yard had been withholding their contributions for the relief of the city's poor. Late in 1632 the Lord Mayor, aldermen and twenty four had announced to the Dean and prebendaries that in future they intended to process as a body from their 'closet' in the nave into the choir, and not to straggle into their places one by one as they had been forced to do since the recent restraint made by the Chapter on walking in the Minster.[3] Consequently when the King reached York in the spring of 1633 ecclesiastics and townspeople already had six years of petty skirmishings behind them. The corporation more and more had come to see itself as under attack from resurgent clericalism while the Chapter felt threatened by powerful and assertive laymen. Behind these apparently trivial disagreements lay fundamental religious differences.

Although in May 1633 Richard Neile had been in possession of his archiepiscopal see for only a little more than twelve months, he had already carried out his primary visitation and his presence at the head of the province had unquestionably strengthened the small band of Arminians who were even before his appointment in the ascendancy in the Minster.[4] Despite the necessary respectful acknowledgement of the Dean in the report of the King's reception, John Scott scarcely qualifies for inclusion in the group, though his weakness prevented him from resisting innovation. Dean in 1625, and a pluralist since 1629 when he acquired the rectory of Barwick-in-Elmet, Scott still found his resources insufficient to finance his gambling. He appeared for the last time at a Chapter meeting in September 1635, thereafter being confined for debt in the King's Bench prison in London where he died in 1644.[5] Impetus for change came rather from the three other Minster dignitaries, Wickham, Hodgson and Stanhope. Unlike Scott who had risen to his present eminence in the church from a family of relatively obscure origin from Richmond in Yorkshire, Wickham had been born into the ecclesiastical purple. His father, William Wickham, had died as Bishop of Winchester in 1595, having held the see of Lincoln for the previous decade, and Henry obtained promotion from another episcopal relation, his uncle by marriage, Toby Matthew, who in succession presented him to the prebend of Fenton in 1614, the archiepiscopal rectory of Bolton Percy three years later, to a prebend in Southwell in 1621 and lastly to the archdeaconry of York in 1624. This abundant patronage notwithstanding, Wickham did not perpetuate his uncle's churchmanship, and after Matthew's death, became in the 1630s one of the leaders of the Laudian party in the Minster where he assiduously attended meetings of the Chapter.[6] In his disciplinary campaigns Wickham could always rely on the support of Hodgson and Stanhope. Phineas Hodgson's appointment as chancellor in 1611 also went back to Matthew's archiepiscopate. Frailty of the flesh may have caused him, too, to adapt himself to the new regime. The father of no less than 24 children, Hodgson had gained notoriety locally for his addiction to food and drink.[7] The last of the quartet who conducted Charles round the Minster, George Stanhope alone owed his preferment to royal intervention. He had been made precentor in 1631 during a vacancy in the see and like Wickham showed exemplary regularity in his appearances in Chapter. In the early 1640s his enemies classed him as 'a cruel but a smooth and smiling malignant.'[8]

Wickham, Hodgson and to a lesser extent Stanhope together formed the party for action both in the Minster and, through their importance in the archiepiscopal courts and in the Northern court of High Commission, in the diocese at large, but they had derived their inspiration from outside, from Neile when Bishop of Durham, from Laud and perhaps particularly from John Cosin, the celebrated, or infamous, Arminian prebendary of Durham who in 1625, after his father-in-law's resignation in his favour, had become Archdeacon of the East Riding. Although rarely resident in York, the Archdeacon made his presence felt through the ecclesiastical lawyer, Edward Mottershed, who performed Cosin's administrative and judicial duties.[9] The member of the Chapter who seems to have sympathised most with Cosin's High Church piety was Timothy Thurscross, prebendary of Langtoft, who after his spectacular conversion to Arminianism gave up his Kirkby Moorside living and the Archdeaconry of Cleveland, being 'much troubled in his conscience for having obtained them through simony.' Antagonistic Parliamentarians in 1644 singled out Cosin, Stanhope, Hodgson and Thurscross as the chief 'idolators' in York, particularly remarking on the self-denial which had reduced Thurscross to 'nothing but skin and bones', he being then 'as lean with his superstition as the other [that is Hodgson] is fed up with his venison.'[10]

The religious interests of the leading citizens could scarcely have contrasted more sharply with those of the resident prebendaries. Already in 1631 Chancellor Hodgson had stored up for future reference the information that one of the two city sheriffs, James Brooke, had been 'standing upon his feet in time of divine prayers' in the Minster, when the clergy had set an example of duly kneeling on their knees.[11] The York aldermen in fact had only very slowly developed an active commitment to Protestantism and had not begun requesting funeral sermons or making explicitly Protestant confessions of faith until the very end of the sixteenth century, but by the accession of Charles I there could be no mistaking their newly acquired zeal. The wills of three former Lord Mayors who died between 1630 and 1633 give a good indication of civic, religious and charitable preoccupations. Besides endowing the corporation with £100 to set the poor on work and making other generous bequests to almshouses and prisoners Thomas Agar asked for a funeral sermon from the chief city lecturer.[12] Elias Micklethwaite, equally in favour of providing work for the poor, left money to five city preachers and put aside £40 'to be paid when there is "feffyers" appointed in this city for buying of impropriations', and he did this in the very month, February 1633, when Laud in the Southern High Commission had dissolved the London feoffees.[13] Drawing up his will within a month of Micklethwaite, William Greenbury included the now virtually obligatory lengthy Protestant preamble and gave £3 6s. 8d. to his incumbent, Roger Bellwood of St. Crux.[14] The theological ethos of the civic governors emerges most clearly from the will of William Brearey, Lord Mayor in 1611 and 1623, who died in 1637. Having commended his soul to the Trinity, he proclaimed his confident belief –

> that all my sins, although never so grievous and heavy, are nevertheless forgiven me, and my election sealed up by the only pure and precious blood and merits of my Lord and Saviour, Jesus Christ, by whom only and by no other means, my redemption is made sure and certain according to the unspeakable love of God towards mankind in his eternal and unsearchable counsel and purpose before the foundations of the world were laid, and which he hath revealed in this latter age of the world for the comfort of his elect by his most holy scriptures, the only ways to know his will and pleasure.[15]

Three days after his reception in the Minster Charles I provided the occasion which brought the already embattled city and Chapter into open confrontation. Writing from his palace at York, and prompted by Laud, the King ordered the ecclesiastical authorities to pull down houses built against the Cathedral and dismantle within the Minster recently erected pews which offered a 'great trouble to the service in the church, and a great blemish to so goodly a choir.'[16] The removal of the offending seats went ahead quickly; they had gone by the last Sunday in September when 'Mr. Doctor Wickham...in the forenoon in sermon time did take [his] place in the Minster two or three stalls above the Lord Mayor which', the corporation indignantly told their legal adviser, 'as yet was never seen before by any man living.' Feeling ran so high at this slight to civic honour that Mr. Justice Hutton in his reply found it necessary to warn the corporation against carrying out its intention of withdrawing from the Minster and patronising instead sermons in St. Michael-le-Belfrey. As an alternative to this act of undisguised provocation he recommended a series of petitions, and the city agreed to write both to the Lord Keeper and the Archbishop of York and, for good measure, to the King. At an acrimonious meeting between representatives of the city and the Minster the Archdeacon disclosed that he had been instructed to sit in the seat by the Archbishop of Canterbury (when Bishop of London) and the Archbishop of York, and Chancellor Hodgson turned the tables on the town clerk by asking sarcastically 'if my Lord Mayor would take it well if they should send to him to know why he dwelt in his house, and withall said that there would two other Archdeacons come and sit there shortly, or else they would be fined.' In the end, however, affidavits from elderly inhabitants convinced the Lord Keeper that the Lord Mayor had indeed once sat where the Lord President's lady's pew had stood and reluctantly Wickham conceded the corporation's prior claim.[17] The city had triumphed in this encounter, but was still far from winning the whole campaign.

The operation for beautifying the Minster, begun in 1633, reached its culmination in the following year when the Chapter purchased in London frontal cloths and new plate for the altar and had the screen behind it coloured and gilt and a magnificent new organ built and set up in the choir, all paid for by a fine of £1,000 imposed by the Northern High Commission on Edward Paler of Thoraldby for the crime of incest with his niece and granted to the Cathedral by the King. Beneath the organ the Chapter in gratitude caused to be inscribed: 'Benedictus Deus patrum nostrum, qui dedit in corde regis ut adornaret domum suam.'[18]

The refurnishing of the Minster, much as it might impress strangers, quite failed to overawe the corporation, and no sooner had the dispute over civic seating subsided than the old conflict over rival jurisdictions broke out anew.[19] In May 1634 the town clerk informed the Dean that since the attempt in York to resolve the differences between the church and the city had had no success the corporation proposed to have recourse for a second time to the Lord Keeper and the Archbishop. Much more was now at stake than injured civic pride. By virtue of their new charter the Lord Mayor, Recorder and aldermen maintained that they had become justices of the peace for all places within both the city and county of York, and that the Dean and Chapter were infringing their privileges by summoning their tenants who were also citizens to do suit in the capitular court. Hearings in London of the case between the city and the Chapter dragged on throughout 1634, 1635 and 1636, both sides making their stand on their respective charters. By 1637, however, the city had been forced on to the defensive and finally agreed to renounce its jurisdiction over certain recently annexed towns in the North and East Ridings.[20]

With this controversy over the rival jurisdictions still unresolved the King once more intervened in a matter of ceremonial, as he had done earlier. In a standard letter, apparently sent to all Cathedral cities, Charles in July 1637 ordered the corporation to 'manifest your conformity to the orders established in the said church' and forbade the Lord Mayor to use his 'ensigns of...authority' within the Minster.[21] Yet again the corporation leapt to the defence of its privileges and sought legal advice as to the precise meaning of 'ensigns of authority'. Resolving that in obedience to the royal command the corporation should attend the Minster in state the civic leaders nevertheless decided that the sword and the mace should be carried before the Mayor as in times past, and that two aldermen and the town clerk should leave for London to petition the King on the matter.[22]

For the second time the Chapter lost the attempt to curtail the city's ceremonial privileges, but in the much more significant question of the competing jurisdictions it eventually gained the victory, albeit a pyrrhic one. Early in 1640 the corporation, the position now totally reversed from what it had been in 1634, was desperately finding reasons why the Archbishop and chancellor should not be appointed justices of the peace in the city: on April 21 it received an ominous instruction to surrender its charter. Fears ran high that the Minster's new charter would prejudice that to be given to the city. Almost certainly the city escaped further curtailment of its jurisdiction only by the summoning of the Long Parliament: it did not get the enrolment of its charter until the much more propitious time of July 1645. Given the city's sensitivity over what it saw as ecclesiastical encroachments upon its liberties in the previous decade and a half it is scarcely surprising that in January 1641 the corporation set up a committee to draft a petition to Parliament 'against episcopacy and ecclesiastical government.'[23]

The dramatic conflicts in the 1630s between the corporation and the Chapter over their respective privileges and jurisidictions took place against a backcloth of mounting mutual suspicion. To a very real degree both bodies considered themselves discriminated against by the other, both felt themselves being pressurised by a superior force. From well before Charles I's accession the corporation had been imposing regulations for Sabbath observance, yet when Neile, through Easdall, Chancellor of the archdiocese, and Wickham, questioned the city's authority in this sphere he obviously thought the city was encroaching upon the Church's preserve.[24] Equally clearly in the increasing harassment of nonconforming and barely conforming civic clergy throughout the decade leading members of the corporation detected the animus of hostile ecclesiastics who had succeeded in monopolising royal favour.[25] Each body anticipated retaliation by the other.

In the event the city won the day. Their triumph must have seemed little short of miraculous to the York aldermen and city ministers who survived the persecution to see the defeat of the Royalist troops at Marston Moor and the city left open to the Parliamentarians. In a series of logical moves the corporation occupied the Minster. In August 1645 the York committee of the Northern Association made an inventory of the Chapter's possessions and commanded Dr. Hodgson to surrender the books. It had the Arminian ornaments and the hated organ removed and, with Parliament's authorisation, established four preaching ministers in the Minster paid out of the capitular revenues. The grant to the corporation in 1653 of the jurisdiction of the lately dissolved liberty of the Dean and Chapter completed the city's victory.[26] For the first time perhaps in its history the Minster seemed to be fully integrated into the city.

While of interest in itself as an illustration of the confrontations between one particular capitular body and its city, the example of York has greater significance in that it appears to have been fairly typical of what was happening in other Cathedral cities at the time of the Arminian revival. At Durham in 1633, and also at Canterbury two years later, Laud took advantage of a ceremonial visit to banish lay pews from the choir, as he had done at York. Divisions between the close and a clique of puritan aldermen reached fever pitch in Salisbury in the 1630s, and at Chichester, Gloucester and Worcester puritanically inclined oligarchies also became embroiled with Arminian Chapters now seized with the desire to assert the rights of the Church. In Norwich and Exeter as well as Chichester and Salisbury civic corporations tried to breach Chapter liberties, and were repulsed in the 1630s in much the same manner as at York. Norwich, like York, for a time had its local feoffees for impropriations. In exactly the same spirit as the York canons Worcester prebendaries in the 1630s launched an attack on corporation pews in the Cathedral where 'senators and their wives sat in more pomp and state than in their guildhall.'[27] More research needs to be pursued at a local level before a national synthesis can be attempted. It is, however, already evident that the eleven years when Charles I ruled without Parliament constituted a particularly turbulent period in the relationship between Deans and Chapters and their Cathedral cities.

NOTES

1. W. Laud, *Works,* 3, Library of Anglo-Catholic Theology (1853), p. 217; J.
    Browne, *The History of the Metropolitan Church of St Peter, York* (1847),
    p. 308; Y(ork) M(inster) L(ibrary), Dean and Chapter Act Book H 4, f.
    735 r-v.
2. G. Benson, *York from the Reformation to the year 1925* (1925), p. 21.
3. Y(ork) C(ity) A(rchives), Housebook 1626-37, ff. 44, 169-70, 186.
4. A. Foster, 'The function of a bishop: the career of Richard Neile
    1562-1640', in *Continuity and Change: personnel and administration of the
    Church in England 1500-1642* ed. R. O'Day and F. Heal (1976), pp. 45-54.
5. J. and J. A. Venn, *Alumni Cantabrigienses* (1922), pt. 1, Vol. 4, p. 32; A.
    G. Matthews, *Walker Revised* (1948), p. 398; YML, Dean and Chapter Act
    Book, H 5, f. 6v.
6. Venn, *Alumni...,* pt. 1, Vol. 4, p. 398; YML, Dean and Chapter Act Books
    H 4 and H 5.
7. R. A. Marchant, *The Puritans and the Church Courts in the Diocese of
    York 1560-1642* (1960), pp. 43, 45, 50-1.
8. YML, Torre Ms. 'Minster volume', pp. 595-6; Dean and Chapter Act
    Books H 4 and H 5; Matthews, *Walker Revised,* p. 398.
9. Marchant, *Puritans and the Church Courts,* pp. 44, 53-4.
10. *Ibid.,* p. 284; Matthews, *Walker Revised,* p. 18.
11. Marchant, *Puritans and the Church Courts,* p. 93.
12. B(orthwick) I(nstitute of Historical Research), York, Prob. Reg. 41, pt. 1,
    ff. 447v-449v.
13. BI, Prob. Reg. 42, pt. 1, ff. 109r-110v; Laud, *Works,* 3, p. 216.
14. BI, Prob. Reg. 42, pt. 2, ff. 375v-376r.
15. *Ibid.,* ff. 711v-713v.
16. *The Fabric Rolls of York Minster,* ed. A. Raine, Surtees Society, 35 (1859),
    pp. 325-7.
17. YCA, Housebook 1626-37, ff. 218-19, 219-20, 223, 224, 229, 230, 231-2.
18. Raine, *Fabric Rolls,* p. 319.
19. *Ibid.,* pp. 319-23.
20. YCA, Housebook 1626-37, ff. 240, 242, 246, 247, 249, 250, 278, 280, 286,
    288-9, 290-1, 294, 303, 324, 327, 329.
21. Raine, *Fabric Rolls,* p. 329.
22. YCA, Housebook 1626-37, ff. 335-6.
23. *Ibid.,* Housebook 1638-50, ff. 40-1, 45, 48, 53, 55, 142, 159.
24. *Ibid.,* Housebook 1626-37, ff. 2, 68, 153, 158, 238, 333, 339.
25. Marchant, *Puritans and the Church Courts,* pp. 74-92, 226-9, 257, 277,
    280-1, 291-2; C. Cross, 'Achieving the Millennium: the Church in York
    during the Commonwealth', in G. J. Cuming (ed.), *Studies in Church
    History,* 4 (1967), pp. 122-35.
26. YCA, E 63, ff. 4, 5, 19; Housebook 1650-63, f. 48.
27. P. Slack, 'Religious protest and urban authority: the case of Henry

Sherfield, iconoclast 1633', in D. Baker (ed.), *Studies in Church History,* 9 (1972), pp. 295-302; P. Clark, *English Provincial Society from the Reformation to the Revolution* (1977), p. 363; M. James, *Family, Lineage and Civil Society* (1974), pp. 112-13, 124; *Victoria County History, Durham,* 2 (1907), p. 47; A. Fletcher, *A County Community in Peace and War: Sussex 1600-1660* (1975), pp. 235-7; J. T. Evans, *Seventeenth Century Norwich* (1979) pp. 84-104; A. D. Dyer, *The City of Worcester in the sixteenth century* (1973), pp. 233-4; W. T. MacCaffrey, *Exeter, 1540-1640* (1958), pp. 200-1; P. Clark, ' "The Ramoth-Gilead of the Good": urban change and political radicalism in Gloucester, 1540-1640' in P. Clark, A. G. R. Smith and N. Tyacke (eds.), *The English Commonwealth, 1547-1640* (1979), pp. 180-7; A. Fletcher, 'Factionalism in town and countryside: the significance of Puritanism and Arminianism', in D. Baker, (ed.), *Studies in Church History,* 16 (1979), pp. 297-300.

Michael Honywood and Lincoln Cathedral library

Naomi Linnell

In spite of civil war, of intense political upheaval, of religious strife, of the withering of University life and formal academic activity, seventeenth century England saw a flowering of poetry and prose, an outpouring of theology and polemic and an ever growing passion for building great collections of books, many to be given to the Universities and to the Church. In 1684, Bishop Morley bequeathed to the Dean and Chapter of Winchester his library of some two thousand volumes, many of them bought in Northern Europe during his Civil War exile. John Knightsbridge, rector of Spofforth in Yorkshire, left in 1677 his not inconsiderable collection of 400 books to the church of his native Chelmsford. This gift was to become the nucleus of the Cathedral's present collection. Wells Cathedral in 1661 had gathered in the library of the neighbouring St. Cuthbert's church, and by 1684 Dr. Richard Busby had given £300 to the Dean and Chapter so that '. . . the library . . . shall be repaired . . . and beautified, as the good Dr. Busby doth desire.' In the County Palatine of Durham, in 1672 Bishop John Cosin endowed what has become one of the most important Cathedral libraries in Europe. The chief benefactor of Ely Cathedral Library, Dean Robert Mapletoft, in his will proved in 1677 stated — 'I give to the Dean and Chapter of the Cathedral Church of Ely and their successors my library of books (the small reserves from the late plundering times with what I have since added to it)'.

It would seem that the priests and prelates of the Interregnum, as with one mind, occupied their enforced idleness and used their private wealth to indulge their passion for the collecting of books. After 1660, returned to a more public and accountable life, many of them gave their extraordinarily important libraries to their own churches and Cathedrals. Amongst the most noteworthy of them, although amongst the least noticed, was Michael Honywood, Dean of Lincoln from 1660 to 1681. Honywood was of particular importance because he not only gave his books to the Dean and Chapter, but also had built the gallery to house them.

To begin the story of this marvellous benefaction at its end: Draft Audit, Dean and Chapter of Lincoln, 1682 '. . . paid for removing the late Dean's books into the Library, 7s. 9d'.[1] Of the late Dean, a contemporary wrote –

> Honywood, Michael D. D. R[ector]. He was a gentleman of very considerable family, brother to Sir Thomas and Sir Peter Honywood of Kent, and one of the 377 descendants which his grandmother saw before she died. He was educated at Christ's College in Cambridge; where he was succcessively scholar, Fellow, Taxer in 1623, Proctor in 1628, and at length a Benefactor; and incorporate A. M. at Oxford in the year 1621. He was very ill used in the time of the Rebellion; insomuch that he went beyond the seas, about the year 1643, and lived at Utrecht during the persecution. In 1660, he was made Dean of Lincoln and died December 7, 1681, in the 85th year of his age. He was an holy and humble man, and a living library for learning; and hath left the Church of Lincoln a well built Library replenished with many rare books.[2]

The Honywood family owned extensive property in Charing, Kent and Marks Hall, Essex. Contemporary records of poor law assessments for Charing show Robert Honywood and his heir Thomas to have consistently been two of the most substantial landowners in the parish. Michael, the sixth son and ninth child of Sir Robert's second marriage, had no place in the management of the family estates, but their prosperity sent him to Cambridge, and to the start of his academic and ecclesiastical career.

Honywood's record at Christ's College was highly successful in University political terms, but not conspicuously scholarly. His extant unpublished writings, other than records of college and later Cathedral administration, amount to a few bad Latin verses and their translations. Published were two Latin odes of dubious quality included in the collection of elegies written to mourn the death of Edward King, one of Honywood's Cambridge friends, a collection famous now only for Milton's *Lycidas.*

Amongst his friends and students were scholars more distinguished than himself: Joseph Mede, fellow of Christ's, lecturer in Greek, mathematician, natural scientist and theologian; William Sancroft, fellow of Emmanuel, theologian and later to become Dean of St. Paul's and Archbishop of Canterbury; Herbert Thorndike, fellow of Trinity, linguist and theologian; John Milton, the poet, also apologist and political writer, and Edward King, fellow of Christ's, drowned in 1637. At the head of the title page of one of his books, Honywood wrote 'Ex dono E. King, ob. 1637'.

In this bookish and largely Royalist circle, Honywood prospered until the comfortable Cambridge world fell about his ears with the outbreak of civil war. In 1643 he fled to Leyden to join the ever increasing numbers of Royalist exiles in the Low Countries, and then to Utrecht where he lodged for a time with Sancroft, did a little teaching, and over the seventeen years of self-imposed exile bought himself a new library. He had left his first collection of books in his college, from where they were later redeemed for him, late in 1646, for £20, by his puritan brother Henry. He never lost touch with his friends or his college or wavered in his loyalty to them. For example, William Power of Christ's College wrote on August 12 1644 –

> Methinks it has been a long eclipse we have suffered in the non-sight of one and another: but we must be content till that which hinders be taken out of the way. I have often wished that either you were here with us, or we there with you; that we might once more enjoy one another before we die. Accept of this short scribbles as a testimony of my love, and so, honest Michael, farewell.
> Cambridge, this 12th of August, 1644.
> Tui, si quis alius vera amantissim J.G.P.[3]

Thomas Bainbridge, Master of Christ's, wrote to Honywood on at least four occasions between 1643 and 1646, often touching on the subject of his library –

> Aug. 14 1643. Yours from Leyden have reached me . . . they tell me indeed what I much desired to know, your welfare, as also what I never doubted, the truth of your affection; whereof my own is evidence sufficient to me, which would had done its best to keep you at home . . .

> Sept. 8 1645. Your Chamber Mr. Widdrington hath as his own, who is now in the South country. But I will write to him and tell him your desire . . . I presume Sir Thomas, your brother hath writ unto you how much I had to do to save [sic] in your pictures and I delivered all into his hands . . .

> May 10 1646. As yet they [the sequestrators] come not. For your books there are none to be found in the library; Mr. Widdrington saith Wilding hath disposed of them; he came home last week; . . . even now Johnson, the Leicester carrier, brings a note subscribed by the committees hands there for the sequestering of your library which hath hitherto been spared; whereupon I have written to your brother Colonel to give him notice that he may take some course for taking the sequestrators off before harvest. He was lately here . . . pray for your ever loving friend.[4]

> June 22 1646. Sir, I received yours of June 4, the 18 of the same; for the

income of your chamber, I find not the sequestrators very hot in pursuit. If they be, so shall wrangle as well as we can; for your books in the library Mr. Widdrington searched, but could find none, whereupon we conceived Mr. Wilding had disposed of them; who is gone into Wales to his father; . . . Leave these at Mr. Pepys his house in St. Bride's churchyard.[5]

The books were found during the next twelve months and were saved. The great importance of them to Honywood was clearly well known to his friends. His correspondence with Power and Bainbridge continued until the death of both in the autumn of 1646, and with Power's son William until at least the end of 1652.

The written record of Honywood's buying in the Low Countries is to be found in Lincoln Ms. 276, 'A catalogue of books bought for myself since my coming out of England, Jul. 6. st. n. 1643'. Books were entered alphabetically, folio 1 — A, folio 2 — B, and so on, mostly by author/title, with a note of the price paid in gilders and stivers. Usually the format was included and sometimes the place of publication and date. Two symbols 'X' and 'g.a.' were used to indicate books bought and then given away. The final leaves were used for entries of books sold, and books lent and to whom.

I have transcribed the whole of the buying part of the book, and some of the lending list, the last with some difficulty, as entries were crossed through as the books were returned. As far as I can tell (some entries are rather laconic, and a very few inaccurate) 1006 items were purchased, and the first 551 of these have been checked against the books on the Wren Library shelves. Of the 551 recorded in the Account Book, 73 were given away and one was sold. Of the titles no longer held in the Wren Library, some have not been identified at all, 'Op. Aug. in fol.', 'Bib. Hisp.', 'Hist. Ang. Lond.', for example. But many of those given away or missing since Honywood's death have been identified with some degree of accuracy, although multiplicities of editions of very popular works make absolute accuracy sometimes impossible. Of the 400 books positively identified as still held at Lincoln, only eight do not have the M monogram — Honywood's mark of ownership — and of these eight, two have lost their title page on which the monogram would have been written.

The Low Countries had long been the centre of the Northern European book-trade — there are extant records of auctions of manuscripts from the beginning of the fifteenth century — and Honywood had ample opportunity to indulge his interests and tastes with the money which obviously his family had no difficulty in sending him from England. He also had books sent to him from home — for example as in folio 28v *Antonini imperator* and *Anonymi . . . in Vet Test;* in folio 30v *Biblia Graeca;* and various items, all sent by W.H. and, in folio 13v, four works by Joseph Mede 'From London' — and no note of any price paid.

A closer look at the subjects and general areas of interest covered by the items recorded in the Account Book show Honywood to have been a man of considerable taste, and with wide fields of interest extending far beyond the classics and theology of his formal education. Particularly notable were the broadsides, some of them Dutch and French, mostly commenting on contemporary events and English political affairs. There were once three Caxtons — *Reynard* and *Jason* sold in 1811, and *Caton* sold in 1814 to T. F. Dibdin; there is the Ortelius *Theatrum Orbis Terrarum* published in 1584 and magnificently hand coloured, which cost twenty gilders, at least ten times more than the average price he paid for a single book; there is Camden's *Britannia* 'of the last edition' (1637), and again a very expensive book; the *Liber Castigationiis Puerorum Dei* and the *Vitas Patrum* published by Wynkyn de Worde in 1493 and 1495, both in their original Caxton binder covers; an illuminated thirteenth century manuscript of the scientific works of John of Holywood; the three volume *Atlas Novus* published in Amsterdam in 1638 by Jansonius and Hondius, with extra maps; four extremely rare printings of Dowland's *Ayres* and *Lachrimae;* the Irish Catechism published for Matthew Parker in Dublin in 1571; and the great 1630 Luther Bible, for which Honywood paid the highest price of all for a single volume — 29½ gilders. He bought a large number of foreign books including contemporary German, Swiss and Dutch theology — Luther, Calvin, Grotius, Arminius, Socinus — and also the Catholic apologists — Bellarmine, for example. He also indulged his literary tastes for poetry, 'romantic' history and philosophy, and for a few livelier items like the French translation of *Leycester's Commonwealth, Discours de la vie abominable, ruses, trahisons etc, de Robert Dudley,* an infamous sixteenth century libel thought to have been written by the Jesuit, Robert Parsons. To accompany these foreign language works he bought grammars and dictionaries and other foreign translations of English contemporary authors. There are also cookery books, mathematical works and medical books.

Ms. 276 represents only seventeen years of a long life-time of book buying, only a percentage of Honywood's total collection. To illustrate further his building of the whole library there is a letter, short enough, and unusual enough from this early period, to be quoted in full –

London Dec. 14th 1674.

Reverend Sir,

I have herewith sent you those books which you wrote for, the prices are usually mentioned in the Catalogue of Books which is the reason I did not particularise them in my letter; but shall be certain to remember to do it for the future as I have here underwritten. Next Thursday you may expect a post letter of news from me. I thought your brother had often wrote to you of that subject, otherwise I should have put you to the charge of a post letter, especially when news is most considerable. Mr. Wood of Oxon. lately published an excellent history of that University and remarks upon all those gentlemen of most note of the several colleges there. The price of it is 30s. in large folio. Sir Winston Churchill also lately published an History of all the Kings of England from Brute to 1660, with the coats of arms in copper of all the Kings thereof. It is in folio, price 12s. Dr. Brevint likewise lately wrote an excellent book against the Church of Rome, which sells well. Its in 8° price 4s. I only mention those three books because they are of most note. The author of *The Whole Duty of Man* hath published nothing since the *Government of the Tongue.* He is now said to be one Mr. Woodard, aged about 60 years, and lives principally upon his own estate in Yorkshire. I forgot what college he was of in Oxon. I humbly remain your most humble servant,

Chr: Wilkinson.

[Here follows the account for books already sent.]

November 30th.	1 Catalogue of Books sent and paid carriage	0. 0. 4
December 10th.	Paid post for the letter received	0. 0. 3
December 14th.	1 Cave's *Primitive Christianity*	0. 6. 0
	1 Cressy's *Epistle Apologetical*	0. 1. 0
	1 Stillingfleet's *Reply* 8° calf's leather	0. 5. 0
	1 Bp Cosin's *Histor. Transubst. Pap.*	0. 2. 0
	1 Catalogus librorum Lat.	0. 0. 6
	1 General Catal. of books	0. 4. 0

Total sum of 0. 19. 1

[Postscript]

Most of the books of note printed after his Majesty's Restoration, have been finer reprinted and included in the General Catalogue of Books.[6]

Amongst many others, three points of bibliographical and book trade history interest arise from this letter. Wilkinson's apology for having neglected to put Honywood on his mailing list, and the reason for having not done so show a proper regard for business expenses, unlike the haphazard mailing habits of modern publishing houses. Rather more important are the titles Wilkinson chose to advertise — Daniel Brevint's work on the Roman Mass was a major work of contemporary Anglican theology, Anthony Wood's *History and*

Antiquities of Oxford and Sir Winston Churchill's *Divi Britannici* were well produced scholarly books of interest to all readers, clerical or lay. The imprint of the Churchill has the date 1675 — Wilkinson was indulging in advance publicity perhaps. Thirdly, the list of books in the account at the end of the letter, which Honywood had already ordered, was very much in the proper and orthodox tradition of an Anglican Cathedral library: Cave's *Primitive Christianity,* Cosin's attack on the Roman doctrine of the Mass, and Edward Stillingfleet's answer to Serenus Cressy's [i.e. the Jesuit, Hugh Paulin's] *Epistle Apologetical* — all good Protestant/Anglican reading, both the Cosin and the Stillingfleet with a 1675 imprint.

Wilkinson continued to send Honywood his catalogues. Lincoln Rr.2.1., which is a collection of catalogues from various London booksellers, includes one of 1680 from Wilkinson and his partner Samuel Crouch: *A catalogue of two choice and considerable libraries, etc.* and there is no reason to suppose that Honywood did not continue to buy from him — Wilkinson would hardly have continued to incur the charges of a post letter for six years if there was no money to be made out of it.

There are two questions which must be asked. Did Michael Honywood actually read his books, and do they then give us an accurate picture of the learning and interests of a late seventeenth century English Dean? I am not wholly sure. Was he a scholar of wide interests and accomplishment, or did he just like books and was he fortunate enough to have sufficient private income to indulge his hobby and fill his bookshelves?

Comparisons with the catalogues of other seventeenth century collectors do not really help to answer these questions. An examination of Pepys's catalogue shows him to have amassed a not dissimilar collection. Amongst his library was a considerable number of books relating to naval affairs, and his personal tastes were closer to the theatre and to the bawdy than were Honywood's, but otherwise there is a notable similarity of author and subjects. Not that Honywood was without the human touch — Lincoln still holds his copy of Aretino's *Ragionamenti,* scandalous enough even to the sixteenth century earthy attitude to sex to have been published with a false imprint. When Honywood bought this book, we do not know — a young man's fancy, or an old man's dream . . .

Pepys's own reaction to Honywood is interesting. Two avid collectors, both men of substance and influential in their own part of society, might have been expected to achieve some sympathy between each other. Peter Honywood lodged with Pepys's brother, Tom, and he, brother Henry and Michael visited Pepys a number of times during the years between 1662 and 1664. Letters from Michael Honywood were sent to Pepys's house for dispatch during Honywood's period of exile. Pepys did not find the brothers ideal guests and Michael especially bothered him –

> Jan. 13 1662. Before 12 o'clock comes by appointment Mr. Peter and the Dean and Colonel Honywood, brothers, to dine with me. But so soon that I was troubled at it . . . but the dinner [did] not please me, and less the Dean and Colonel, whom I find to be pitiful sorry gentlemen, though good-natured.
> June 1 1663. To my brother's, where I dined (being invited) with Mr. Peter and Dean Honywood — where Tom did give us a very pretty dinner — and we very pleasant but not very merry, the Dean being but a weak man, though very good.
> June 3 1663. Up betimes and studying of my double horizontal dial [an instrument for astronomical calculation] against Dean Honywood comes to me, who dotes mightily upon it and I think I must give it him.
> June 4 1663. By and by comes Dean Honywood and I showed him my double horizontal dial and promise to give him one, and that shall be it.
> Aug 6 1664. And here lay Dean Honywood last night: I met and talked with him this morning, and a simple priest he is, though a good well-meaning man.
> June 29 1664. By water to Westminster to see Dean Honywood, whom I had not visited a great while. He is a good nature, but a very weak man; yet a Dean and a man in great esteem.[7]

Pepys was a generous man both in hospitality and friendship. He appreciated wit and learning, he loved company and good conversation, but although he gave much to the acquisitive Dean of Lincoln, including the sought after double horizontal dial, he got little back in return. The conversation did not flow and Pepys was puzzled, I think, by a man who was 'good', 'in great esteem', well meaning, fascinated by the astronomical calculator, but who was to Pepys so obviously dull. If Pepys, who knew him well, could offer no explanation for this, who can? The portrait of Honywood which hangs in the Wren Library shows a face quiet and observant, and extremely withdrawn, a man who fundamentally lacked something. Honywood had achieved some academic success, as an administrator he was extremely able, he enjoyed the care of a close-knit family, but appreciation of and sensitivity to poetry, to drama, to music, to philosophy, to emotion showed only in his choice of books.

There are, however, at least two pieces of evidence for Honywood's interest in what would now be called textual bibliography and in contemporary scholarship. First, excerpts from another letter to Dean Honywood –

> Sir, your letter was exceeding welcome . . . Mr. Mede's conjecture upon Gog and Magog was printed with the second impression of the *Key of the Apocalypse* bound up at . . . the end thereof. Examine your book, and if it be not there, I will either get you a sheet or have it transcribed for you . . . His *Respons. Epistol-arii ad Ludovicum de Dieu* is imperfectly printed in his *Opuscula* set out at Cambridge . . . *Opuscula Latine . . . Cambridge: T. Buck, 1652*. In my former letter I have signified the author of Mr. Mede's life to be Dr. Dow . . . yet was it supervised and additions put thereto by Mr. Brereley . . . His additions are, that passage in the fifth leaf of (Zz) touching the influence which the celestial luminaries have on subluminary bodies; which after the italic begins thus . . . In the fourth leaf of Aaa that whole passage beginning at a break thus . . . *The Ending of Unchristian Animadversions* was also Mr. Brereley's . . . However it will please God to dispose of me I know not; but so long as I have any being, I am, and shall continue your true friend to serve you. 28th of Sept 1657, J.C. [8]

The identity of the writer has been difficult to trace — J.C. could have been the initials of more than a dozen of Honywood's contemporary fellows at Oxford and Cambridge, but none of these was of the right persuasion, the right age, in the right place at the right time. The most likely candidate was John Cheyney, a very distinguished Anglican divine whose life's work was to publish extraordinarily abusive pamphlets against the Quakers. His initials do appear at the end of the introduction to the collected sermons of Mede's editor, Brereley, and the *British Library Catalogue of Printed Books* has entered his name with a question mark. This is the slimmest of evidence, but it is all that is known at the moment. But, whoever the author of the letter was, it is the communication of one scholarly man to another whom he obviously knew or believed to be receptive to such analysis and comments.

Second, and much more significant, was Honywood's relationship with Richard Crakanthorp. Crakanthorp was an Anglican — a staunch Anglican — with a highly developed puritan theology. He taught at Oxford and was theologian, philosopher and apologist for the established Church. Honywood owned copies of most of his published works, and two of those still held at Lincoln have the inscription 'Sum Michaelis Honywood, ex dono Authoris'. Honywood's copy of Crakanthorp's *Logicae libri quinque,* published in 1622, is one of the most interesting books in the Cathedral library, for it contains emendations, corrections and comments by both Honywood and the author.[9] The other small volume which Crakanthorp gave to Honywood, his *Introductio in Metaphysicam* published in 1619, was also corrected by him before it was sent. And again it reflects the esteem in which Honywood was held by his distinguished and scholarly friend.

Whatever his claims or otherwise to scholarship, whatever his motives for collecting, of Honywood's care for his books there can be no doubt. The meticulous accounting, the binding up of his own important items — the Byrd part books, for example — and his concern for the order and housing of Lincoln Cathedral's library in the 1660s all bear witness to this. Honywood was installed as Dean of Lincoln on October 12 1660. He was faced with a daunting situation: a dilapidated Cathedral and close, no choir, no organist, an enormous diocese where, over seventeen years, Cathedral and decanal rights had been largely eroded, and — perhaps the least of the Dean's troubles — a dilapidated fifteenth century library room never adequately repaired since the fire in the early part of the century. Some time in the 1660s Honywood made a copy of the Recorder of Lincoln, Charles Dallison's text of an *Appeal for the Fabric Fund* –

> The joys and comforts, which God of his infinite mercy bestowed upon this kingdom and people, by that happy restoration of his sacred Majesty to his just right and government, are inexpressible . . . Due consideration taken hereof, prudent men will find it a duty incumbent upon them, vigorously, with heart and hand, to endeavour the continuation of these blessings . . . For our religion, it is too apparent, that the carrayer *[sic]* thereof in the late sad times were not satiated by their abolishing (as much as in them lay) the doctrine and discipline of the Church of England; but (driving at root and branch) the churches and buildings erected, built and dedicated for the service of God (especially the Cathedrals) must down . . . most of the Cathedrals escaped total destruction, yet many of them miserably rent, torn and defaced. And particularly the Cathedral Church of the blessed Virgin Mary of Lincoln, and that not only, but the dwelling house and habitations of the churchmen, the vicars, the singingmen, and other officers belonging to that Cathedral, pulled down, and the materials sold, and converted to profane uses . . . the present Dean and Chapter of Lincoln have, out of their own purses, not only begun the work but have made some progress therein; nor do they want affections to pursue, and would themselves finish it, if the rents and profits of the church, or their own private fortunes would complete it. But having exhausted themselves, they find it impossible without assistance to finish that blessed work: and upon these grounds they implore the consideration and assistance of all such as shall voluntarily contribute hereunto.[10]

By December 5 a choir of seven men and five boys had been formed.

Some initial problems were caused by the alcoholic tendencies of the new organist, Mr. Mudd. A letter sent on March 16 1662 from the precentor, John Featley, to Honywood stated –

> Sir, Although I wrote to you on Saturday last yet I must trouble you with another letter. Yesterday Mr. Mudd showed the effect of his last week's tippling. For when Mr. Joynes was in the midst of his sermon, Mudd fell asinging aloud, in so much as Mr. Joynes was compelled to stop. All the auditors gazed and wondered what was the matter, and at length some near him stopping his mouth silenced him, and then Mr. Joynes proceeded. But this continued for the space of near half a quarter of an hour, so that now we dare trust him no longer with our organ. [11]

A new and totally undistinguished Dutch organist, Dr. Hecht, was engaged, and divine service was sung properly and decently again in the Cathedral. On May 11 1661 the Chapter had voted £1,000 'of lawful money of England towards the repairing of the Cathedral Church of Lincoln which is to be put in the chest of the common chamber', and in 1662 a memorandum was sent to the Archbishop of Canterbury, a copy of which survives — 'Expended by the residentiaries in common and equally for the fabric of the Cathedral Church out of their purses £1,000 . . . in all £5,302. Divided by four, to each £1,258.' Honywood always seemed to have enjoyed sums, as other of his papers show. A note at the end of the memo reads — 'Besides, the needful reparations of the cloister will ask £300' — very significant for the future of the library.

In 1660 the Dean and Chapter library consisted of somewhat less than 100 manuscripts and little else. On September 20 1662 the Common Council of the City of Lincoln, meeting in the Guildhall, decreed as follows –

> Dean and Chapter books: whereas we are informed from the Dean and Chapter of Lincoln that they having their library called great St. Mary's formerly in the unhappy war plundered, some books of which library is conceived by them to be in our custody, it is therefore propounded and enacted that the said Dean and Chapter shall have a view of what books are in the school library and such of them as they shall sufficiently make appear did belong to their library to be forthwith restored unto them. [12]

The recovery of these 600 or so items from what Sir Francis Hill suggested to me was the Greyfriars school, was effected. Item in the Fabric Accounts for 1662/3 –

> Several disbursements. Imprimis for the fetching of three loads of books from the schoolhouse below the hill to the Common Chamber at 1s. 6d. the load, 4s. 6d. [13]

The titles were listed by the Dean himself in Lincoln Ms. 296. This is a list of approximately 650 volumes, in Honywood's hand, entered by author and/or title and with date of publication and a preceding mark of class or arrangement — possibly designation of press or classis in the Greyfriars school library. The first 31 entries from this list have been checked against the shelves of the Wren Library: 25 are still in Lincoln, four have been positively identified, but are no longer at Lincoln, two are unidentifiable. A fair copy of this list was made in 1668 — Lincoln Ms. 251 — by a clerk of the Common Chamber when the old fifteenth century library was brought back into use. The same hand had recorded in the Fabric Accounts for 1668 –

> For ordering and cleansing the library: and for the wages of labourers and servants employed in it £1 10s. 0d.[14]

The entries, made in a very stylish and individual formal hand, include details of 'classis', 'book' or 'bundle' — that is shelf or trough, and each volume's position within it. The contents of these two manuscripts, the significance of which has never been considered before (Ms. 296 is not included in Anne Reade's *Checklist of . . . catalogues . . . relating to the Cathedral Libraries of England)*, should make it possible to reconstruct both the contents and physical arrangement of the Cathedral library before Honywood's building of the Wren library and the bequest of his own magnificent collection to the Dean and Chapter. The first eight and ten pages of the two manuscripts show a library of writings of the Early Fathers of the Church, Bibles, liturgy and other works generally found in early seventeenth century parochial and Cathedral libraries. If Michael Honywood's personal collection had not been added to it in 1682 Lincoln Cathedral library would not be of such outstanding interest today.

Not only did Honywood amass the great collection of printed books and manuscripts which he bequeathed to the Dean and Chapter, but he also had built and furnished a magnificent gallery to house their library –

> May 18, 1674.
> Memorandum that an agreement was made to be expressed more fully in articles hereafter to be made between Mr. Dean of Lincoln and Mr. Evison wherein Mr. Evison did undertake to build the library over the decayed cloister according to Mr. Surveyor's direction and Mr. Thompson's model, and to cover it by the feast of St. Martin Bishop next ensuing or as much before as he can. For which works, Mr. Dean does undertake to pay Mr. Evison seven hundred and fourscore pounds.
> It is also agreed that the said Mr. Evison must for the same sum and within the same bargain make a staircase at the West end of the building according to his own model, and the entrance into the old library at the East end, with steps and rails and banisters, and folding doors, and when

he covers the roof with lead make leaden spouts necessary for the conveyance of water.

Transacted in the presence of
William Wyatt, pr[ecentor]
Samuel Fuller, chan[cellor]
James Gardiner, Subdean[15]

This, the first item in a bundle taken from the muniments of the Dean and Chapter of Lincoln, is the opening of the story, albeit a brief and incomplete one, of the reconstruction of the North cloister arcade and the stone shell of the Wren library, its furnishing and decoration. Light is thrown on contemporary building practices, on prices, and here and there is a glimpse of the men who actually did the work. This is the first of a group of papers which I believe to be Michael Honywood's personal file concerned with what was to be his most permanent memorial in Lincoln Cathedral — the great stone arcade in the cloister and the marvellous gallery above it which houses the Dean and Chapter's priceless collection of early printed books and Medieval manuscripts. On the reverse of this short memorandum, in Honywood's writing, is its date, May 18 1674, and a brief statement and estimate of how the £780 was to be spread out in instalments over the next seven months. How widely established payment by instalment was by the end of the seventeenth century is not known, but there is nothing in the text of the memorandum or in the subsequent legal agreements to suggest that this was in any way an unusual practice, and no sign of interest being charged on the extended payments. Another agreement made earlier in 1673 between the Dean and Chapter and Evison for repairs to the Cathedral choir also prescribes payment on the instalment system — four quarterly payments of £30 and two further of £20 each.

For his part, in the 1674 agreement, Evison contracted to make good damage to Cathedral property, and to remove builder's rubbish, provide specified materials, make proper drainage pipes and spouts and to follow in every detail Wren's directions and Thompson's model. He also agreed [c. 10] −

He doth covenant and promise to and with the said Dr. Honywood, that he will maintain the stone wall with arches and pillars upright and good for ten years, that is against such defects as may proceed from ill workmanship or bad materials and no other.[16]

This has a curiously modern sound about it.

Another file had begun. During the two years from 1674 to 1676, eleven more documents were added — or, rather, eleven more remain

— others may well have been included, and subsequently lost. Those extant include the lawyer's indented articles for 1674 for the building of the shell of the library and staircases, those of 1676, for the construction of shelves and panelling the new gallery. There are bills and estimates for painting and gilding, and for the measure of wood to be used by Evison in the library interior, and memoranda from the Chapter clerk's office.

Two of the most interesting items are from 1676. First, a letter from Sir Christopher Wren to the Subdean, James Gardiner, listing the rates for gilding and painting, which gives precise details of the original decoration of the library. For example –

> Veined work like black and white marble . . . Veined like walnut tree or Indian woods, well performed . . . Ranse marble and Indian woods extraordinarily well done so as to deceive the eye and be taken for natural.

Since the early nineteenth century when the marbled panels were refurbished in their original style, the library has been painted several times, but no account has been taken of the original architect's intentions.[17] The second item is a page of notes made by Honywood, a list of measurements and costs apparently checking Evison's estimates and measurements for the wood he used. It gives us yet another example of the Dean's carefulness and attention to detail, which are shown throughout his life and faithfully mirrored in all his papers. There was incidentally a discrepency of 1s. 7½d. between the original estimate and the painter's final bill — £61 6s. 1d. instead of the £61 4s. 5½d. endorsed by Honywood. But there is no record of any lasting dispute.

By the end of 1676, Michael Honywood had paid for the building and furnishing of the great Wren library the not inconsiderable sum of £1,030 8s. 8½d. Of this, £780 had already been paid in 1674, and, since I believe the file Ciii/31/1 in the records of the Dean and Chapter of Lincoln to have been Michael Honywood's private collection of library records which would only have become part of the official muniments after his death in 1681, it seems that Honywood paid the balance of £250 8s. 8½d. to Evison and to the painter, Thomas Rowley, out of his own funds. The Fabric Accounts of 1676 did record a payment made to Mr. Evison of £5 4s. 0d. 'for work done above cloisters and old library,'[18] but I have been unable to find any other evidence of the Chapter either corporately or individually contributing to the building expenses of the Dean and Chapter's library. Michael Honywood was only one of the many seventeenth century bibliophiles who so well enriched the Cathedrals and parish churches of England, but the story of his benefaction should be given its due credit and his memory should be held in the same high esteem as that of his illustrious friends and contemporaries — Morley, Matthew, Cosin, and the other bright stars in the murky firmament of seventeenth century church and politics.

NOTES

This paper was first published in *The Library* (June 1983) and was based on an earlier version read at the Lincoln Cathedral Colloquium on December 4 1981. Acknowledgement is made to the Dean and Chapter of Lincoln for permission to quote from Dean and Chapter muniments.

1. L[incolnshire] A[rchives] O[ffice], Bj/4/1.
2. J. Walker, *An attempt towards recovering an account of the numbers and suffering of the clergy of the Church of England, etc.* (1714), pt. 2, p. 269.
3. LAO, Dvij/3/B(3).
4. *Ibid.,* B(1).
5. *Ibid.,* B(9).
6. *Ibid.,* Dvij/1/65.
7. *The Diary of Samuel Pepys,* ed. R. C. Latham and W. Matthews (1970–83), 3, p. 9, 4, pp. 167, 171-2, 173, 5, pp. 233, 192.
8. LAO, Dvij/70.
9. For an account of this book and of Honywood's scholarly relationship with Crakanthorp, see N. Linnell, 'A unique copy of Richard Crakanthorp's *Logic*', *The Library,* VI, 4 (1982), pp. 323-6.
10. LAO, Dvij/2/19.
11. *Ibid.,* Dvij/1/5.
12. *Ibid.,* L/1/1/1/6.
13. *Ibid.,* Bj/1/8.
14. *Ibid.,* Bj/1/9.
15. *Ibid.,* Ciij/31/1.
16. *Ibid.*
17. In the 1980s the Library was redecorated in a style which reflected Wren's original intentions.
18. LAO, Bij/1/8.

Norwich Cathedral under Dean Prideaux, 1702–24

Patrick Mussett

Humphrey Prideaux became a prebendary of Norwich in 1681. In 1688 he became Archdeacon of Suffolk as well, and in 1702 he vacated his prebend on becoming Dean. He died on November 1 1724. His biography[1] portrays him as dominating the Norwich Chapter from the moment of his installation in 1681, imposing efficient administration and firm management on a Cathedral which was being run in a very lax fashion. This paper sets out to investigate the topics of the alleged laxity of administration at Norwich before Prideaux, his efforts to raise standards and the personal characteristics which enabled him to achieve improvement.

Was Norwich Cathedral run in a lax fashion before Prideaux's time? The Benedictine chapter at Norwich had never been distinguished by any remarkable virtues,[2] and when in May 1538 a royal charter[3] transformed the Convent into a secular Chapter there was a greater degree of continuity of personnel than in any other of Henry VIII's New Foundations: every monk of Norwich was given a place in the new community.

Thirty years after its foundation the secular Cathedral was facing serious problems, and in 1568 Bishop Parkhurst and five others commissioned by the Queen to visit the Cathedral reported their findings.[4] They had had to disentangle a good deal of conflicting testimony, and had not been helped by Dean Salisbury's sudden departure for London on what was said to be church business. The Dean had taken with him Edward VI's patent of refoundation, even though the commissioners had only just begun reading it; this patent had turned the 1538 community into a standard New Foundation Cathedral on the lines of Rochester or Peterborough, for example. The commissioners could find no statutes,[5] no proper record of Chapter decisions and no accounts for the timber or lead from three major buildings, two of them demolished and one, the Lady Chapel, recently collapsed. Three of the six prebendaries were not priests. There was no divinity lecturer, and no copy of the Bible or the *Paraphrases* in the church. The Cathedral plate ought to have weighed 271 oz. but weighed only 19½ oz. The library was not properly cared for, slackness in attendance at sermons was very common, and there was a tippling house in the close. The important financial posts of receiver and treasurer, which should have been held by prebendaries, had been given to John Hoo, a layman whose friendship with the Dean's wife had given rise to a graffito on the cloister wall reading, 'My Lord Dean is a very cuckold, witness John Hoo.' There were a few other minor points. Yet in spite of this visitation the Queen still had reason for complaint as soon as 1570.[6]

In 1613 the prebendaries wrote to Dr. Thomas Ridley, Vicar General to Archbishop Abbot, explaining that they could not submit to the Archbishop's visitation as by Edward VI's foundation they could not be visited by anyone not commissioned by the Crown. They were willing nevertheless to reply to Ridley's enquiries, and confessed that only one prebendary, Hugh Castleton, was resident, although Edmund Suckling and Nicholas Bate lived only five and twenty miles away respectively and so were able to take some share in church business. The other three prebendaries seldom or never came to Norwich, and Dean Montgomerie, Bishop of Meath and of Clogher, had visited Norwich only four times in eleven years. Because of the Dean's absence and the cost of communicating with him they were sometimes unable to get authority from him to deal with pressing business, and as a result suitors and tenants were sometimes not given satisfaction, 'which much grieveth us.' The Dean's absence also made impossible an annual audit; the last audit had dealt with three years' accounts and had taken place three years before. The Chapter owed at least £1,600, and of this debt £400 was the fault of the Dean, who at the end of an audit which had shown a deficit of about £255 had demanded £400 for himself for his trouble and expenses in church business and had offered to resign the deanery if paid the £400. Chapter had given in to his demand, but he had not resigned.[7]

The criticisms of the Dean and Chapter of Norwich produced by Archbishop Laud's Vicar General in 1635 were routine and modest;[8] it was a rare Cathedral which could live up to Laud's standards.

In the late 1660s the Cathedral was again suffering under a difficult

Dean, John Crofts. Violence was Dean Crofts' special fault. On one occasion, having during service in the Cathedral, 'in the presence of a great congregation', hit one of the sub-sacrists on the mouth, he offered his victim money on condition that he would fight with him. More relevantly to our theme, he often acted without Chapter's consent, kept the Chapter records to himself, received rents and fines personally, employed workmen without consulting the treasurer and obstructed business by preventing the sealing of leases agreed to by himself and the Chapter and paid for by the tenants.[9]

The Dean and Chapter's reply to Archbishop Sheldon's circular of 1670 asking what they had spent since the Restoration on the fabric, gifts to the King and other worthy causes admits to one very serious problem in that 'a very great part of the lands are out on leases which will not determine until about 50 years hence.'[10] An examination of the Chapter's Private Register shows that 'a very great part' is an exaggeration, but investigations in the 1670s and 1680s revealed eleven properties most of whose leases were not due to expire until the eighteenth century and two which would not fall into the Chapter's hands before the twenty-first century.[11]

Norwich does indeed seem to have been a Cathedral inclined to run into difficulties.[12] Its prebendaries were a small body, numbering only six, tending to non-residence and therefore often hardly out-numbering the Dean. Perhaps the support of a strong bishop would have helped, but at the critical moments in the Chapter's history between 1538 and Prideaux's appointment the bishops of Norwich were not strong figures. Was this somewhat accident-prone Cathedral any worse than other Cathedrals of its time? A definitive answer must wait for further research, but for comparisons with Norwich the natural places to look are the other Henrician foundations or re-foundations with Chapters as small as that of Norwich: Bristol, Chester, Gloucester, Peterborough, Rochester. For Bristol and Rochester I have been able to read the Chapter Acts from the Restoration until the early eighteenth century, for Chester we have Archdeacon Burne's study, for Gloucester the *Victoria County History* and an article by Dean Evans, and for Peterborough Gunton's volume, the *Victoria County History* and the editions of records published by Mr. Mellows;[13] although these published records of the Peterborough Chapter are all from the sixteenth century they help to confirm the impression given for the seventeenth century by Gunton and the *Victoria History*. These sources all suggest that Norwich was a more troubled Cathedral than its obvious comparisons, even allowing for the fact that a Cathedral with a large surviving collection of archives, such as those at Norwich, is likely to reveal more of its past difficulties than a Cathedral whose surviving records are less full.

How did Prideaux tackle Norwich's problems? According to the *Life*[14] there were no rentals or treasurer's books to provide a guide to the receipt of rents and the payment of salaries, wages and stipends, and the resultant inadequate information enabled the seniors to impose on the juniors. Norwich had had rentals and treasurer's books in the 1620s and 1630s,[15] but after the Commonwealth a new series of rentals begins only in 1683, not long after Prideaux's arrival. These new rentals adopted an alphabetical arrangement of properties, instead of using the old pre-Commonwealth order.

Rentals and treasurer's books are necessary tools of tidy administration, but since they record income and expenditure of fixed amounts it is hard to see how their absence enables the senior members of Chapter to impose on the junior. A more fruitful source of opportunities for malpractice was in the choice of tenants for the better parts of the Cathedral's estates and in the negotiations about the fines to be paid by tenants for their leases. The Norwich estates were let, like almost all ecclesiastical estates up to the 1850s, on long leases at low and static annual rents, with the Chapter making up some of the gap between these low rents and the full annual value by taking a fine each time a lease was renewed. By the late seventeenth century the establishing of the proper level for a fine was in principle a matter of almost mechical routine. The gross annual value of the property was ascertained and the rent deducted to give a net annual value. In fixing the fine allowance was made for the fact that the Chapter gained by being paid in advance. Thus if the Chapter were paid a rent of £10 *per annum* for a property worth £50 *per annum,* then over a 21 year period they would need £840 (21 times the difference between £50 and £10) to make up the balance; but if the tenant paid £840 in a lump at the beginning of the period then the Chapter, by investing such part of the £840 as was not needed immediately to make up one year's rent to the full annual value, could make a profit. And so it was customary to make allowance, at a set interest rate, for this potential investment. A very common interest rate towards the end of the seventeenth century was £11 11s. 8¼d.% (about 11.6% in modern terminology), and a tenant taking out a new 21 year lease with this interest rate allowed would pay for his fine just over 7¾ times the difference between his annual rent and the full annual value of the property. If after seven years of his lease had expired he renewed it he would be required, if the 11.6% interest rate were again employed, to pay a fine equal to one year's difference between the rent and the full annual value. This may seem a very small amount to cover the difference between the rent and the annual value over a period of seven years, but it must be remembered that in renewing his lease the tenant was surrendering a lease with fourteen years left in it and receiving a new 21 year lease in exchange, and so the period to be covered by the fine was only the last seven years of that new period and would begin fourteen years after the date of the renewal.

The Norwich Chapter in the late seventeenth century used the £11 11s. 8¼d. interest rate in setting fines for almost all their 21 year leases; the use of this rate, much higher than the then general level of interest rates for reasonably safe investments, represented not a conscious decision that such a rate was the most appropriate but rather a following of a custom dating from the period of high interest rates around 1600. Fines were normally, at Norwich as elsewhere, expressed in some such words as 'one year's value', this value being the property's annual net worth to the tenant, assuming that he was able to sub-let it for its full value and that he paid the Chapter's rent out of that income. Printed tables of fines were published, under the name of Sir Isaac Newton as well as of lesser mathematical luminaries, and in 1711 the Norwich Chapter seem to have begun using the tables in Edward Hatton's newly-published *An Index to Interest*. Tables from some other source were copied into the front of the Private Register, presumably at its inception in 1682; some of these tables are quite anonymous, but some are said to be taken from Mr. Pearson and to be used by other Chapters. Mr. Pearson's work does not seem to have been published. A powerful and confident Chapter, as at Durham, might often require and receive a fine at the correct level.[16] At Norwich a document which may be unique among Cathedral archives shows how very often the fine received fell well below the amount set. This document is the Private Register, created by Prideaux in 1682[17] but containing as much information as Prideaux could collect about capitular leases from December 1660. For a number of years Prideaux kept the Private Register in his own hand, recording the date of each lease renewal, the name of the tenant, the nature and location of the property, the date of the previous lease, the amount of the rent and, where possible, the gross annual value. There follows a note of the correct amount of the fine, the fine paid and the reason for any difference between the two. This reason is often stated very briefly, as in December 1700 when Alice Harwood, widow, came to renew her 40 year lease of three tenements in the Cathedral close. Her previous lease dated from December 1686 and so the fine, on the 8% interest-rate table then used at Norwich for 40 year leases of urban housing, ought to have been one year's net value. The gross value was ascertained very easily, as Mrs. Harwood was known to sub-let the tenements for a total of £12 *per annum*. The rent paid to the Chapter was 6s. 8d. *per annum,* plus two fat hens or 2s., and so the net annual value was £11 11s. 4d. and the fine should also have been £11 11s. 4d. But a fine of only £10 was set and paid, since Mrs. Harwood was a daughter of John Hassall, Dean of Norwich 1628–54. [18]

Similarly, when in December 1709 Thomas Pyle of King's Lynn, clerk, came to renew his 21 year lease of land in Outwell, Upwell and Welney his fine on the 11.6% table should have been 1¼ times the net annual value, as his previous lease had run for eight years. The property was 150 acres of marshland, situated in the Fens and therefore liable to great expenditure on maintenance of banks, dikes and drains. The annual value, after allowing for this expenditure, was no more than £20. Deducting £4 for the rent paid to the Chapter left a net annual value of £16 and so the fine should have been £20, but only £12 was taken –

> The tenant being a clergyman of worth and lecturer at Lynn where the Dean and Chapter are patrons abatement was made him on this account. [19]

Sometimes a long and detailed account is made necessary by the unco-operative behaviour of a tenant over quite a small amount. In June 1700 Henry Framingham of King's Lynn, merchant, having bought the tenant's interest in Fring rectory from Lady Purbeck, whose lease from the Chapter was dated December 1696, came and told the Chapter that he wanted –

> to have it [the lease of the rectory] in his own name and therefore paid an half fine [viz. half of one year's net value] for it, that is £20. It was objected that to renew at three years and a half is not worth an half fine which we readily acknowledged but told him if he renewed for half it would be to our prejudice to renew it till seven years are expired for then we must have a whole fine that is £40 for the renewal and if he had a desire to renew it now he must do it on such terms as would not be to our damage or else leave it alone till the seven years are expired there being no reason we should damage ourselves to please him but since by his lease he had the recommendation of the curate we offered that if he

would quit that we would abate him £10 . . . but this he would not do
. . . although he covenants with us to pay the curate £20 *per annum* he
hath contracted with the present curate for £15 *per annum* and so puts
the other £5 fraudulently into his own pocket.[20]

Framingham, a baker who had made good and become an alderman
of King's Lynn and sheriff of Norfolk, was disliked by Prideaux as
being a miser and a parvenu with social ambitions.[21]

In both the choice of tenants and the results of negotiations about
fines one can see in the Norwich archives the expression of various
preferences and some weaknesses. Favour is shown to the corporation
of Norwich in their capacity as managers of the Boys' Hospital,[22] and
occasionally to neighbours in the close, particularly when, as in
December 1708, they had to deal with a neighbour who was 86 years
old and bore the surname Townshend; 'the Chapter thought fit to deal
tenderly with him.'[23] More frequent beneficiaries of the Chapter's
kindness were clergymen, such as Edward Beckham, who in 1695 was
allowed to renew his lease of Barford rectory, the fine for which should
properly have been £44, for £10. The Private Register notes that he is
'a Dr. of Divinity and not in so good circumstances in the world as his
degree and worth do deserve.'[24] Chapter employees were also
sometimes favoured, and the relatives of members of Chapter;[25] this
last group may be larger than is realised, as it is only helpful asides in
the Private Register which make it clear that Mrs. Alice Harwood, a
tenant of property in the close, is a daughter of John Hassall, a former
Dean, and that the Rev. Mr. Croshold, the tenant of West Beckham
rectory, is the son-in-law of prebendary John Hildyard.[26]

Tenants who improved their Chapter leaseholds by building or
rebuilding were also treated favourably in that at the first renewal after
any such improvement the resulting increase in the value of the
property was ignored in the setting of the fine. This policy was
obviously necessary to avoid discouraging tenants from improving, and
it was a policy adopted by a number of other Cathedral Chapters.[27]

A particularly prominent family in the Norwich Chapter archives in
the late seventeenth and early eighteenth centuries are the Astleys. It
has recently been pointed out that Herbert Astley, Dean of Norwich
1670–81, was born the son of Herbert Ashley in Plymouth and went
to the trouble of adopting the name of his Norfolk relatives.[28] The
Astleys were already important tenants of the Cathedral before Herbert
Astley became a member of Chapter; in 1662 Sir Jacob Astley renewed
a 21 year lease of Hindolveston manor and rectory which had been last

renewed in 1648.[29] Herbert Astley's other Norfolk relatives were the Hobarts, the family from whom came his wife Barbara. The Hobarts also had been Chapter tenants since at least the 1640s.[30] The first occasion on which the Astley interest came into conflict with the Chapter's interest was in 1680, when Dean Astley's wife, a difficult woman with a temper bad enough for it to be rumoured that she had beaten a footboy to death –

> apprehending the Dean her husband to be in a dying condition got as many leases as she could to be renewed even at any rate rather than lose her share in the fines which were to be paid for them.[31]

This accusation is made by Humphrey Prideaux and may be exaggerated; Prideaux does not substantiate it in detail by his accounts of leases renewed in 1680, and he was not a member of the Norwich Chapter until 1681, but the story does at the least point to a weakness in the position of any Chapter granting beneficial leases. There are likely to be occasions in the history of any Chapter when a powerful member of the body, feeling that he is near death or suspecting that he is near promotion to a different place, presses his colleagues to renew leases immediately for small fines rather than to spend time negotiating for larger ones. At Norwich this happened not only in 1680, as has been mentioned, but also in 1697, when Dean Fairfax was in a hurry for cash, and in 1700, when Dean Fairfax was thought to be dying.[32]

In another place Prideaux makes another charge against Dean Astley, or perhaps against Mrs. Astley if we accept Dr. Miller's suggestion that she may have hen-pecked her husband.[33] In an account of the Cathedral's financial state which can probably be dated to 1684 or 1685 Prideaux complains that, whereas Dean Crofts, who was not in some ways a model of self-restraint, refused to let houses for the full term of 40 years allowed by law and insisted, to the annoyance of the tenants, on 21 year leases of such property, his successor Astley reversed this cautious policy. He –

> without having any respect to the benefit of the church . . . for his own advantage renewed all those leases for 40 years which brought them in great sums of money which was all divided among them [viz. the members of the Chapter] and thereby as long as this lasted (which was two years) they made their places advantageous to them.[34]

Whether or not Dean and Mrs. Astley behaved as badly as Prideaux claimed, the Norwich Chapter certainly had difficulty with Dean Astley's extended family. In 1700 or 1701 Hobart Astley renewed his 21 year leases of the manor and the rectory of Eaton, and Prideaux complained that the Chapter were 'kept in the dark' about the value

of their Eaton estate. Astley claimed that part of Eaton was his own
freehold, 'but if he hath any it is not above an acre all the rest is
copyhold or leasehold.'[35] The Private Register also grumbled that the
leases to Hobart Astley both omitted the covenant, required by the
Cathedral statutes, binding the tenant to produce a terrier. It is only
fair to Astley to note that a few other Chapter leases omitted this
covenant, but Prideaux's Private Register said sourly –

> I suppose the covenant was omitted first by Dean Astley in favour of his
> father-in-law Mr. Hobart [Hobart Astley's predecessor as tenant of
> Eaton manor and rectory] and his own interest after him, for it hath been
> a policy among them to conceal our estate thereby to swallow as much
> of it as they can.

A later note added by an unidentified hand records that the leases of
Eaton before Dean Astley's time omitted the covenant.[36] In 1714
Hobart Astley was still irritating Prideaux by claiming to own a
significant amount of freehold in Eaton, and in 1721 Prideaux's last
years were not made more peaceful by the claim of Hobart Astley's
successor as tenant of Eaton, alderman John Riseborough, that some
of the parish was freehold.[37]

The only other instance that has been noted of the Astley family
benefitting at the expense of the Cathedral is the payment by the
Chapter of £20 *per annum* to a bailiff to look after the 181 acres of
woodland at Hindolveston, where the Chapter's tenant was Sir Jacob
Astley; 'a needless expense', said Prideaux in the Private Register. 'The
office was made of purpose by Dean Astley to compliment Sir Jacob
in giving such a salary to one of his servants.'[38]

How did Prideaux tackle the problems presented by this Cathedral
and its unsatisfactory, though hardly scandalous, business affairs? His
Life records his settling permanently in Norfolk in 1686, five years after
he became a prebendary, when he exchanged his rectory of Bladon,
Oxfordshire, for that of Saham in Norfolk.[39] Until then he had been,
like some of his contemporaries on the Chapter, resident in Norwich
for not much more than two months a year, but Prideaux had in July
of the previous year written of his weariness of life in Oxford (where
he was still a student and librarian of Christ Church) and his decision
to retire to his parish with a wife. He was then, at the age of 37,
apparently too mature to be carried away by passion; he says he has
'hearkened to proposals that have been made to me of marriage', and
that these proposals are very advantageous. He has already sealed
articles securing himself £3,000 at his marriage and expects at least

£1,500 more when his prospective parents-in-law die. He refers to his bride-to-be (Bridget, the only child of Anthony Bokenham of Helmingham, Suffolk) as a gentlewoman, but refrains from any word about either her appearance or her temperament.[40] They married in February 1686 and had at least three children, and Bridget seems to have died by August 1714, when Prideaux made a will mentioning only his son Edmund.[41] How happy this businesslike marriage was it is impossible to say. The *Life* says that when Prideaux settled at Norwich in 1686 the whole management of the Cathedral's business at once fell into his hands[42] –

> he found all matters there in the utmost disorder and confusion; for they had no rentals, whereby to receive their rents, nor any Treasurer's Book, whereby to pay the salaries of their officers and other outgoings; but the Audit Book of the former year was the only guide . . . and that was very confused and defective.

To read through the Norwich Audit Books from the Restoration to the 1680s does not really produce an impression of great disorder; the Receiver's Charge section contains an adequate statement of what rents are due, from whom and for what outside the city of Norwich, although the practice of listing all the Norwich rents in a single entry is very unsatisfactory. Similarly the Treasurer's Discharge section of the Audit Books wants only the quarterly signed receipts of the members of the foundation to be as good a record as, say, the Treasurer's Books at Durham Cathedral, and these signed receipts are wanting not only at Norwich but also at Bristol, Ely and Rochester Cathedrals.

As has been mentioned above, the *Life* goes on to argue that inadequate financial recording allowed the seniors to impose on the juniors. The mention of seniors and juniors is puzzling. In one of those University colleges where the senior fellows had more power than the juniors this sort of imposition would be quite possible, but in a New Foundation Cathedral, where the only member of Chapter with more power or a larger share of the income was the Dean, opportunities for this sort of malpractice were very limited. But Prideaux's *Life* is believed to be based partly on information from Prideaux's son Edmund,[43] and there is some evidence among the Norwich archives to support the argument. In 1707, 1714 and 1722 prebendary Thomas Littel persuaded the Chapter, much against the wishes of Prideaux, to accept low fines from members of the Bell family of King's Lynn.[44] It was Littel also who in 1710 helped the Chapter out of a difficulty by becoming its tenant of the mediety of Fordham rectory. He paid a fine of 60 guineas, and Prideaux pointed out not only in the Private Register that the Chapter had been 'kind' to Littel but also elsewhere that the Chapter had asked Littel to find a tenant at any fine over £80. The suggestion seems to be that Littel could have tried harder to find a tenant before offering 60 guineas (perhaps equivalent to £66 at that time) on his own behalf.[45]

It is not clear who on the Chapter had an interest in the grant in September 1683 to John Taylor and his executors and assigns of complete control over the office of Cathedral porter for 21 years. Prideaux was presumably in Oxford at the time of the grant, as in those early years of his membership of the Chapter he usually resided in Norwich for late November, December and January and visited Norwich more briefly for the General Chapter in June. When he heard of it he disapproved strongly and argued at length and in detail for the illegal and indeed invalid character of the grant.[46] Certainly, as Prideaux pointed out, there was a great deal of difference between the normal procedure, which would have been for the Dean to appoint Taylor as porter for life, and this 21 year grant, which if Taylor were to die before 1704 would enable his executors to appoint as porter anyone they chose, quite irrespective of the wishes of Chapter. Whether any member of Chapter was bribed to arrange the sealing of this grant is not known. At any rate by 1700 the Chapter had recovered the right to appoint their own porter. An enquiry held by Prideaux in 1703 decided after examining witnesses that in 1700 Thomas Cudden had paid Dean Fairfax twenty guineas for his appointment as porter and that Fairfax had kept the money for his own use.[47]

It seems likely that the Cathedral's business affairs did not completely, in spite of the claim in the *Life*, fall into Prideaux's hands in 1686. He himself recorded in 1696 the negotiation by Henry Fairfax, then Dean, of a very satisfactory agreement with Lady Purbeck, tenant of Fring rectory;[48] and in a document about the state of the Cathedral said to have been written in July 1697 Prideaux devoted a long paragraph to arguing that 'the whole business of the church is entrusted in him.' [the Dean].[49] Prideaux got on well with John Sharp, Dean of Norwich 1681-9, and Sharp, in the short period in 1681 between his own appointment as Dean and Prideaux's appointment as prebendary, was actually planning to ask prebendary William Smyth to run the Cathedral's affairs for him.[50] While therefore it is easy to envisage Prideaux as influential in the Cathedral's affairs in Dean Sharp's time, for Prideaux to achieve a friendly or even rational relation with Sharp's successor Henry Fairfax was much more difficult. Fairfax's appointment to the deanery was probably at first welcome to Prideaux. Prideaux had worked hard against popery in James II's reign, and Fairfax was famous for his resistance to James's attempts to turn Magdalen College, Oxford, into a Roman Catholic college. But Fairfax as Dean of Norwich was an alcoholic. In October 1691, in an emotional letter in which he told his friend John Ellis that he had decided to refuse the chair of Arabic at Oxford (which he had at one time rather hoped for) Prideaux described Fairfax as 'good for nothing but his pipe and his pot, and we are wretchedly holpd up with him.'[51]

Nevertheless Prideaux did manage some improvements. By December 1681, during his first residence as a prebendary, he was working in the muniment room. He investigated the early history of the Cathedral, partly with a view to restoring the funeral monument of its founder Herbert Losinga, sorted and arranged the documents, and had the fabric of the room repaired.[52] He reformed the receiver's accounts, as we have already seen. He instituted the Private Register, beginning in 1682 but gathering information from the Audit Books, the Ledgers (the registers into which leases were copied) and the memories of his colleagues so that this record of the renewals of leases could be as complete as possible from 1660 onwards. The plan for keeping the Private Register seems to have been originally that each year the prebendary who held the office of receiver for the year should also keep the Private Register and should be paid an extra £5, the same as the fee for the receiver's post, for the work. Thus the Audit Books record as receiver and keeper of the Private Register Joseph Loveland for 1683–4, Richard Kidder for 1684-5, John Hildyard for 1685–6, Richard Kidder for 1688–9 and Joseph Loveland for 1689–90; in the other years from 1682–3 to 1689–90 Prideaux was receiver and keeper of the Private Register. After 1689–90 the Audit Books do not give the name of the receiver or the keeper of the Register, and after 1701–2 the Audit Books record no payment to the keeper of the Register, as in July 1702 Prideaux offered to be its permanent and unpaid keeper.[53]

The Private Register as it survives today is in two volumes. The first volume covers the years 1660 to 1744, and from 1660 to 1718 Prideaux's hand fills the great majority of the pages. On page 355, in June 1718, a new hand appears, coinciding with the spread of palsy from Prideaux's left to his right hand.[54] Whose this new hand is we do not know, but whoever he was he was supervised by Prideaux, who read over his work and occasionally made a correction.[55] In 1720 Thomas

Church, perhaps the same man who was junior sub-sacrist from 1719–20, and very probably the man who surveyed estates for the Chapter between 1725 and 1742, took over the writing of the Private Register; in October 1724 he was paid 16s. for writing 32 pages of the Register.[56] It is not only the hand which shows the continuity of Prideaux's interest in the Private Register. During the 42 years of Prideaux's Norwich career the Register covered over 400 large pages, and the tone and attitudes are consistent throughout. There is a constant diligent search for and recording of information, with references to the Commonwealth surveys of the Chapter's estates and occasionally a sensible reminder of the low valuations contained in those surveys.[57] Other surveys are used when available, such as the survey of Bawburgh rectory made in Henry VII's reign and copied into the Register in 1694.[58] New surveys are sometimes made; Thomas Martin, one of the Cathedral's lay clerks, surveyed Surlingham Marsh in 1681 and Aldeby rectory in 1683, and in 1696 prebendary Hildyard went to survey Fring rectory in the hope that fresh information would enable the Chapter to attract a new tenant, as the former tenant, having allowed his 21 year lease to run for twenty years, refused to pay more than £80 for a renewal. Dr. Hildyard's work bore fruit, as Fring rectory was leased to Lady Purbeck for a fine of £250.[59] Sometimes, particularly with properties a long way from Norwich, the only information available was such as the tenant provided, and the accounts in the Private Register sometimes admit to being defective.[60] The Chapter's most distant property of all was the rectory of Scalby, just North of Scarborough in Yorkshire. This rectory was leased for lives (as were a few other rectories and manors), and a covenant in its lease bound the tenant to inform the Chapter if the vicarage became vacant, so as to avoid the risk of a long vacancy causing the Chapter's right of presentation to lapse to the Archbishop.[61] Just as the tenant of Scalby provided the Chapter with information about their patronage there, so the vicar provided information about their estate. In September 1700 the vicar wrote to give Prideaux some facts affecting the valuation of the rectory, and in February 1701 he wrote that two of the lives in the lease of Scalby were dead.[62]

It is no surprise to find the Private Register very concerned to preserve all the Chapter's rights, but Prideaux's diligence in the collecting of documents with which to resist attack sometimes rivals that of Prior John Wessington of Durham in the fifteenth century. In 1703 the diocesan Chancellor, Thomas Tanner, for whom Prideaux felt great respect, began an attempt to take away the Chapter's peculiar jurisdiction. The Bishop supported the attempt, in the Chapter's view because Tanner was his son-in-law and the diocesan Registrar was the Bishop's son. The Chapter's defence was based on a specially-compiled section of the Private Register, 49 pages devoted to texts of papal bulls, both originals and registered copies, from the Cathedral's archives, texts of agreements with previous bishops, references to Hostiensis, Lyndwood and other canon law authorities, legal opinions, accounts of earlier episcopal attacks on the jurisdiction from the fourteenth century onwards, and affidavits sworn in January 1704 by elderly people who had known the jurisdiction as the Chapter had exercised it over the past few decades. The business was settled, to the Chapter's satisfaction, in October 1705.[63]

A more personal and less important dispute in which Prideaux was also victorious was against prebendary Nathaniel Hodges. Hodges was a former Professor of Moral Philosophy at Oxford and was Dean Fairfax's only friend on the Chapter. As such Prideaux despised him, and when Hodges was unwise enough to object to Prideaux's claiming, as Archdeacon of Suffolk, a stall in choir indicating superiority to any simple prebendary Prideaux appealed to the Bishop and received a solemn declaration, with costs, that Hodges must yield precedence.[64]

Another characteristic of the Private Register is its freedom of language. The Chapter had a number of tenants who were difficult and aggressive in negotiations with their landlords, and the Private Register on occasion records the language in which they address the Chapter, and also describes the tenants in terms which recall the *Dictionary of National Biography*'s judgment that Prideaux's letters 'exhibit him as a man of more frankness than refinement of mind'.[65] Perhaps the very nastiest of the tenants was John Norris, elected Recorder of Norwich in May 1680.[66] In November 1681 he came to negotiate for the renewal of his lease of Bawburgh rectory. His old lease dated from Elizabeth's reign and was within ten years of expiry; it must therefore have been a 99 year lease and the Chapter will have had no fine from the property for 89 years. Norris admitted that the estate was worth £70 *per annum,* and the Chapter's reserved money and corn rent was about £20 *per annum,* so that the rectory's clear annual value was about £50. A fine for three years' value seemed to the Chapter to be the least that they could reasonably expect after 89 years, but they proposed to reduce this amount for two reasons. The first was that this new lease would be the first lease of this rectory granted since the receipt by the Cathedral of its new statutes in 1620. An outstanding and valuable feature of these statutes was that they made the Dean and Chapter of Norwich subject in effect to an Act of Parliament, 18 Eliz. cap. 6, which specified that one third of the reserved rents paid by tenants of the Oxford and Cambridge colleges and of Eton and Winchester colleges should be paid in wheat and malt at 6s. 8d. a quarter of wheat and 5s. a quarter of malt. That is, of a reserved rent of, say, £20 *per annum* one third or £6 6s. 8d. would be expressed as ten quarters of wheat and thirteen quarters three bushels of malt; and the tenant would be required each year to pay £13 13s. 4d. of his rent in cash and in addition to produce either the specified quantities of wheat and malt or a cash equivalent at the prices paid in Norwich market on the quarter days on which the rent was due. In practice all the Norwich tenants paid their corn rents in cash.[67] As a result of this inflation-proofing clause in the statutes Mr. Norris's reserved rent was now to be increased: in 1681 the average prices of wheat and malt at Norwich were not, as in 18 Eliz. cap. 6, 6s. 8d. and 5s. a quarter respectively but £1 1s. 6d. and 8s. 9d. Since his reserved rent was being increased the Chapter proposed to reduce Mr. Norris's fine by £50. They reduced it further, to a mere £20 –

> out of the consideration of the eminency of the person in the profession of the law and the hope we had that he might be serviceable therein to us as being our counsel.

Norris was far from pleased at the Chapter's suggestion of a fine of £20 –

> he called us Jews and gave us besides very reproachful language, telling us that no church in England would deal so with him but us, and that he was worth us all and knew things better than us all, and that we dealt unworthily and Jewishly with him.[68]

Nine years later Mr. Norris had not mellowed –

> having an equitable fine set him [he] out of dislike of the same rose up pulled his hat over his eyes turned his back upon us in a very disdainful manner and went away without saying as much as a word to us.[69]

The Private Register merely records Mr. Norris's words and actions without commenting on them. About other tenants it is more outspoken, describing one as 'exceedingly troublesome and clamorous', another as 'intolerably importunate and troublesome' and a third as 'this most notorious knave.'[70] Two other tenants who were very attached to their money were described respectively as 'a man much upon the shark', and 'a covetous griping man who parts with every penny of his money as with so many drops of his blood.'[71] More surprising is the clear criticism of a present member of Chapter in a

note of August 1685 which points out that a 40 year lease to John
Coats of a house in the sextry yard in the close should not have been
renewed, as statute 21 forbids the leasing for terms of years of the lesser
houses in the close, but –

> This was done when Dr. Prideaux absent by the management of Mr.
> Hodges who had some obligations to Coats for service done him.[72]

Prideaux's other major innovation among the records of the
Cathedral was his Diaries. These survive in three volumes, covering the
period from 1694 to the end of Prideaux's life. The first volume,
covering 1694 to 1703, contains a good deal of the material about lease
renewals that fills the Private Register, as well as other material most
of which one might expect to find in the Chapter Books (in which the
acts of Chapter are entered). Prideaux's purpose in creating these
volumes was that they might be useful to himself and to members of
Chapter after him.[73] He therefore recorded decisions and occurrences
of which he thought a reminder would be useful. In January 1699 he
recorded agreements with Christian Smyth of London for restoration
and thereafter for maintenance of the Cathedral organ, and with Mr.
Downes for a six-year programme of tree-planting in the close.
Similarly the notes on different timbers which could be used to support
lead roofing, including their costs and expected lengths of life on both
the North and South slopes of a roof have an obvious use.[74] It is less
easy to see why he chose to record the Chapter's refusal to help the
Dean and Chapter of Ely with the cost of restoring the West front of
their Cathedral in 1700.[75] The second and third volumes of Prideaux's
Diaries relate entirely to his time as Dean, and before we turn to that
period we ought to assess his achievement as a prebendary. His energy
and thoroughness in organising the existing records, resurrecting useful
records which had gone out of use and devising new ways of recording
valuable information produced a great improvement in the machinery
of management, and in spite of his statement that the Dean had not
only 'a negative in all matters debated in Chapter' but also 'the sole
power of proposing things to be debated of'[76] some business went
through Chapter of a sort which one cannot easily envisage Dean
Fairfax taking an active interest in. The agreement already mentioned
with Mr. Downes for the planting and care of lime trees in the close
was doubtless proposed to Chapter by the Dean but seems to show
more care for the Cathedral environment than one would expect from
a Dean who –

> comes little to church and never to the sacrament, though we have a

sacrament every Sunday; and as for a book, he looks not into any from the beginning of the year to the end.[77]

Moreover, Prideaux's Diaries show him acting as the Chapter's representative in negotiations, not only during his period of formal office as treasurer, receiver or Vice Dean (and he held these offices more often than did any of his colleagues) but also occasionally when he had no formal responsibility. In May 1699, when he was treasurer, the corporation of Yarmouth asked Prideaux to recommend to Chapter that the corporation be given leave to demolish the chancel of Yarmouth church and to use its materials for a new church.[78] And in June 1700, when Prideaux was again treasurer, a tenant and the agent of another tenant came to talk to him about two lease renewals of a complicated nature. In June 1695 Prideaux was neither treasurer nor receiver when he was used as the Chapter's envoy in negotiations about a lease with their powerful neighbours the corporation of Norwich, the third largest city in England.[79]

Prideaux was a strong personality who will not have been surprised when at a General Chapter in June 1697 he persuaded his colleagues that the lease of Westhall rectory should not be renewed; instead the appropriation was to be united to the vicarage. In November of the same year all he could do was to protest when his colleagues ignored their own decision and decided to renew the lease.[80] But the greatest weakness of Prideaux's position as a prebendary was, in his own words, that the Dean 'hath the sole power of putting in and putting out the minor canons lay clerks and all other officers and ministers of the church',[81] and the Norwich archives show much less disciplinary action against the choir members and other men on the foundation under Dean Fairfax than under Dean Prideaux.

Prideaux became Dean of Norwich in 1702. He had a couple of years earlier tried to get for himself the deanery of Ely, when he had been a prebendary of Norwich for eighteen years and had, he said, run the church's business for seventeen years, putting up with intolerable treatment from the Dean. He was now the senior of both the prebendaries and the archdeacons except for prebendary Hodges, who was too ill to be capable of work, and he felt that for him not to be offered the deanery of Norwich at the forthcoming vacancy (Fairfax was ill) would be humiliating; to be given the deanery would be no great benefit, as it was worth hardly £220 a year.[82]

As a prebendary Prideaux had improved the Chapter's administrative machinery but had lacked the power to dismiss those members of the foundation whose behaviour was totally unacceptable. As Dean he now had this power: the fourth of James I's Norwich statutes, *De Officio Decani,* allowed the Dean to expel any of the lower officers and ministers who after two admonitions for his conduct offended a third time. Prideaux was installed as Dean on June 8 1702, and on August 22 he expelled John Stukeley, a minor canon and curate of St. John de Sepulchro, Norwich, for 'a very abominable practice of lust.' Stukeley's behaviour was not recent; Prideaux had begun examining witnesses on oath in the previous November, but it was only on becoming Dean that he was able on his own authority to expel Stukeley, who initially appealed to the Bishop against his expulsion but failed to pursue his appeal and instead annoyed Prideaux by becoming a pet of the Jacobite party in Norwich.[83]

In October 1704 Prideaux eased out the Cathedral porter Thomas Cudden, whose patent had been bought from Dean Fairfax and had now expired. Prideaux wanted the porter's place vacant so that he could give it to Stephen Searle, the Chapter clerk, who had served Chapter adequately for a number of years, having been appointed in 1683,[84] but had in recent years become incompetent as a result of drunkenness. Searle managed to keep the post of Chapter clerk until 1706, and he then avoided dismissal by resigning, having received two admonitions, one for not attending the Eucharist for several years and the other for frequenting ale houses and other places of debauchery.[85] At the same time as he eased Cudden out from the porter's place Prideaux expelled William Pleasants, a lay clerk and the master of the choristers, for talking atheism and sexually molesting a chorister, but Pleasants was reinstated, after a formal admonition, when one of the witnesses against him withdrew his evidence.[86]

These demonstrations in Prideaux's early years as Dean that he would investigate and punish misbehaviour either weeded out all the worst characters on the foundation or at least frightened the remaining ones into more satisfactory conduct, for disciplinary proceedings and notes of misconduct by members of the foundation became less frequent. In 1711 a minor canon, John Blagrave, was gaoled for debt. In 1713 another minor canon, Charles Tillet, confessed to adultery and promised in future to avoid the company of Mrs. Sarah Bayly, wife of a Norwich waggoner.[88] About 1689 Richard Kidder, who in that year added the deanery of Peterborough to his prebend at Norwich, had persuaded the Norwich Chapter to appoint as a minor canon Francis Folchier, a Frenchman who was at that time a minor canon of Peterborough. In 1715 Folchier was allowed by Prideaux to resign his minor canonry after his maidservant had given birth.[89] Later in 1715 Charles Tillet, having been accused of continuing his affair with Mrs. Bayly, ran away.[90] In 1718 minor canon Philip Burrough died after falling off his horse while either drunk or at least under the influence of alcohol.[91] And that is the sum total of disciplinary problems in a record so detailed as to make arguments from silence less dangerous than usual; Prideaux was painstaking enough to note the death of a lay clerk from a broken heart after his father had fled to Holland to avoid being imprisoned for debt, and it is difficult to believe that he recorded only some of the disciplinary problems among his staff.[92]

We have already noticed Prideaux's energy in the collection of evidence for the defence of the Chapter's rights. In order to be able to continue this activity more easily and effectively he persuaded Chapter almost as soon as he became Dean to buy for the Cathedral library all future Acts of Parliament and such past Acts as were needed.[93] With the library thus reinforced, and with the Cathedral muniments in good order, Prideaux was ready for any attack, and when a letter from the Chapter of Westminster Abbey in June 1712 asked the Norwich Chapter to prove their right to the annual pension they claimed from Westminster's impropriate rectory of Swaffham, Prideaux replied in devastating detail, drafting a letter the composition of which must have been as much pleasure as effort.[94] Since Prideaux so much disliked his predecessor Fairfax he must also have enjoyed writing to Fairfax's executors to point out that the monument erected over his grave had the date of death wrong and that the reference in the inscription to Fairfax's kinsman, the Parliamentarian general, was praise of a rebel.[95]

Another opportunity for the defence of a privilege the loss of which might have had important practical consequences came in 1715. The then mayor of Norwich, Peter Attlesey, lived in Bishopsgate Street (now Bishopgate) and so his route from home to the town hall passed through the close. As he went through the close the mayor had the city sword carried before him, and Prideaux objected to this as being a practice which might suggest that the close was subject to the authority of the mayor and corporation. Arthur Branthwait, the Chapter's counsel and deputy steward, was instructed to negotiate with the mayor and corporation, with satisfactory results. It was agreed that the city would ask for permission to carry the sword through the close, and that the Chapter would grant permission; and Branthwait was paid an extra £2 3s. 0d. for 'adjusting the carrying the sword through the close.'[96]

When Prideaux became Dean in 1702 the Cathedral was in financial difficulties. In 1704, when the workmen maintaining the Cathedral fabric had not been paid for months, he noted that many of the tenants were in arrears with their rent;[97] this was true, but it had been so since the financial year 1698/9, and there were serious deficits revealed at the annual audit in November in each of the years 1699, 1702, 1703 and 1704. Clearly some action was needed to increase income or reduce expenditure. A century later at Rochester Cathedral, where in normal times all the income from fines for leases was divided among the Dean and prebendaries, the Chapter at times of financial strain either gave or lent the Cathedral some of this income.[98] The introduction at Norwich under the 1620 statutes of corn rents had increased the regular annual payments by Chapter tenants and reduced the amounts which they paid in fines,[99] and at Norwich only some of the fines were divided among the members of Chapter.[100] Prideaux's first reaction to the Cathedral's accounting deficits was therefore to borrow £250 not from the Chapter but from his mother-in-law, at 5% simple interest.[101] This money was borrowed in September 1704, near the end of the 1703/4 financial year, and in the following financial year the Chapter had all the fines received credited to the Cathedral account, the 'public account' as it was occasionally called.[102] This self-denial was wise but should not be exaggerated; crediting all the fines, totalling £248 18s. 0d., to the public account produced a surplus on the money rents account of over £192, and this surplus was, in accordance with normal practice, divided among the members of Chapter, the Dean receiving a quarter of it and each prebendary an eighth.[103] In 1706/7 the Chapter was again reducing outgoings, by assigning an accounting surplus of £95 to the reduction of the amount owed to Prideaux's mother-in-law, and by 1710 the Chapter's financial situation was comfortable and stable; it remained so for the rest of Prideaux's life.

A class of expenditure worth mentioning is that of repairs to the Cathedral fabric. Like other Cathedrals Norwich suffered damage and neglect during the Commonwealth, although the damage would have been worse but for the trouble and money expended by a resident of Norwich, Christopher Jay.[104] During the first decade after the Restoration £2,800 was spent on repairs to the church and cloister, together with a new organ and other interior fittings.[105] This may well have been sufficient to restore the fabric to its proper state, but under Dean Fairfax it deteriorated again. Prideaux suggested in a paper of

1697 that Fairfax had deliberately minimised expenditure on repairs so as to enable the accounts to show larger surpluses and so benefit the pockets of the members of Chapter when the surpluses were divided among them.[106] Blomefield says the fabric was neglected from soon after the Restoration until the time of Dean Bullock in the 1740s,[107] but Prideaux's *Life* claims that he had the fabric regularly surveyed and repaired as required by statute 22.[108] The *Life* is supported by the records. A Chapter act of June 1713 ordered that surveys and repairs be carried out as specified by the statute, and every year from 1691/2 onwards £10 was spent on 'surveying the church work.'[109] In most years while Prideaux was Dean £100 or thereabouts was spent on repairs to the Cathedral, and in each of the years 1702/3 and 1714/15 over £200 was spent.[110]

Prideaux was a diligent and successful Cathedral administrator, methodical and clear-headed, with sufficient strength of character to be able to impose his policies on Chapter as a body. There is also evidence that he was a devout churchman, but there is no space here to discuss that aspect of his life.[111] One problem which he did not solve with total success was that of controlling his individual colleagues on the Chapter. On at least two occasions he was unable to hold the annual General Chapter because too few prebendaries attended,[112] and he later reduced his dependence on his colleagues' co-operation in the administration of the Cathedral by virtually abolishing the posts of receiver and treasurer. Each of these positions was filled by one of the prebendaries, elected annually and paid £5 *per annum* for the responsibility. In December 1710 Prideaux persuaded his colleagues to agree that in future the receiver and treasurer would each year pay their salaries plus an extra £2 10s. 0d. each to Mr. Ferrer, the Chapter's porter and former auditor, so that he might with the help of his successor as auditor Roger Smyth act for them as receiver and treasurer.[113] Although the *Life* records that Prideaux never had the least difference with his Chapter, the records of his time as Dean seem rather to support another statement in the *Life*,[114] that he 'generally spoke his mind with freedom and boldness, and was not easily diverted from pursuing what he thought right', so that one can imagine that the handing over of the receiver's and treasurer's duties to a paid servant pleased the prebendaries almost as much as it did the Dean. It was perhaps to further this policy of running the Cathedral through people he could control, as well as to provide an income for a relative, that in 1717 Prideaux appointed as the Chapter's counsel and under-steward his son Edmund, a graduate of Clare Hall, Cambridge, and a student at the Middle Temple. There is no evidence that Edmund was not a competent under-steward, but he did not receive from the Chapter the warm praise given to his predecessor Arthur Branthwait.

Prideaux must have been a difficult man to like and an intimidating colleague to work with; his intelligence, moral integrity and determination were not sufficiently tempered by tact. In his Cathedral he achieved a great deal in improving the tools of administration and in controlling the conduct of his subordinates, but he failed to inspire his colleagues on the Chapter with much of his devotion to the work of the Cathedral. He is best briefly characterised, as forceful, frank and persevering in his attempts at improvement, in a few sentences from one of his letters, dated September 29 1722[115] –

> about thirty years since Dr. Fairfax, then Dean of Norwich, put one Mr. Richardson to be minister of the parish of the close, with a permission to serve it once a fortnight. This I then protested against as contrary both to former usage and to the service of God Almighty, and have ever since many times expressed my dislike of it, and have as often promised that it should be remedied whenever it should fall in my power. About a year since, Richardson dying, Dr. Clark [who later became Dean of Salisbury] applied to me for the place, and would serve it no otherwise than Richardson did. But, not being able to comply with him herein, I did put another in the place. This is the whole reason of his quarrel with me. I told him I denied him nothing but what I would deny to a brother or a son; that I thought the obligation for doing the best for God's service to be greater than any obligation whatsoever for the acting contrary thereto, and neither his brother nor his father think I did otherwise than my duty herein.

NOTES

I am grateful to the Dean and Chapter of Norwich for permission to publish quotations from their archives. I am also indebted to Barbara Dodwell, of the University of Reading, who introduced me to the Norwich Cathedral archives; to the past and present staff of the Norfolk Record Office, especially Jean Kennedy, Paul Rutledge, Diane Parsons and Ian Dunn, for producing documents, microfilm and information and for reading a typescript; to the Keeper of Rare Books at the University of St. Andrews; and to my colleagues Alan Piper, who has worked to make my English intelligible, and Ann Robinson, who typed a manuscript which was posted to her in penny numbers.

1. *The Life of the Reverend Humphrey Prideaux, D.D. Dean of Norwich* (1748).
2. F. Blomefield, *An Essay towards a Topographical History of the County of Norfolk,* 3 (1806), p. 617; *The Victoria History of the County of Norfolk,* ed. W. Page, 2 (1906), p. 326.
3. It cost the Prior and Convent over £1400, about two years' income; Norfolk Record Office, Dean and Chapter Records, Liber Miscellaneorum 3. Documents in the Dean and Chapter Records are hereafter cited simply as DCN followed by the appropriate detailed reference.
4. DCN, Liber Miscellaneorum 1, item 3.
5. There had been some draft statutes issued by Henry VIII; their text is preserved in DCN, Liber Miscellaneorum 2, pp. 23-56.
6. *VCH Norfolk,* 2, p. 267.
7. DCN, Liber Miscellaneorum 2, pp. 129-31.
8. *VCH Norfolk,* 2, p. 283.
9. DCN, Liber Miscellaneorum 4, item 25.
10. *Ibid.,* item 29; Oxford, Bodleian Library, Tanner Ms. 134, f. 139 (cited hereafter as Tanner Ms.); DCN, Liber Miscellaneorum 2, pp. 296-9.
11. DCN, Private Register 1660-1744, pp. 31, 50-3, 55-8, 75-6, 82, 99; cf. a list of 43 long leases, from 50 to 500 years, in DCN, Liber Miscellaneorum 4, item 19.
12. A further accusation made by Blomefield, *History of the County of Norfolk,* 4 (1806), pp. 433-4, is of long-term mismanagement of Norman's Hospital.
13. Bristol Record Office, DC/A/8/1; Kent Archives Office, DRc/Ac 2-4; also useful for Rochester is the Red Book, Vol. 2, DRc/Arb 2; R. V. H. Burne, *Chester Cathedral. From its Founding by Henry VIII to the Accession of Queen Victoria* (1958); S. J. A. Evans, 'Cathedral Life at Gloucester in the Early Seventeenth Century', *Bristol and Gloucestershire Archaeological Transactions,* 80 (1961), pp. 5-15; S. Gunton, *The History of the Church of Peterburgh* (1686); *The Foundation of Peterborough Cathedral A.D.1541,* ed. W. T. Mellows, Northamptonshire Record Society, 13 (1941); *Elizabethan Peterborough. The Dean and Chapter as Lords of the City,* ed. W. T. Mellows and D. H. Gifford, Northamptonshire Record Society, 18 (1956).

The ecclesiastical history sections of the Victoria Histories of the counties of Chester, Gloucester and Northampton make very little mention of the Cathedrals; *VCH Cheshire*, ed. C. R. Elrington, 3 (1980), pp. 12-49; *VCH Gloucestershire*, ed. W. Page, 2 (1907), pp. 1-48; *VCH Northamptonshire*, ed. R. M. Serjeantson and W. R. D. Adkins, 2 (1906), pp. 1-75.

14. *The Life of the Rev. Humphrey Prideaux*, pp. 19-20.
15. DCN, Liber Miscellaneorum 3, *ad fin.*
16. DCN, Private Register 1660-1744, p. 332. Durham Chapter tenants could nevertheless make large profits from their leaseholds; see D. Marcombe, 'Church leaseholders: the decline and fall of a rural élite', in *Princes and Paupers in the English Church, 1500-1800*, ed. R. O'Day and F. Heal (1981), pp. 255-75. See also more generally C. Clay, ' "The Greed of Whig Bishops?"': Church Landlords and their Lessees, 1660-1760', *Past and Present*, 87 (1980), pp. 128-57.
17. DCN, Chapter Book 1, f. 176v.
18. DCN, Private Register 1660-1744, p. 210.
19. *Ibid.*, p. 322.
20. *Ibid.*, pp. 148, 206.
21. DCN, Dean Prideaux's Diaries, Vol. 2, p. 213.
22. DCN, Private Register 1660-1744, p. 320, December 5 1709.
23. DCN, Dean Prideaux's Diaries, Vol. 2, p. 242; Private Register 1660-1744, pp. 315-16.
24. *Ibid.*, p. 139; cf. Private Register 1660-1744, p. 49, December 10 1682, p. 213, January 24 1701.
25. *Ibid.*, pp. 166-7, December 10 1698, pp. 208-9, December 14 1700, p. 308, December 9 1707, p. 19, June 5 1667, p. 210, December 17 1700, pp. 232-3, December 5 1702, p. 209, June 6 1704.
26. *Ibid.*, pp. 210, 232-3.
27. *Ibid.*, p. 318.
28. A. C. Miller, 'Herbert Astley, Dean of Norwich', *Norfolk Archaeology*, 38, 2 (1982), p. 149.
29. DCN, Private Register 1660-1744, p. 9.
30. *Ibid.*, p. 8.
31. Miller, *Norfolk Arch.*, 38, 2 (1982), p. 155; Tanner Ms. 133; DCN, Private Register 1660-1744, p. 164.
32. DCN, Dean Prideaux's Diaries, Vol. 1, p. 109; Private Register 1660-1744, p. 160.
33. Tanner Ms. 134, f. 21; Miller, *Norfolk Arch.*, 38, 2 (1982) p. 155.
34. Tanner Ms. 134, ff. 20ᵛ-21.
35. DCN, Private Register 1660-1744, p. 196; Dean Prideaux's Diaries, Vol. 1, p. 105.
36. DCN, Private Register 1660-1744, p. 197.
37. *Ibid.*, pp. 341, 397-400.
38. *Ibid.*, p. 291.
39. *The Life of the Rev. Humphrey Prideaux*, p. 16.
40. *Letters of Humphrey Prideaux sometime Dean of Norwich to John Ellis sometime Under-Secretary of State, 1674-1722*, ed. E. Thompson, Camden

Society, New Series, 15 (1875), pp. 143-4.
41. Norfolk Record Office, N.C.C. Wills 1725, 200 Gregson.
42. *The Life of the Rev. Humphrey Prideaux,* p. 19.
43. Alexander Gordon in *Dictionary of National Biography,* s.v. Prideaux, Humphrey.
44. DCN, Private Register 1660-1744, pp. 311, 345, 406-7.
45. *Ibid.,* pp. 324-5; Dean Prideaux's Diaries, Vol. 2, p. 277.
46. DCN, Private Register 1660-1744, p. 84; Ledger Book 5, f. 330v.
47. DCN, Dean Prideaux's Diaries, Vol. 2, pp. 8-14.
48. *Ibid.,* Vol. 1, p. 25.
49. Lambeth Palace Library, Ms. 930, item 80.
50. Thompson, *Letters of Humphrey Prideaux,* p. 89; Tanner Ms. 134, f. 57; neither Sharp nor the Bishop of Norwich knew that Prideaux was about to be given a prebend.
51. Thompson, *Letters of Humphrey Prideaux,* pp. 135, 150-1; cf. Tanner Ms. 134, f. 94v, and Thompson, *Letters of Humphrey Prideaux,* p. 160.
52. *Ibid.,* p. 122; *The Life of the Rev. Humphrey Prideaux,* pp. 20-1.
53. DCN, Dean Prideaux's Diaries, Vol. 1, p. 167.
54. *The Life of the Rev. Humphrey Prideaux,* p. 141; Thompson, *Letters of Humphrey Prideaux,* p. iv.
55. DCN, Private Register 1660-1744, p. 355.
56. DCN, Audit Book 1723-4, Extraordinaries; Audit Book 1719-20; Private Register 1660-1744, pp. 391-422.
57. *Ibid.,* pp. 50-3, 226-7, 235, 297, 305-6, 366-73, 382-3, 393-4.
58. *Ibid.,* pp. 123-8.
59. *Ibid.,* pp. 148-9.
60. *Ibid.,* pp. 97, 140, 382-3.
61. *Ibid.,* pp. 237-8.
62. DCN, Dean Prideaux's Diaries, Vol. 1, pp. 112-13, 135.
63. DCN, Private Register 1660-1744, pp. 239-87; Chapter Book 4, ff. 124-125v contains the text of a fine threatening letter from the Chapter to the Bishop in January 1705.
64. Tanner Ms. 134 ff. 37-8, 118-19; Thompson, *Letters of Humphrey Prideaux,* pp. 34n., 161.
65. DCN, Private Register 1660-1744, e.g. pp. 132, 134, 137, 159, 163-4, 206, 211, 235-7, 305.
66. F. Blomefield, *History of the County of Norfolk,* 3, p. 416.
67. DCN, Dean Prideaux's Diaries, Vol. 2, p. 228.
68. DCN, Private Register 1660-1744, p. 45.
69. *Ibid.,* p. 129.
70. *Ibid.,* pp. 134, 163-4, 206.
71. *Ibid.,* pp. 235, 350-1.
72. *Ibid.,* p. 89.
73. *Ibid.,* p. 415, marginal note; Dean Prideaux's Diaries, Vol. 2, p. 306.
74. *Ibid.,* Vol. 1, pp. 61-3.
75. *Ibid.,* Vol. 1, pp. 97-8, 101.

76. Lambeth Palace Library, Ms. 930, item 80, f. 2.
77. Thompson, *Letters of Humphrey Prideaux,* p. 160.
78. DCN, Dean Prideaux's Diaries, Vol. 1, p. 70. The corporation a little later decided not to build a new church but to go on repairing the existing one; Dean Prideaux's Diaries, Vol. 1, p. 76.
79. *Ibid.,* pp. 105, 14.
80. *Ibid.,* p. 40; BL Add. Ms. 28929, item 136.
81. Lambeth Palace Library, Ms. 930, item 80, f.2.
82. Tanner Ms. 22, f. 167.
83. DCN, Dean Prideaux's Diaries, Vol. 1, pp. 168, 170, 173; Private Register 1660-1744, p. 142; Tanner Ms. 134, ff. 1-2v.
84. DCN, Chapter Book 3.
85. *Ibid.,* Chapter Book 4, ff. 128v, 130v, 132v.
86. DCN, Dean Prideaux's Diaries, Vol. 2, pp. 42, 44-5.
87. *Ibid.,* p. 322.
88. *Ibid.,* Vol. 3, p. 9.
89. *Ibid.,* pp. 27-31.
90. *Ibid.,* p. 37.
91. *Ibid.,* p. 61; Burrough had been helping to drink a bowl of punch.
92. *Ibid.,* p. 68.
93. DCN, Chapter Book 4, f. 91, June 23 1702.
94. DCN, Dean Prideaux's Diaries, Vol. 2, pp. 339-44.
95. *Ibid.,* Vol. 1, pp. 222-3.
96. *Ibid.,* Vol. 3, p. 32; Audit Book 1714-15, Extraordinaries.
97. DCN, Dean Prideaux's Diaries, Vol. 2. p. 32; Audit Book 1703-4.
98. Gave in, e.g., 1801-2 and lent in, e.g., 1825-6; Kent Archives Office, DRc/FTb 133, p. 1; DRc/FTb 157, p. 1.
99. Tanner Ms. 134, f. 21.
100. How it was decided which fines should be divided among the Chapter and which credited to the Cathedral's accounts is not clear. A note to a 'Summary List of Money from Corn, Hen and Timber Rents 1671-1760' among the Dean and Chapter Records (Q229B) suggests a regular custom of dividing the fines paid at the General Chapter each June and crediting to the Cathedral accounts the fines paid at or soon after the audit each November. Comparison of the complete lists of fines, which can be compiled from the Private Register, with the lists of fines credited to the Cathedral accounts in the Audit Books, suggests that the note is a simplification; but it is all we have.
101. DCN, Dean Prideaux's Diaries, Vol. 2, p. 32; Audit Book 1707-8, Extraordinaries.
102. *Ibid.,* Audit Book 1704-5, Forinseca Recepta; Private Register 1660-1744, pp. 293-300; Audit Book 1705-6, Extraordinaries.
103. *Ibid.,* Audit Book 1704-5.
104. Tanner Ms. 134, f. 140r-v.
105. *Ibid.,* f. 139.
106. Lambeth Palace Library, Ms. 930, item 80, f. 2.
107. Blomefield, *History of the County of Norfolk,* 4 (1806), p. 6; cf. Blomefield,

3 (1806), p. 630, where the Cathedral before Bullock's time is said to have been in a condition 'not only nasty but ruinous'.
108. *The Life of the Rev. Humphrey Prideaux,* p. 146.
109. DCN, Chapter Book 4, f. 163; Audit Books, Extraordinaries.
110. *Ibid.*
111. *The Life of the Rev. Humphrey Prideaux,* pp. 97-8, 118, 150, 151-60; Thompson, *Letters of Humphrey Prideaux,* pp. 185, 205; Tanner Ms. 36, f. 126.
112. In 1707, DCN, Chapter Book 4, f. 138; and 1709, DCN, Dean Prideaux's Diaries, Vol. 2, p. 250.
113. DCN, Dean Prideaux's Diaries, Vol. 2, p. 301. Prideaux thereby re-created John Hoo's post of the 1560s and was fortunate not to have his action seriously questioned.
114. *The Life of the Rev. Humphrey Prideaux,* pp. 149-50.
115. Thompson, *Letters of Humphrey Prideaux,* p. 206.

Winchester Cathedral in the Nineteenth Century

Philip Barrett

William Cobbett visited Winchester Cathedral on Sunday, October 30 1825 and attended matins. He was not impressed by this experience and wrote –

> The 'service' was now begun. There is a *Dean* and God knows how many *prebends* belonging to this *immensely rich* bishopric and Chapter: and there were at this 'service' *two or three men* and *five or six boys* in white surplices, with a congregation of *fifteen women and four men!* Gracious God! . . . it beggars one's *feelings* to attempt to find *words* whereby to express them upon such a subject and such an occasion.[1]

Cobbett was not the only visitor to Winchester in the early nineteenth century who was critical of what he saw. Another recorded in 1806 that –

> in several parts of the nave, the rain poured through in such torrents as to leave no doubt that the roof was in a deplorable state . . . There is in this church a kind of griping, avaricious propensity with the officers deputed to show the nave to strangers.[2]

E. W. Garbett, the Cathedral architect, confirmed these impressions in 1834. Describing the condition of the Cathedral in 1809, he said that –

> the idle public had access to all parts of the building by paying a small sum at the entrance; the consequences were that innumerable depradations were committed, the walls defaced by obscene writing and architectural ornaments deposed . . . the transept was in great dilapidation, some of the Northern part being used as a common workshop and depot for the coarsest materials; the windows were unglazed; many of the staircases and galleries were choked up with accumulations of rubbish of every description.[3]

From these accounts, it might be supposed that the Dean and Chapter were unconcerned for the great building in their care. In fact, as Canon Bussby says, the period between 1775 and 1825 was a time of '50 years of feverish building, repair and alteration'.[4] The key figure in the Chapter was Prebendary George Frederick Nott, who took a lively interest in the repair of the fabric, but in many ways Winchester was served by a Chapter that possessed considerable style and distinction.[5]

Newton Ogle was Dean of Winchester until his death in 1803. Father-in-law of the dramatist Sheridan, he spent little time at Winchester, finding his golden prebend at Durham more attractive. He spent much of his time at Kirkley, where he had 'a very good house with very fine offices, gardens and grounds laid out in pleasing taste'.[6] Ogle was briefly succeeded by Robert Holmes, editor of a monumental version of the Septuagint,[7] and then by Thomas Rennell, who was Dean from 1805 until 1840.[8] Rennell was a gifted preacher, whom William Pitt the Younger described as 'the Demosthenes of the pulpit', though Sydney Smith thought he was 'a ponderous limner'. Philip Williams, one of his canons, had little respect for him, describing him as 'our miserable Dean', and noting that Dr. Gabell, the headmaster of Winchester College, 'complains of the Dean stinking at church and desires much an intervening prebendary in the stalls'.[10]

Philip Williams was an engaging and urbane clergyman. He became a canon of Winchester in 1797 by exchanging his stall at Canterbury Cathedral with the Honourable Edward Legge,[11] and remained a member of the Chapter until his death in 1830. In addition he was a canon of Lincoln, a fellow of Winchester College, and incumbent of Compton and Houghton in Hampshire and Gosberton in Lincolnshire.[12] Like many of the Chapter, Williams leased out his house in the close and lived at his rectory at Compton, coming in from there to fulfil his Cathedral duties. In 1803 he wrote to his daughters –

> I received a note from Dr. Sturges on Monday sen'night to intimate that he was laid up with the gout, that the Archdeacon was gone to town on business, and that Mr. Poulter, whose month it was, had left things to shift for themselves. So that I trotted over to breakfast the greater part of the week.[13]

Eighteen months later he wrote –

> I am in residence and move to Winchester every morning, of course, but by great good fortune my brother Hawtrey is staying there likewise, which excuses me from attending matins and lightens the business exceedingly.[14]

Even when he was eighty years old he was still commuting from Compton –

> I kept my strict residence last month and am the only member of the church upon the spot or likely to be till the latter end of the present one. I have a chaise at the gate every morning at seven (as our prayers begin at eight) and return on horseback, vespers not being over till five, so as to sit down to dinner about half after six . . . I have been very little

annoyed by the extreme heat; my mornings to the extent of five or six hours are uniformly spent in the college library . . . I breakfasted this morning with Mrs. Audrey *[sic]* and three of her girls.[15]

Williams' letters, carefully preserved at Winchester College, contain fascinating comments on the life of the close in his time. A fleeting visit to Winchester by King George III, the arrival in the Cathedral of new monuments carved by John Flaxman, the concerts of the Hampshire Music Festival, the local celebrations over the defeat of Napoleon Bonaparte, as well as gossip about the elderly clergy widows in Bishop Morley's College, all attracted his attention. The two ladies who rented his prebendal house were friendly with Jane Austen, who admired the 'sagacity and taste' and large dark eyes of his daughter Charlotte.[16]

George Frederick Nott was a prebendary of Winchester from 1810 until 1841. He was an expert on Italian art and poetry, and sixteenth century literature in general. He produced editions of the complete works of Henry Howard, Earl of Surrey, and of Sir Thomas Wyatt the elder, as well as an Italian translation of the Prayer Book. He amassed a vast library of over 12,000 books and a notable collection of coins and gems. He supervised the opening of Bishop Fox's tomb in 1820, designed new ceilings for the Cathedral transepts, and, despite a serious fall when ascending a ladder in 1816, continued to be the most active member of the Chapter.[17]

Another prebendary of distinction was Frederick Iremonger. He was a member of the Chapter for only two years until his sudden death in 1820 aged 39, but he had already established himself as a leading figure in education and philanthropy. His cortege was escorted by many schoolchildren and the *Hampshire Chronicle* commented: 'Wherever there was poverty, affliction or disease, there was Frederick Iremonger'.[18]

Bishop Brownlow North died in the same year as Iremonger. Many of the Chapter belonged to his family, including two sons, two sons-in-law and three other relatives. His successor, Bishop Pretyman Tomline, was thus only following an established tradition when in 1825 he appointed his son George Pretyman to a canonry. He was one of the last of the great pluralists. In addition to his stall at Winchester, which he held until 1859, he was also chancellor of Lincoln Cathedral and prebendary of Biggleswade, and incumbent of three parishes. By the 1850s he was something of a relic of a bygone age, as he still gave 'great dinners and fills the close with servants in the brightest yellow liveries'. Pretyman's interests were not confined to ecclesiastical affairs. At

Lincoln, he frequently dashed from Cathedral services to the Doncaster races.[19]

The seventeenth century statutes of the Cathedral made provision for six minor canons, one of whom held the office of precentor, and another that of sacrist. In 1807, the minor canons asked for an increased stipend, 'the necessary expenses of life having become enormously exorbitant', but their request was refused. Five years later, however, their stipend was increased to £200 each, and they were awarded an extra £15 in 1825.[20] They were in a difficult position, as no houses were provided for them and the cost of renting accommodation in the city was heavy.[21]

The Cathedral choir was in a poor state in the early nineteenth century. This appears to have been the fault of the organist, George William Chard. In March 1814, the Dean and Chapter insisted that he should rehearse the choristers every Saturday.[22] Less than a year later, they decided that as Chard had been –

> so generally remiss in attending to his duties as organist and master of the choristers, a remonstrance be addressed to him stating the determination of the Dean and Chapter to enforce the statutes and regulations of the church in order to remedy the evils which have resulted from his neglect of duties.

In particular, they asked Chard to ensure that the choristers –

> make the responses and etc. in a decent, uniform manner, and not at the highest pitch of their voices, as at present, which resembles a street cry rather than a religious rite.[23]

The Dean and Chapter were concerned about the 'neglect and inattention' amongst the choir, which was still in a bad state three years later.[24] Chard continued to be neglectful of his duties. He attended only fourteen practices in the year ended December 1818 and was frequently absent, even on Sundays.[25] For a time he was mayor of Winchester and appears to have been less interested in music than in outdoor pursuits, such as fly-fishing and hunting. His choristers were clearly ill-disciplined as well as ill-taught. In 1814, some of them were caught throwing stones in the churchyard and in 1820 two of them were observed 'cracking and eating nuts during the service'. Altogether, Chard's long reign of 47 years was a story of slackness and inefficiency.[26]

The Dean and Chapter, however, were not slack in their charitable work. As well as maintaining Bishop Morley's College for clergy widows and Dr. Hoadly's charity for helping in the education of deserving children, they also distributed coal to the poor and sometimes they also gave them blankets.[27] In 1809 they pressed the mayor to call a public meeting 'to consider of a proper mode of relieving the poor inhabitants of the said city and suburbs at this inclement season'.[28] In 1815 they gave £50 to help soldiers wounded in the battle of Waterloo, while in 1833 they gave £125 to help poor clergy in Ireland.[29]

The charitable work of the Chapter, together with the maintenance of the Cathedral, its staff and its services, was largely financed by the income from the capitular estates. In the early nineteenth century, it was common for Chapters to lease nearly all their property, whether farms, tenements or tithes, for a number of years. A small annual rent was paid to the Chapter for each property rented, but the leases were renewable every seven years. The bulk of the income from property came from substantial fines paid when a lease was renewed. The Dean and Chapter of Winchester were generous hosts to their tenants. Audit dinners were held on three consecutive days — the Thursday, Friday and Saturday in the week preceding November 25, which was the day of the November Audit and General Chapter Meeting. One of the canons, who held the office of receiver, and as such was the member of the Chapter responsible for the administration of the capitular estates and the funds which they produced, entertained successively 'the gentlemen of the close', the minor canons and the farmers. The menus for these dinners in 1839 and 1840 have survived and they provide a fascinating (and possibly unique) insight into capitular diets in the nineteenth century.[30] The Dean and Chapter retained their estates until 1860, when they were commuted for an annual sum of £6,450.[31]

By the 1830s, there was a strong feeling in the country for reform, and the Church of England was not excluded from this. Sir Robert Peel, in his brief first ministry in the spring of 1835, proposed the establishment of an Ecclesiastical Commission, but the majority of the work was done when the Whigs, under Lord Melbourne, came back to power. Five years and three Acts of Parliament later, the Ecclesiastical Commission was an established fact of church life, empowered to take money from episcopal and capitular sources and use it to endow new parishes and build new churches in the rapidly growing industrial cities. Henceforward, nearly all Cathedrals would be served by a Dean and four canons, whose income would be limited, and the separate endowments of the remaining stalls would be taken over by the Commissioners as they fell vacant. So far as Winchester was concerned, the extra stalls were gradually suspended over a period of 25 years, leaving an establishment of a Dean and five residentiary canons, to which were added a number of honorary canons. [32]

In common with nearly all Cathedral Chapters, the Dean and Chapter protested vigorously against this 'act of spoliation' –

> We do not make light of our daily services of prayer and praise . . . neither do we deprecate the value of our Sunday services, nor distract from the benefits derived from them by the large and attentive congregations on that holy day; nor yet again, would we overlook the advantage which has been derived in Cathedral towns from the support afforded by the members of the Chapter, both individually and collectively, to the various local charities, which cannot but suffer in proportion to the diminution of the number of residentiaries. But we beg leave to state it as our entire conviction that the utility of Cathedral institutions is not to be measured by considerations of this nature alone, and that their vast importance is to be traced, not only in the outward magnificence of the venerable fabrics, in the sanctity which attaches to them as repositories for the ashes of the illustrious dead, and in the sacred and imposing effect of the choir service, co-evel and co-extensive with the establishment of Christianity itself, but in addition to these, in the aid which they give to the theological learning of the country and in the opportunities which they afford for its public development. [33]

But this protest was ineffective and Winchester was reformed, together with all other Cathedrals.

In 1840 Dean Rennell died and was succeeded by Thomas Garnier. [34] Already a member of the Chapter, Garnier was a scion of a well known Hampshire family whose seat was at Rookesbury Park, near Wickham. Universally known as 'the good old Dean', Garnier's greatest interests were horticulture and helping those in need. The rectory garden at Bishopstoke, which he tended for 62 years, achieved a wide fame. He was also a long-standing member of the Linnean Society. Whenever he walked into the city from the close, he would be 'followed by applicants for relief, none of whom, deserving or undeserving, went away empty handed'. If he had a full purse in the morning, it would be empty by the evening. [35]

The Chapter over which Dean Garnier presided included several notable personalities, including Samuel Wilberforce (who was Archdeacon of Surrey until 1845), Philip Jacob, George Thomas Pretyman, William Wilson, David Williams, William Dealtry, Charles James Hoare and William Carus. Wilberforce's main work, of course was as Bishop of Oxford, but he returned to Winchester as Bishop towards the end of his life, and the South transept of the Cathedral is still dominated by his huge cenotaph. Philip Jacob's long connection with Winchester was commemorated by the restoration of the Great Screen towards the end of the century. David Williams, who had a 'powerful and melodious voice', was headmaster of Winchester College and later Warden of New College, Oxford. Both Dealtry and Carus were notable evangelicals.[36]

Perhaps the best known person on the Cathedral staff in the mid nineteenth century was the organist, Samuel Sebastian Wesley. The most famous Cathedral organist of the century, Wesley came to Winchester in 1849, after appointments at Hereford Cathedral, Exeter Cathedral and Leeds Parish Church. Wesley had already outlined some of the aspects of Cathedral music which he felt were in need of reform in the preface to his E major service, published in 1845.[37] He followed this in 1849 with a pamphlet entitled *A Few Words on Cathedral Music and the Musical System of the Church with a Plan of Reform,* and a further paper in 1854.[38] But Wesley himself fell short of the standards he advocated. In 1859 the Dean and Chapter of Winchester admonished him for neglect of duty, as he had attended only 397 services out of a possible 780 in the course of a year, frequently leaving the organ in the hands of a fourteen year-old pupil. He had also neglected the training of the choir –

> The present state of the choristers, two only being qualified to sing solos and the none *[sic]* proficiency of many others are a proof that this provision has been sadly neglected.

Thirdly they criticised his lack of respect and courtesy –

> The Dean and Chapter would remind Dr. Wesley that a kind of threat that he might put the note addressed to him by a member of the capitular body into the hands of his solicitor was utterly at variance with both the letter and the spirit of Dr. Wesley's engagement.[39]

Two years later, he was again admonished, especially for neglecting the choristers' practices and for his sudden absences. He had also been very truculent at a recent audition of lay clerks.[40] It was no doubt a relief to the Chapter when Wesley moved to Gloucester in 1865.

Wesley's choir must have been fairly rough, even by contemporary standards. The Dean and Chapter were so concerned about it in 1857 that they asked three of the canons to make a full enquiry.[41] The lay clerks were obliged to attend all three Sunday services and sufficiently frequently on weekdays to ensure that there were always two of each voice present at the daily services of matins and evensong.[42] This meant that each lay clerk was present for 576 services a year, for which he was paid £72 or 2s. 6d. a service. At the beginning of the century the lay clerks were paid £30 *per annum* plus augmentations, rising to £63 *per annum* by 1853 and £100 in 1873.[43] New sets of rules for the choir were introduced in 1887, 1891 and 1897.[44] In common with many other Cathedral choirs, there were occasional cases of drunkenness among the lay clerks, and certainly none of them could be admitted without promising never to keep a public house.[45] Several lay clerks, including William Simonds and George Richards, were drunkards.[46] The lay clerks were expected to be regular communicants and considerable pressure was put upon them to be diligent in this respect. No new lay clerk who was in debt would be admitted.[47] In 1860, a lay clerk by the name of Corps was in trouble with the Dean and Chapter. He had deliberately taken a different note from that given by a minor canon during the course of a service, and later, in the presence of the Dean and two of the canons, had spoken of the incident 'in a very rude and unbecoming manner'.[48] In 1889 a lay clerk called John Phillips defied the precentor by impertinently refusing to stay to a special rehearsal.[49] Lay clerk Gardiner was a persistently insolent and difficult character.[50] Towards the end of the century a lay clerk was dismissed after being imprisoned for contempt of court.[51] An outstanding lay clerk was Penuel Cross, who was appointed in 1847 and retired in 1890. S. S. Wesley wrote some of the famous bass solos in his anthems for Cross, who had a splendid voice. The Dean and Chapter gave him £10 in 1870 to enable him to purchase a set of false teeth.[52] Eight supernumerary lay clerks were appointed in 1895 to sing at the Sunday services for £5 *per annum,* provided they attended the newly established weekly practice on Saturdays.[53]

Wesley's time at Winchester was not entirely unproductive. He secured for the Cathedral part of the famous Willis organ which had been built for the Great Exhibition in 1851, and in 1853 he published a volume of his anthems, many of which are still among the most popular in the repertoire of English Cathedral music.[54] His organ playing, of course, was outstanding, his extempore playing being particularly famous. This took place after the psalms, before the anthem and at the end of the service.[55] The Dean and Chapter asked Wesley to play a voluntary before every service on Christmas Day, Easter Day, Ascension Day, Whitsunday and Trinity Sunday –

> The organ to commence playing when the clock strikes and to continue until the clergy have taken their places in the choir.[56]

Following the 1840 Cathedrals Act, the number of minor canons was reduced to four and later to three.[57] They were responsible for conducting the choral services according to a rota, and for reading the epistle at communion services in the absence of a canon. Later in the century, two of them were required to be present on a Sunday morning, but they were rarely asked to celebrate communion services. C. H. Thompson told Bishop Davidson in 1900 that he had celebrated only three times in the previous five years.[58] Precentor Henry Wray was said to be 'unusually zealous', conducting choir practices even when S. S. Wesley was present.[59] In 1879 Precentor Crowdy had a lively correspondence with Dr. G. B. Arnold, but the matter was settled over the dinner table.[60]

The virgers (*sic,* local usage) at Winchester were assisted by subsacrists. They were responsible for the daily covering and uncovering of the altar. The senior subsacrist was responsible for all the arrangements for the early morning celebrations, with the assistance of the junior subsacrist at the midday celebrations –

> This includes the changing of the altar cloth when necessary, spreading the fair linen cloths, placing the kneeling cushions, cleansing the vessels, marking the collect, and etc.

The senior subsacrist also presented the service register to the Dean and canon for signature after each service, drew up statements of the quarterly and monthly monies due to the lay clerks and others, and of the monies placed in the offertory boxes, and the fees from the college. The junior subsacrist found the lessons and the music to be sung for the precentor, minor canons and lay clerks at each service. He changed the weekly schemes (or bills) of services, presented the new ones for signature and took them to the printers. He gave necessary assistance to the senior subsacrist, especially at special services such as confirmations.[61]

In 1874, a charge of 6d. was introduced for each visitor who wished to see the Eastern part of the Cathedral. The virgers were not allowed to receive personal gratuities from visitors. Instead, they were invited to put donations into a special box, the income from this source being used to augment the virgers' salaries, to pay for incidental expenses involved in inserting new statues into the Great Screen, and to augment the Fabric Fund.[62] Some of the virgers could be troublesome. George Crupper was strongly reprimanded and fined 10s. for using coarse language towards a visitor in 1844, and James Dennett was accused of using 'improper language' in 1862, while showing two ladies to their seats before a service.[63] William Bond, however, who served the Cathedral (apart from a brief interval of two years) from 1868 to 1913, was described by the *Hampshire Chronicle* as 'one of the oldest and most highly esteemed residents of Winchester'.[64] There were also twelve old men who acted as bedesmen.[65] By 1900 their number had been reduced to six. In addition to their sweeping, weeding and cleaning duties, they took turns to sit by the iron gate leading into the South transept and supervised the admission of visitors to the Eastern part of the Cathedral.[66] There was also a porter who guarded the gates of the close and was responsible for posting and delivering letters within the close.[67] In 1802, Mr. Man, the close porter, was rewarded by the Chapter for catching a thief red-handed.[68]

The ringers practised on Wednesday evenings at 7 p.m. At least eight bells were rung each Sunday before the services, and ten bells on special occasions. There was muffled ringing on New Year's Eve and during Lent.[69] But the ringers could also be troublesome. In 1835, one of them was accused of using 'disrespectful and offensive language' to a member of the Chapter, and another was reprimanded for a similar offence towards a visitor in 1856.[70]

The pattern of Cathedral worship began to alter in the middle years of the century. In addition to the daily choral services of matins and evensong, a choral Eucharist on great festivals was introduced in 1864. An early celebration of the holy communion was started in 1874.[71] In 1866, no less than 956 singers from the United Choirs of the North and South Hampshire Association for the Improvement of Parish Psalmody came to two big services in the Cathedral. There were 480 trebles, 110 altos, 144 tenors and 195 basses. 2,500 tickets were issued and some 4,000 persons were estimated to be in the Cathedral.[72]

Processional entries to services were rare in the early nineteenth century. At most Cathedrals the choir and clergy donned their surplices and found their own way to their stalls. In 1856, Dean Garnier said that he was in favour of making the choristers and lay clerks enter the choir in procession on weekdays as well as Sundays.[73] Any lay clerk who was not ready to join the procession was liable to a fine of one shilling.[74] Two virgers walked together before the clergy.[75]

The precentor at Winchester was responsible for the choice of music. He generally managed to resist –

> the very erroneous views of the canons and Dean as occasionally expressed by them at the instigation of *ladies* and idle people of *distinction,* who visit Cathedrals and ask for pretty, showy things to be sung.

When S. S. Wesley arrived as organist –

although the precentor claimed, and had conceded to him an absolute power here, I found him desirous to consult me in every way. He urged me to always express my views to him and whatever I said was attended to.[76]

Some years later, Precentor Wray had an unpleasant dispute with Archdeacon Jacob about the choice of music for services. Jacob asked another minor canon to substitute on the list music by Wesley for a setting by Aldrich, and wrote to Wray as follows –

> I confess when I saw the bill I expected Mr. Beckwith would have yielded the service as he had done the anthem. For I had asked the substitution of Wesley for Aldrich, not only the grounds of my dislike of Aldrich generally, but that for persons coming from the country as I expected the congregation of Tuesday to be, Wesley was more intelligible and appropriate. Mr. Beckwith remarked that this of *Aldrich in E* was peculiarly suited to country people; it was the very class of music which one would submit as a sample of Cathedral music. I expressed my dissent. Now I quite believe Mr. Beckwith's word, that had he understood my wish to be persevered in for Wesley's service, he would have changed the service as he did the anthem. But conceiving that he adhered to Aldrich on a principle, I resolved to act on a principle also, or to quote my own saying, to 'try the right' – and I substituted Wesley for Aldrich. I claim to do again what I did last week.

Wray protested to the Dean and Chapter, adding that if individual canons could exclude composers at whim –

> the result would be that Anglican church music would sink to the popular taste instead of those tastes which require formation being raised to the best style.[77]

In 1878 the Dean and Chapter made the organist responsible for the first choice of music to be sung. He was to submit this to the precentor and then to the Dean or canon in residence. In the event of a disagreement between the precentor and organist, the Dean or canon in residence had the final decision. No subsequent alteration could be made without the approval of the organist, precentor and Dean or canon in residence. There was a further dispute about the choice of music in 1889.[78]

In 1872, Dean Garnier resigned at the age of 96. His successor, John Bramston, was a very experienced parish priest from Essex. When he was installed, Bishop Samuel Wilberforce was keen to make it an occasion of joint significance both to the Cathedral and the diocese, and asked the Vice Dean to invite as many as possible of the clergy from the diocese to the service. Bramston was an energetic Dean and a memorandum of all the changes he made during his first year in office has been preserved. These alterations indicate a man with a considerable eye for detail, who was anxious to improve the conduct and dignity of the Cathedral's services.[79] Bramston, like Garnier, took an active interest in the Royal Hampshire County Hospital. Several canons served as governors and the hospital chaplain was often one of the minor canons.[80]

Soon after Bramston's arrival, Bishop Wilberforce died suddenly in a riding accident. His successor, E. H. Browne, who had previously been Bishop of Ely, decided to make a formal visitation of the Cathedral. His enquiries were mainly factual, and in his articles he asked a long series of questions about the statutes and constitution of the Cathedral, the number of canons and their residence, the number and employment of the lay clerks and so on.[81]

Within a few years of this visitation, the Dean and Chapter found themselves in considerable financial trouble. Between 1879 and 1882 they had an excess of expenditure over income of £5,586, and in 1883 they were forced to suspend all their customary donations to charity.[82] In 1884 the Dean and Chapter told the Ecclesiastical Commissioners that the £6,450 *per annum* which they were receiving under the 1860 agreement was insufficient.[83] Many Cathedrals were in a similar position at the time, having suffered during the great agricultural depression. In 1883 the accounts of the Dean and Chapter were found to be inaccurate and subject to delay. The duties of Mr. Comely, the Chapter agent, were therefore taken over by a firm of land agents, Messrs. Clutton, but they proved to be unsatisfactory. In 1886, the Dean and Chapter engaged Messrs. Castle, Field and Castle of Oxford, who also acted for the Dean and Chapter of Gloucester Cathedral.[84] Archbishop Benson tried hard to obtain additional funds for Winchester Cathedral, pointing out that the Ecclesiastical Commissioners were receiving immense sums from the former estates of the Cathedral. Dean Kitchin and the Deans of Peterborough and Canterbury, together with three canons, formed a committee to lobby the Prime Minister, Lord Salisbury, in 1886, but the capitular income at Winchester was still greatly reduced in 1894.[85]

Wesley's successor as organist was Dr. G. B. Arnold. He had been a pupil of Wesley and became a Doctor of Music at Oxford at the age of only twenty. He remained at Winchester until his death in 1902.[86] There was, however, little improvement in the condition of the choir. Shortly after his appointment, Arnold had an altercation with precentor Wray, who complained that an anthem had been sung 'discreditably'.[87] In 1869, that redoubtable champion of Cathedral music, Miss Maria Hackett, visited Winchester, but she recorded that the service which she heard was 'shamefully performed.'[88] In 1880, one of the minor canons told the Cathedrals Commission –

> our services at this Cathedral are most unsatisfactory . . . the men hold foundation appointments for life. Of the nine, two or three manage to mar all the music of our services and they cannot be removed.[89]

Ten years later, Precentor Marshall complained that the services were 'tuneless and slovenly'.[90] Difficulties were caused in the same year when some of the congregation started to join in the music sung by the choir.[91] The Dean and canons used to intone the collects on Saints' days, but abandoned this 'unedifying' custom in 1897.[92] Precentor Wray had complained in 1869 that the canons always wanted to intone 'when they thought there was an opportunity of showing off'.[93] Canon Warburton, however, told Bishop Davidson in 1900 that he thought that the daily choral services –

> leave little to be desired in the way of carefulness and brightness and reverence, though the attendance is so lamentably small that it is necessary constantly to bear in mind the altruistic and intercessory character of these services.[94]

There were sixteen choristers by 1891, six of whom were regarded as foundation boys. There were also between four and eight probationers, who occupied seats adjacent to the choristers and attended one service daily as well as all practices.[95]

For over thirty years the Dean and Chapter had struggled to provide the choristers with a proper education, but a variety of temporary expedients failed to provide a permanent solution to this problem. In 1884 the Dean and Chapter told the Ecclesiastical Commissioners –

> The choir is not what it might be and the school arrangements are very defective and unsatisfactory.[96]

The Cathedral's responsibility for the encouragement of learning was taken seriously during these years and several important developments were made. Precentor Wray did much good work in cataloguing the library and Dean Bramston took an interest in the Sunday afternoon lectures, which for many years had been the responsibility of the minor canons. Bramston introduced a wider range of preachers for these lectures.[97]

This side of the Cathedral's life was further developed when Dean Bramston was succeeded by an Oxford historian, George Kitchin, in 1883. During Kitchin's time at Winchester, he edited and published many of the Cathedral's records,[98] but his greatest work was the restoration of the Great Screen behind the high altar.[99] Despite considerable controversy, new statues for the empty niches were commissioned and the work was finally completed in 1899.[100] Soon after Kitchin became Dean, a Cathedral Advisory Committee was appointed, consisting of the Bishop, the Dean and Chapter, one honorary canon and four laymen from the diocese. The purpose of this committee was to give advice to the Chapter on matters affecting the fabric and furnishings of the Cathedral.[101] In 1887, a diocesan chapter was held, the Dean and Chapter being joined by the Archdeacon of the Isle of Wight, many honorary canons, all the minor canons and several rural deans, to advise the Bishop to find ways of helping poor clergy. In 1892 the Bishop used a meeting of the Greater Chapter to discuss affairs affecting the whole diocese.[102] In 1893 the Cathedral's financial arrangements were overhauled and the Chapter appointed three of their number to act as a finance committee. Meetings of this committee were held before every Chapter meeting, so that a monthly check could be kept on the Cathedral's finances. The accounts of the receiver and treasurer were merged, so that all money due to the Chapter was paid into their joint account. The agents on the capitular estates and the Chapter clerk were obliged to submit quarterly statements, and separate accounts were kept for the General Fund, the Charities Accounts, the Offertory Account and for special funds of a temporary nature. The General Fund income was derived from copyholds, dividends, rents, tithes, interest, boxes in the Cathedral, rents of houses in the close and sundry other payments.[103]

In 1898/99, the capitular estates at Winchester were exchanged for tithe rent charge. In 1900 Dean Stephens told Bishop Davidson that 'the result has so far been satisfactory, even with tithe in its present depreciated condition'. The capitular income had fallen steadily since 1879, so that the members of the Chapter had been receiving only half what they were due, but he now expected the income to rise again.[104] Comprehensive new regulations were drawn up for the lay clerks and choristers, and the architect was asked to inspect the Cathedral twice a year and the houses in the close annually.[105] The year 1893 was the 800th anniversary of the Norman Cathedral. A great musical festival was held in celebration of this event. The Stock Exchange orchestra played with the Dean's nephew as conductor (much to the chagrin of the Cathedral organist, Dr. Arnold) and the precentor acted as secretary. Singers came from all over the diocese to take part, but the festival ended with a considerable deficit.[106]

The late nineteenth century saw a considerable increase in the number of special services in the Cathedral. In 1871, the colours of the 101st Royal Bengal Fusiliers were entrusted to the Dean and Chapter.[107] The Lent Assize service in 1873 included some novel features. The choir, as well as the clergy, went to the West door before the service to greet the judges and lead them in procession to the choir, singing the anthem *O How Amiable* by Richardson –

> The clerical procession was kept distinct from the secular one, the clergy not walking with the judges as formerly. By this arrangement, the talking and levity which formerly characterised these ceremonies was avoided.[108]

In 1879 and 1881, quiet days for the clergy and churchwardens of the diocese were held.[109] In 1890 and 1891, evensong on Christmas Eve was postponed until eight o'clock, so that there could be a carol service (including an address by the Dean) in the afternoon. Carols were sung after evensong on Christmas Eve 1893 and the following three days.[110] In 1892 there was a special service for cyclists, while the first Three Hours' service at Winchester took place on Good Friday, 1895. During the Boer War, special services of intercession were held each week in the Lady Chapel.[111] During the year beginning August 1 1899, eighteen special services were held in the Cathedral.[112]

When Dean Kitchin was appointed Dean of Durham in 1895, his successor was another historian, William Richard Wood Stephens. Stephens was the son-in-law of Dean Hook of Chichester. Although he was Dean for only seven years, his time at Winchester was busy. The restoration of the Great Screen was brought to a triumphant conclusion, new stained-glass windows were inserted in the Lady Chapel, substantial repairs were effected to the nave roof and other parts of the Cathedral roof, and great festivities were held in 1901 to mark the millenary of the death of King Alfred and the unveiling of his imposing statue in the Broadway.[113] Dean Stephens was a great champion of the choir, and told *The Guardian* in 1898 –

> I can confidently assert that a healthier and happier set of boys than our choristers could not be found anywhere. Notwithstanding the time spent in musical practice, they are amongst the most proficient in the school of 80 boys which they attend, carrying off a large proportion of the prizes, and some of them are also our best cricket players.[114]

Two years later he told Bishop Davidson that he had added eight Sunday men and two full-time choristers to the choir at his own expense. The choristers had a daily practice and there was a weekly rehearsal for the full choir.[115]

Towards the end of the nineteenth century, the close at Winchester contained two very distinguished canons' wives. In 1882, George

Butler, the headmaster of Liverpool College, became a canon. His wife, Josephine, had already made herself famous for her courage in tackling prostitution and other social problems in Liverpool. Three years later, George Sumner, son of a former bishop of the diocese, became suffragan Bishop of Guildford and a canon of the Cathedral. He had previously been rector of Old Alresford, where his wife Mary had founded the Mothers' Union. [116]

In 1900, Bishop Randall Davidson held a visitation of the Cathedral. After eliciting the necessary facts he needed, he asked the members of the foundation only three general questions. It is clear from these questions that he was looking for ideas to bring the Cathedral 'into fuller practical connexion with diocesan work', for a more central role in diocesan affairs for either the Dean and Chapter or the Greater Chapter as a whole, and for new ways to promote 'the corporate unity and life of the Cathedral'. The replies of Canon Lee and Canon Stenning showed that there had been considerable developments in the links between the Cathedral and the diocese in the closing years of the nineteenth century. Lee pointed out that three of the canons were archdeacons, another was an examining chaplain and director of higher religious education, while the remaining canon was diocesan missioner –

> It is hard to suggest what more they could do, especially as we know they are personally interested in all kinds of societies, institutions, religious and philanthropic movements.

Stenning was equally pleased with this new relationship –

> Many years ago the Cathedral appeared to hold itself aloof from the diocese and to have no sphere of activity and few interests outside its walls. Gradually, and of late increasingly, it has entered largely into diocesan life, as opportunities have been given. [117]

Winchester was by no means the most outstanding of Cathedrals in the nineteenth century. Although there were some able members of its Chapter, for the most part they lacked the distinction and energy to be found among the clergy at St. Paul's or Worcester in the closing decades of the century. In addition, Winchester escaped the substantial restorations which so transformed the appearance of Cathedrals such as Ely, Worcester or Hereford. There was no sudden and dramatic catastrophe such as the calamitous collapse of the spire at Chichester. The music of Winchester, despite the fitful efforts of S. S. Wesley, was generally indifferent and the worship often dull. But there was a tradition of sound scholarship, civilised life and religious earnestness which sustained the Cathedral throughout the years between 1800 and

1900 and well prepared it for the fresh opportunities and challenges of the twentieth century. By 1900, as Canon Bussby has said –

> The Cathedral was finding its new role and was conducting the *Opus Dei* better than it had done for many years. Indeed, the Cathedral had reached a turning point in its long history. [118]

Although Winchester was not the most outstanding of Cathedrals in the nineteenth century, it has a good claim to be one of the most typical.

NOTES

1. W. Cobbett, *Rural Rides,* ed. G. Woodcock (1967), p. 253; F. Bussby, *Winchester Cathedral 1079-1979* (1979), pp. 214-15. Bussby checked Cobbett's description with the attendance registers and found that the Dean was present at the service, together with three prebendaries and four lay vicars. It it not known how many choristers were there, but there were only six in the choir at the time.
2. Quoted in D. N. King, 'Winchester Cathedral under Deans Rennell and Garnier', W(inchester) C(athedral) A(rchives), Winchester Cathedral Chronicle, 1972, p. 1.
3. Report by E. W. Garbett in Winchester Cathedral Chronicle, 1800-1865, pp. 1-21.
4. Bussby, *Winchester Cathedral,* p. 194; cf. J. Crook, 'Winchester Cathedral, 1079-1905: a brief history', pp. 31-4 in I. T. Henderson and J. Crook, *The Winchester Diver* (1984).
5. For Nott, cf. Bussby, *Winchester Cathedral,* pp. 200-1.
6. Philip Williams to his daughters, June 9 1803. W(inchester) C(ollege) M(uniments), Williams Letters, M/PW/105.
7. For Holmes, cf. Bussby, *Winchester Cathedral,* pp. 196-8 and the same author's 'Winchester Cathedral, 1789-1840', *Winchester Cathedral Record,* 44 (1975), pp. 26-7.
8. For Rennell, cf. Bussby, *Winchester Cathedral,* pp. 198-9, and G. H. Blore, *Thomas Rennell, Dean of Winchester, 1805-1840* (1952).
9. Bussby, *Winchester Cathedral,* pp. 198-9.
10. WCM, Williams Letters, M/PW/139, 123.
11. J. M. Horn (ed.), *Le Neve, Fasti Ecclesiae Anglicanae, 1541-1857,* 3 (1974), pp. 37, 98.
12. For Williams, cf. P. L. S. Barrett, 'Philip Williams - the acceptable face of pluralism', *Winchester Cathedral Record,* 57 (1988), pp. 13-26. The following quotations from his letters are also published in that article.
13. *Ibid.,* p. 19. WCM, Williams Letters, M/PW/102. John Sturges held the 8th prebend from 1759 until his death in 1807 (Horn, *Fasti,* p. 101). Edmund Poulter was a canon from 1791 to 1832 (*ibid.,* p. 95).
14. *Ibid.,* p. 19. WCM, Williams Letters, M/PW/110. John Hawtrey held the 11th prebend from 1803 to 1817 (Horn, *Fasti,* p. 105).
15. *Ibid.,* pp. 22-3, WCM, Williams Letters, M/PW/174, June 13 1822.
16. *Ibid.,* p. 20; cf. V. A. Clanchy, 'Jane Austen and the Williams family', *Hampshire* (December 1976), p. 56; Bussby, *Winchester Cathedral,* pp. 211-13, and the same author's *Jane Austen in Winchester* (1973).
17. Cf. fn. 5 above.
18. *Hampshire Chronicle,* May 22 1820, quoted in Bussby, *Winchester Cathedral,* p. 206.
19. King, 'Winchester Cathedral'; P. C. Moore, 'The Development and organisation of Cathedral Worship in England, with special reference to choral services, from the Reformation to the 19th century', unpub. D.Phil. thesis, Oxford University, 1954, p. 355, quoting a letter of Maria Hackett,

November 22 1853; J. W. F. Hill, *Georgian Lincoln* (1966), p. 301.
20. A. W. Goodman and W. H. Hutton, *The Statutes governing the Cathedral Church of Winchester* (1925), pp. 43-4, 49-51; WCA, Act Book of the Dean and Chapter (hereafter ABDC), November 25 1807, November 25 1812, November 25 1825.
21. WCA, ABDC, November 25 1863, June 25 1864.
22. *Ibid.,* March 24 1816.
23. *Ibid.,* February 2 1815.
24. *Ibid.,* February 2 1815, November 25 1818.
25. *Ibid.,* November 25 1818.
26. B. Matthews, *The Music of Winchester Cathedral* (1975), p. 21; WCA, ABDC, June 23 1814; Choristers' Book, 1819-1822, September 2 1820. Cf. also J. Crook, *A History of the Pilgrims' School* (1981), pp. 14-16, and two articles by the same author: 'Half-a-century of choral indiscipline: George Chard and his choir, 1802-1849', *Southern Cathedrals Festival Programme* (1981), pp. 11-13 and 'Fifty years of choral misrule: George Chard and the choristers of Winchester Cathedral', *Winchester Cathedral Record,* 56 (1987), pp. 30-6.
27. WCA, ABDC, November 25 1820, November 25 1830.
28. *Ibid.,* January 19 1809.
29. *Ibid.,* June 23 1815, February 8 1833.
30. *Ibid.,* Winchester Cathedral Chronicle, 1800-1865, p. 62.
31. *Ibid.,* ABDC, February 1, May 4, June 23, October 1 1860; March 25, April 25 1861; September 29 1864.
32. Horn, *Fasti,* p. 107; WCA, ABDC, May 8 1844.
33. *Parliamentary Papers* (henceforward PP), 1837, xli, p. 62.
34. Cf. A. E. Garnier, *The Chronicles of the Garniers of Hampshire* (1900); B. Carpenter Turner, *Winchester* (1980), pp. 172-3.
35. King, 'Winchester Cathedral'.
36. Bussby, *Winchester Cathedral,* pp. 216-18, 223-4. For Wilberforce cf. A. R. Ashwell and R. G. Wilberforce, *Life of the Right Reverend Samuel Wilberforce* (1883); S. Meacham, *Lord Bishop: the life of Samuel Wilberforce, 1805-1873* (1970); D. Newsome, *The Parting of Friends* (1966).
37. Cf. M. P. Chappell, *Dr. S. S. Wesley* (1976), p. 55.
38. S. S. Wesley, *Reply to the Inquiries of the Cathedral Commissioners relative to the improvement in the Music of Divine Worship in Cathedrals* (1854).
39. WCA, ABDC, November 25 1859.
40. *Ibid.,* September 28 1861; cf. also May 5 1854, November 25 1858, June 29 1864.
41. *Ibid.,* September 29 1857.
42. *Ibid.,* February 1 1860; cf. November 25 1856 and November 25 1859.
43. *Ibid.,* November 25 1801, November 25 1802, November 25 1853; cf. June 23 1809, November 26 and 29 1810, November 26 1853, October 4 1873.
44. *Ibid.,* August 2 1887, December 29 1891, January 1 1892, June 1 1897.
45. *Ibid.,* June 23 1856, June 23 1857, November 25 1864, April 5 1887; De Precentore, p. 36. There were nine lay clerks in 1875 (PP, 1876, lviii, pp. 539-49). In 1884 the secular occupations of the lay clerks included keeping

a music shop, acting as a clerk in a house of business, teaching singing in parish schools, and acting as schoolmaster to the choristers. Bishop Browne's Visitation Mss., 1884; Winchester Cathedral Chronicle, 1873-1891, p. 86.

46. WCA, ABDC, June 23 1855, June 23 1856, June 23 1857, November 25 1862.
47. *Ibid.,* De Precentore, p. 13; ABDC, November 25 1874, November 25 1879.
48. *Ibid.,* October 1 1860.
49. *Ibid.,* De Precentore, June 1889.
50. *Ibid.,* December 24 1894; ABDC September 28, December 28 1896. February 25 1898; cf. also De Precentore, November 25 1879.
51. *Ibid.,* ABDC, July 30 1890, March 25 1891; De Precentore, April 1891.
52. E. H. Fellowes, *English Cathedral Music from Edward VI to Edward VII* (1941), p. 226; WCA, ABDC, June 23 1870.
53. *Ibid.,* De Precentore, 1895, p. 116.
54. For two recent studies of Wesley's music, cf. K. Long, *The Music of the English Church* (1971), pp. 340-51; W. J. Gatens, *Victorian Cathedral Music in Theory and Practice* (1986), pp. 128-46. The Willis organ is described in B. Matthews, *The Organs and Organists of Winchester Cathedral* (n.d.), pp. 8-11.
55. Fellowes, *English Cathedral Music,* p. 35; cf. B. Matthews, p. 24, quoting W. A. Fearon, *The Passing of Old Winchester* (1924), p. 78.
56. WCA, ABDC, March 30, 1864.
57. WCA, Cathedralia Winton: Minor Canons 1860-1918, (hereafter MCB), July 15 1890.
58. *Ibid.,* ABDC, June 23 1858; June 22, August 3, November 26 1878; January 7 1879; MCB, July 15 1890; Davidson Visitation Mss., 1900.
59. Chappell, *Wesley,* pp. 98-9, quoting *Musical Times* (June 1899), pp. 377-8.
60. WCA, De Precentore, 1879, p. 71.
61. *Ibid.,* ABDC, August 1 1882; cf. February 3, September 29 1874.
62. *Ibid.,* February 3 1874, November 25 1889.
63. *Ibid.,* June 23 1862.
64. R. A. Godfrey, 'Cathedral Virgers through the centuries', *Winchester Cathedral Record,* 24 (1978), quoting Winchester Cathedral Chronicle, 1854-1916, p. 131.
65. Goodman and Hutton, *Statutes,* pp. 56-7; WCA, ABDC, November 25 1874.
66. WCA, Bishop Davidson's Visitation Mss., 1900.
67. *Ibid.,* ABDC, June 23 1839.
68. *Ibid.,* November 25 1802.
69. *Ibid.,* April 6 1899.
70. *Ibid.,* November 25 1835, September 29 1856.
71. *Ibid.,* De Precentore, March 29 1864; King, 'Winchester Cathedral'.
72. WCA, De Precentore, June 5 1866; Bussby, *Winchester Cathedral,* p. 237.
73. WCA, ABDC, November 25 1856.
74. *Ibid.,* March 30 1864.
75. Goodman and Hutton, *Statutes,* p. 52.
76. S. S. Wesley to H. E. Ford, September 19 1858, quoted in Moore, thesis

p. 357.
77. WCA, De Precentore, June 1-2 1864.
78. *Ibid.*, ABDC, November 26 1878, January 7 1879; De Precentore, May 21-2 1889.
79. *Ibid.*, Winchester Cathedral Chronicle, 1873-1891, p. 71; *ibid.*, opp. p. 1.
80. C. Moxley, *Cathedral, College and Hospital* (1986), p. 71.
81. WCA, Bishop Browne's Visitation Mss.; cf. also Winchester Cathedral Chronicle, 1873-1891, pp. 85-9 and Bussby, *Winchester Cathedral*, pp. 232-4.
82. *The Guardian*, 1885, p. 645; WCA, ABDC, March 3 1883.
83. *Ibid.*, Ecclesiastical Commissioners' Box, February 5 1884.
84. *Ibid.*, ABDC, March 6, October 3, December 11 1883; January 8 1884; Bishop Davidson's Visitation Mss., Dean's reply.
85. Lambeth Palace Library, Benson Papers, I, f. 399; Norwich Cathedral Library, Dean Goulburn's Diary, November 30 1886; *Church Congress Report 1894*, pp. 32-3.
86. Bussby, *Winchester Cathedral*, pp. 237, 266-7.
87. WCA, De Precentore, p. 40.
88. Quoted in Moore, thesis, pp. 306-7.
89. PP, 1884-5, xxi, p. 54; W. O. Chadwick, *The Victorian Church*, 2 (1970), p. 376.
90. WCA, De Precentore, September 22 1890.
91. *Ibid.*, November 1890.
92. *Ibid.*, MCB, March 12 1897.
93. *Ibid.*, De Precentore, 1869, p. 49.
94. *Ibid.*, Davidson's Visitation Mss.
95. *Ibid.*, ABDC, January 6 1891.
96. *Ibid.*, Ecclesiastical Commissioners' Box, Dean Kitchin to Commissioners, February 5 1884; cf. also Choristers' box file; ABDC November 26 1860, November 25 1868; J. Crook, *A History of the Pilgrims' School* (1981), pp. 18-20.
97. F. Bussby, *Winchester Cathedral Library* (1972), p. 9; Goodman and Hutton, *Statutes*, p. 31; WCA, MCB.
98. Bussby, *Winchester Cathedral*, pp. 237-8.
99. G. W. Kitchin, *The Great Screen of Winchester Cathedral* (1899); Bussby, *Winchester Cathedral*, pp. 245-9.
100. For a detailed account, cf. F. Bussby, 'The Great Screen — part II', *Winchester Cathedral Record*, 48 (1979), pp. 12-17.
101. WCA, ABDC, January 8 1885.
102. *Ibid.*, MCB, July 15 1890; Winchester Cathedral Chronicle, 1866-1894, p. 46; Winchester Cathedral Greater Chapter Minutes, 1892-1907.
103. WCA, ABDC, October 31 1893.
104. *Ibid.*, Bishop Davidson's Visitation Mss.
105. *Ibid.*, ABDC, November 25 1893, May 29 1894.
106. *Ibid.*, De Precentore, 1893-4.
107. *Ibid.*, Winchester Cathedral Chronicle, 1873-1891, p. 72.
108. *Ibid.*, De Precentore, 1873.
109. *Ibid.*, Winchester Cathedral Chronicle, 1873-1891, p. 91.

136   *Close Encounters*

110. *Ibid.,* De Precentore, 1893.
111. *Ibid.,* Winchester Cathedral Chronicle, 1866-1894, p. 41; *ibid.,* 1895-1932, pp. 4, 66.
112. *Ibid.,* Davidson's Visitation Mss., Dean's preparatory answers.
113. Cf. Bussby, *Winchester Cathedral,* pp. 249-51, 266, and J. B. Colson, *The Reparation of the Nave Roof* (1898).
114. *The Guardian,* 1898, p. 1143.
115. WCA, Davidson's Visitation Mss., Dean's reply (preparatory).
116. Cf. G. W. and L. A. Johnson, *Josephine Butler — an autobiographical memoir* (1928) and J. Coombs, *George and Mary Sumner* (1965).
117. WCA, Davidson's Visitation Mss., replies of Canons Lee and Stenning; Bussby, *Winchester Cathedral,* pp. 250-2; G. W. Kitchin, *Edward Harold Browne,* (1895), p. 356.
118. Bussby, *Winchester Cathedral,* p. 252.

The Nineteenth Century Revivification of Salisbury Cathedral: Walter Kerr Hamilton, 1841 – 1854

Arthur E. Bridge

Walter Kerr Hamilton arrived to take up his new duties at Salisbury at Easter 1841, as one who had moved from Evangelical to Tractarian discipleship –

> He was a hard working parochial clergyman, whose sympathies at an early date were certainly 'Evangelical' but who developed before long into advanced Tractarian, and remained in that place to the end of his life. Such instances often remind one of that fine but mournful couplet of Pope: 'And middle natures reach, and long to join yet never pass the insurpassible line.'[1]

The general popularity and security which he had enjoyed at Oxford made it at first difficult for him to settle into his new position as canon of Salisbury. The depression of the situation was only lifted through his personal friendship and association with Bishop Denison and his wife Louisa. On September 22 1841, Mrs. Denison died. Hamilton was devastated. The effect of her death upon him was so great that he seriously contemplated resigning his canonry and returning to Oxford.[2] In July, 1841, Hamilton was collated to the Prebendal Stall of Calne, to which was attached the office of Cathedral treasurer.[3] The duties of this office were not at first burdensome, for in respect to pastoral duties he merely acted as 'curate' to the residents of the close. When it eventually became possible to do so, Denison offered to Hamilton the office of precentor. Hamilton was, at first, unwilling to accept the position. He was, however, eventually persuaded of the merits of accepting such an offer, although he did so with some reluctance.[4]. Hamilton was installed in January 1843 as precentor of Salisbury and collated to the prebendal stall of Forleton.[5] He was above average in his attendance at Chapter meetings.[6] The office of precentor gave Hamilton the unique opportunity to set about a series of reforms in respect to the services and general character of the

Cathedral. The Cathedral was the bastion of the faith against the assaults of the world. Much of what he achieved in the performance of his duties as precentor of Salisbury was of such a pioneering kind, that to many his reforms must have seemed radical, if not revolutionary.

It is hardly surprising to understand why Hamilton needed to improve the situation at Salisbury when you read about the Cathedral's life at that time –

> The Cathedral and its Services. The fittings of the church were most lamentable. Wyatt, in the eighteenth century, had destroyed much that was beautiful; 'Neat, cold, unmeaningly symmetrical, the interior of Salisbury' (so writes Dr. Liddon in sketching Bishop Hamilton's life)[7] 'chills the soul more cruelly than does the roofless nave of Tintern'. No other English Cathedral suffered so desolating a scourge. Many who came to worship in the winter brought horse rugs with them to prevent them shivering with cold, for the only attempt to warm the big church were three charcoal braziers, that stood upon the choir floor, looking, perhaps, somewhat cheerful, and emitting sparks which sometimes settled upon the surplices of the alarmed choristers.
>
> But I turn to the living body of the Cathedral. There was a Dean and six canons, and four vicars choral. The Dean alone kept residence for the three summer months. There were two canons resident for three months each during the rest of the year. There was only one sermon on a Sunday, except on Easter Day and Assize Sunday. An afternoon sermon was introduced in Dean Pearson's time during the summer months. There was no way of lighting the Cathedral, so that there was no sermon during the winter afternoons. The holy communion was celebrated on the first Sunday in the month and on the great festivals. Alms were only collected when the holy communion was celebrated. There were seven lay vicars, the organist being one of them, and eight chorister boys. These were natives of Salisbury, who lived in the town with their parents or friends, and never had a holiday from the Cathedral. The lay vicars were not very competent singers, and only three attended at a time, except on Sundays. The precentor was master of the Charterhouse, and was rarely seen in the Cathedral. The chancellor, holding a well-endowed office, was Bishop of Carlisle. His business was to preach Saints' day sermons. This he did by deputy, paying one of the minor canons £25 *per annum*. The prebendaries were all endowed, many of them with considerable emoluments and preferments, and many living beyond the diocese. A few preached in their statutory turns, but many of them never came to the Cathedral. We can hardly wonder that an Act of Spoliation passed through Parliament in 1837, depriving all clerical holders of Cathedral preferments of their salaries, except the Dean (whose salary was greatly reduced) and four canons. Existing interests were respected. The vicars choral were a separate corporation.[8]

Music was a social statement of mid-Victorian life, so it was to things musical that Hamilton first applied himself. Although he was not a musician by training, he did have a right sense of order and dignity, and in the light of his Oxford experiences,[9] soon set about re-ordering the musical presentation of the services. In regard to his musical endeavours, Hamilton was a visionary –

> Here this ardent reformer was able to exert a wide and then beneficient influence; other Cathedrals slowly came into line.[10]

> Wakeling in his *Recollections of the Oxford Movement,* drew particular attention to Hamilton's pioneer activity in the reform of Cathedral music, remarking that, once he had shown the way at Salisbury, 'Cathedral after Cathedral carried on the way of improvement'.[11]

The unwillingness of the vicars choral to chant the services or even to be present at the services was, to say the very least, disappointing. Dr. Rainbow notes, although not entirely accurately –

> Although not gifted with a cultivated ear, nor much natural inclination to study music, Hamilton endeavoured to supply these defects by conscientious effort. Disappointed to find that the residentiaries at Salisbury were largely unable or unwilling to chant the services, he resolved that he would 'contribute nothing to the unseemly discord of the prevailing practice'.[12]

The Cathedral organist was Arthur Thomas Corfe (1773-1863), and his observations about the choristers' poor record of attendance is most alarming –

> 'Well, Sir,' said the organist, 'I daresay you are right, but you must know that the rule at Salisbury has always been, "let everybody get off everything he can"'.[13]

Hamilton believed that the musical settings and anthems used at each service must either emphasise the Church's liturgical seasons, or point to some noteworthy features of her teaching as presented in the services of the Church.[14] His zeal for reform did not pass unnoticed in the diocese. Some of the parochial clergy sought his advice.[15] He laboured by example and constant teaching to impress upon his colleagues, and more especially the lay vicars and choristers, the importance and significance of conducting and singing the daily services with dignity. He showed the importance of the office by wearing his cassock for the greater part of the day –

> The general reappearance of the cassock probably owes something to Bishop W. K. Hamilton of Salisbury, who as canon of that church between 1841 and 1847 'by way of keeping before him a reminder of his work ... used to wear his cassock all day, and it was not until after the afternoon (Cathedral) service that he put on his coat for a walk'. Such a practice shows that the practice of wearing the cassock was returning.[16]

Regularity of attendance was the standard he required for both clergy and choir alike, and was without compromise in its enforcement.

Hamilton, who as precentor was master of the choristers, moved through the Cathedral Chapter a series of rules for lay vicars and supernumeraries –

1. Each lay vicar and week day supernumerary shall attend morning and evening service each day in the week, unless he have leave of absence.
2. Leave of absence shall be given to every lay vicar and week day supernumerary for one day during each week – but the absence cannot take place either on a Sunday or Tuesday afternoon or Saint's day or other festival or holy day of the Church or public day without a special sanction.
3. There shall never be fewer than four laymen present at divine service and of these, there shall be always at least one bass, one tenor, one counter tenor. NB. In the case of illness or other absence of some of the laymen it may be necessary to suspend *pro tempore* the above rules about leave of absence.
4. No layman or supernumerary can by exchange of leave of absence be absent for more than one day in the week without special sanction.
5. The lay vicars and week day supernumeraries shall practice with the choristers at the singing school on one day in each week to be agreed upon with them by the precentor and organist. [The] services and anthems shall be appointed for the following Sunday and other music which the precentor and organist shall select.
6. The fines for absence without leave shall be as was fixed Dec. 5 1815 viz. 10/6 – ten shillings and sixpence on Sundays, Christmas Day, Holy Thursday, the Anniversary of the Infirmary and other Public Days. [And] on other days 1/6 for each service.
7. Each member of the choir shall choose his day of absence by seniority.[17]

Hamilton categorically fixed those days when the whole choir was expected to attend services in the Cathedral. Namely, 'Sundays, Tuesday afternoons, Christmas Day, Holy Thursday, Monday and Tuesday in Easter week, Monday and Tuesday in Whitsun week, Circumcision, Epiphany, Purification, Annunciation, St. Michael and All Angels, Ash Wednesday, Holy or Passion Week, All Saints Day, Martyrdom, Ascension, Restoration, November 5, Anniversary of the Infirmary, Public Days, such as meetings of Church and Diocesan Societies, etc'.[18]

> During his precentorship at Salisbury, Hamilton made it his duty to select all the music of the services. Every anthem sung in the Cathedral was chosen by him to illustrate the progress of the Church's year or some salient feature of her teaching. He also made the intimate acquaintance of the choristers and lay vicars and sought to convince them of the high privilege of their offices – encouraging them to abandon the perfunctory attitude then common in most Cathedral choirs.[19]

The choristers in most cases were inhabitants of the city, living in dwellings scattered about Salisbury. They were often quite unruly and of very poor ability. Hamilton's practical interest in the education of the choristers eventually resulted in the establishment of a choir who resided together in the close, under the care and direction of a priest.[20] In this regard –

> Salvation for the school was heralded by the appointment, in 1841, of Walter Kerr Hamilton, as a member of the Chapter.[21].

Hamilton proposed funding the choristers through a series of choral exhibitions. He further promoted an idea of his friend Dr. Arnold about the establishment of choral colleges at Oxford and Cambridge. Dora Robertson notes –

> Elaborating the question of exhibitions in his letter, Canon Hamilton says that he would 'be very thankful to see some exhibitions founded in connection with our choristers' school, both for the continuation of the choristers' education when their voices break, and also for the giving a gratuitous education to other poor scholars in this city.
> Why should we not also look forward [he continues] to the time (for it is surely coming) when our two great Universities shall adopt the plan which was always so fondly cherished by my dear and honoured friend and tutor, Dr. Arnold, and which is perhaps the very best of all the valuable suggestions of the Oxford tutors, and we shall be able (if we can in the meanwhile secure funds for the purpose) to open a hall at Oxford or Cambridge for the most meritorious of our choristers and other grammar scholars.'[22]

Hamilton's intervention removed a 250 year neglect of Cathedral choristers. His visionary endeavours set firmly the foundations for all future Cathedral choir schools in Britain.

In 1846 Hamilton and the new Dean, Francis Lear, worked together to effect more sweeping internal Cathedral reform. Some have described this contribution as heralding an 'epoch in Cathedral reform'.[23] Hamilton firmly believed that the Cathedral was the 'Mother Church' of the diocese and as such should be open daily and be accessible to everyone. Access was made easier in 1847 with the arrival of the South Western Railway link to Salisbury. During a visit to the Continent in 1849, Hamilton was greatly inspired by the large numbers of ordinary people that he saw gathered in the naves of the great Cathedrals for services.[24] Upon his return to Salisbury, he was personally responsible for seeing that the nave of the Cathedral of Salisbury was open to the public between morning and evening service each day, and that a member of the Chapter was present.[25] In 1847, Hamilton resurrected the much neglected daily office of morning prayer, taking upon himself almost sole responsibility for the performance of this service. During 1849 he effected the introduction of a weekly celebration of the holy communion at eight o'clock on Sunday morning.[26] Again, as with other of his initiatives, he took the burden upon himself in carrying out this duty, without allowing it to interfere with his other commitments.

He worked continually for the improvement of the Cathedral furnishings and fabric. He provided, at his own expense, a pair of candlesticks,[27] and altar cloths, as well as a side chapel altar curtain. He bought new prayer books to enable more people to have a copy of the service, thereby increasing the participation of the congregation at services[28] – a fairly simple thing, with profound implications. The restoration of the Cathedral building was thought necessary; and so with ceaseless effort he worked with the architect and his brother canons to facilitate this endeavour. When appointed keeper of the Cathedral muniments, he saw to the safe keeping and cataloguing of the archives, as well as the ordering of the library. He completely restored and refilled the muniment room.[29] At this time it was the custom for the canon in residence to preach on holy days. The clergyman concerned was of some advanced age; so Hamilton took upon himself the task of preaching.[30] In respect of the influence he exhibited, Hamilton was ahead of all others.[31]

In the first half of the nineteenth century, Cathedrals were regarded as 'white elephants' in the ecclesiastical world. The situation was well noted –

> In the early part of the nineteenth century a government commission enquired into the affairs of the Cathedral bodies, and some of the worst financial scandals were removed. It was not, however, until the Oxford Movement made its influence felt that there came a real change over the life and work of the Cathedrals. They were cleaned, restored and gradually brought into use as centres of worship.[32]

The Cathedral Chapters were in great want of reform. So much so that in 1840, a bill was passed in Parliament requiring Cathedral Chapters to report to the Church Commissioners on their present state of affairs, and to submit schemes of reform, whereby they proposed to put their houses in order. In respect to the work of the Cathedral Commission, Dr. Best notes –

> The Cathedrals Commission, for all its antiquarianism and despite the self-interestedness which showed through the statements of some Chapters, had much to report that was worthwhile, and its recommendations respecting the overhaul of Cathedral statutes were

sound. But nothing came of it. It was of too esoteric a character for the general public or the ordinary member of Parliament to take note of. Church extension and religious education, subjects that would have attracted attention, hardly appeared in its pages.[33]

Hamilton was such a Tractarian, who was at this time strategically placed to be able to influence and affect Cathedral reform. Salisbury Cathedral was, as we have already noted above, no exception to the current situation.

It fell to Hamilton, as precentor, to make a report on behalf of the Chapter. This took the form of an open letter to the Dean, which was printed and circulated at the request of Bishop Denison in April 1853.[34] It was 36 pages in length and was the result of much careful thought and study, in the light of much practical experience gained in the life of Salisbury Cathedral.[35] This document was to have a profound influence throughout the Church. Hamilton would have been aware of contemporary writings concerning the reform of Cathedral institutions and the Church generally. Firstly, there was Lord Henley's 1832 plan for *Church Reform*. Henley put forward the idea of the re-circulation of ecclesiastical property and finances in order that certain endowments could be properly used make the whole Church's task of evangelism more effective. The Cathedrals he believed were to be in the vanguard for the re-distribution of wealth. Secondly, there was Thomas Arnold's 1833 *Principles of Church Reform*.[36] Hamilton was a pupil of Arnold and a close personal friend. Arnold called for the commutation of tithes, the remodelling of the episcopate to obtain a more effective Church government, the splitting up of dioceses to extend the influence of the Church into every town and village, the annexation of prebendal stalls to unpaid livings, the enforcement of compulsory residences, and the creation of new parishes in the larger and more populous towns throughout the nation. In the summary he called for a more 'Comprehensive National Church'. Thirdly, there was the pamphlet of the Tractarian divine Edward Pusey of 1833 entitled *Remarks on the Prospective and Past Benefits of Cathedral Institutions*, written in response to Lord Henley's letter on Cathedral reform. In this document Pusey advocates the prominence of Cathedrals as centres of theological learning with special interest for those training for holy orders in the Church of England. He felt that the traditional centres at Oxford and Cambridge were neglecting theological education. He further felt that Cathedral institutions should contain suitable libraries for theological students and that the Cathedral environment was an exemplary setting for young men training for the ministry because of their close proximity and easy access to the Bishop and senior clergy resident in the close.[37]

> But Pusey came forward as the defender of Cathedrals, giving evidence of their past work as centres of theological learning from which sprang the best of English theology, and suggesting the means by which they could be preserved and their educational task continued and extended.[38]

Finally there was Henry Manning's published letter to the Bishop of Chichester in January 1838 entitled the *Principles of the Ecclesiastical Commission Examined,* in which Manning advocates an increase in the episcopate and the infusion of a new life into all Cathedral Chapters in order that they should become centres of theological learning in which the canons serve as instructors to those preparing for ordination.[39] While at Oxford Hamilton was a close associate of both Pusey and Manning. A contemporary view of one associated with the Cathedral life and its reforms remarked –

> There is sound common sense in the pamphlet, founded as it is upon precentor Hamilton's views of Cathedral reform – but going, needless to say, a long way beyond them.[40]

Hamilton's letter to the Dean covers the whole ground on which the Cathedral reform was to be constructed, in order to eliminate the abuses of the existing system, and the steps which, in his opinion would rectify the many problems and deficiencies. In short a grand re-ordering of men and facilities.

An analysis of Hamilton's reform proposals bear close examination. The *Problems,* as Hamilton saw them, were, 'the condition of the property of the Cathedral bodies is in every way most inconvenient and disadvantaged.'[41] Chapters were confronted with working inadequacies of past systems, which simply had no practical relevance in the nineteenth century. The system was such that, 'annual incomes are very *unequal* in amount and very *uncertain.*'[42] They resulted in all sorts of inequalities and anomalies. Furthermore, Hamilton points out other conditions which, 'impair the life and usefulness of Chapters' – namely, 'the division of authority ... the uncertainty of limits, and so the habitual neglect of all attempt to exercise it.' Also, 'the shortness of residence, the holding of other preferment with our canonries, and so residing at the Cathedral only a few months in the year.' And, 'the discontinuance of the Pentecostal meetings of the prebendaries, and so their exclusion from the counsels of the Chapter.'[43] Finally, the size of the 'Great Chapter' needed to be substantially reduced. For it seemed to him that any body 'consisting of five or six members, is both too large and too small for the good conduct of business, and for the influence upon them of a keen sense of responsibility.'[44] And it was further alleged that 'Deans and canons and vicars choral have no *definite* duties,' which resulted in accusations of idleness being levelled against such members of the Cathedral institutions.[45]

For Hamilton the *Solutions* were as follows, 'that the whole of the property should be placed for a time in the hands of the Commissioners for its better management.'[46] This would then facilitate the property being 'more productive' and thereby prevent 'misemployment of means' and 'management' of properties.[47] In order to meet the two principal purposes of any Cathedral foundation, namely, 'the celebration of divine worship and the promotion of religious education',[48] Hamilton suggested that –

> we should have four canons and four vicars choral always resident, that the number of our laymen (who are seven including the organist) should be increased to thirteen, and that of our choristers to sixteen, and should wish to provide that there should be at all services two canons, two vicars choral, eight laymen, and twelve choristers present and on Sundays and other holy days the whole body, except when hindered by illness or absent with permission.[49]

This would remove a good many of the complaints levelled at the canons and choir of the Cathedral. The education of the choristers he believed required, 'an improved system of management', whereby 'some exhibitions founded in connection with our choristers' school, both for the continuation of the choristers' education when their voices break, and also for giving a gratuitous education to other poor scholars in the city.'[50] Hamilton desired the incorporation of an idea of Dr. Thomas Arnold, which would facilitate the opening of a 'hall at Oxford or Cambridge for the most meritorious of our choristers and other grammar scholars'.[51] Furthermore, other educational reforms might come about if more money were available, whereby –

> adequate stipends should be paid to the under masters of our grammar school, in addition to their proportionate share of the profits of the school – that a salary of a school inspector for the diocese, or small stipends to the many school inspectors, who according to the present arrangements fill this office, should be paid from the same sources – and that the training school for school mistresses, and a first rate elementary school, and infant school should be mainly supported in the same way, I think that all Church educationists would be satisfied that we desired faithfully to fulfil the wishes of our founders, and had really at heart the sacred course of religious education.[52]

Hamilton further felt that there was a need to extend the spiritual jurisdiction to those districts adjoining the close. There were three city parishes (St. Thomas, St. Edmund and St. Martin), as well as schools, hospitals, and other sacred and secular institutions. This would mean –

> by extending our district and including within it some portions of the adjoining parishes, we should be bringing our ministrations to bear more directly on the spiritual condition of Salisbury.[53]

The Cathedral library would also be another area to benefit from the availability of money, whereby, 'we shall have a librarian with a proper salary and have the means of adding to our valuable collection of books'.[54]

Improvement in the status of Cathedral prebendaries and payment of laymen was keenly advocated.[55] Hamilton wanted a fund to be established to meet the expenses of the canons in fulfilling their preaching commitments, and an increase in the salary for the organist and lay vicars, subject to attendance and good conduct.[56] The endowments of the three city parishes needed to be substantially improved, in addition to which there ought to be provision made for the chaplaincy of the city workhouse and the Bugmore Hospital.[57] Hamilton did not favour a current proposal to attach large parishes to particular canonries, because it would impede the very progress it intended.[58] He pointed out that it would –

> be far better, as a general rule, to provide adequate endowments for the parishes of the Cathedral city out of the Chapter funds, and to connect with canonries definite duties, distinct from the work of the parish priest, and almost as necessary as his to the well-being of the Church. If canons have parochial duties beyond the precincts of their Cathedral, they will be generally tempted to look at the Cathedrals through their parishes, and thus making them secondary objects.[59]

Hamilton went on to outline a scheme for the regulating and defining of the different duties of the Dean, the Chapter, and the vicars choral. This was perhaps his most valuable contribution of all to the whole reform issue –

> The Dean should stand in the same relation to the whole body, as that in which the head of a house in our Universities stands to his fellows, and should have the exercise of his authority cleared of all unnecessary trammels.
> Under the Dean and his Chapter, the precentor should regulate the choral services and be responsible for all parish duties and early and other services, and should always be ready to take the sermons which are not specially provided for, and which neither the Dean or the canon in residence wish to preach.
> The chancellor should be the head master, or principal of the grammar

school, and have, as his house of residence, the adjoining canonical house, which was occupied by Mr. Marsh. The house, now held under lease, on the South side of the school, should at the expiration of the lease, be connected with the grammar school as a boarding house. The garden at the back of this house and of the master's present house should be the play-ground instead of the square.

The treasurer should discharge the duties of secretary to the Board of Education and of chaplain to the training school; the fourth canon should be also vicar of St. Thomas.

One of the vicars choral should be the curate of the precentor.

Another should be a lecturer at the grammar school and training school.

A third should be chaplain of the city workhouse and Bugmore Hospital, and secretary to the elementary and infant schools in connexion with the Cathedral.

The fourth should be the librarian.[60]

Hamilton further pushed the question about, 'proper endowment of the vicarages and perpetual curacies of those parishes where we are the impropriate rectors'.[61] These parishes, he maintained, should receive the responsible care and attention of the Cathedral, because –

the parishes, where we have property, have claims on us not only for providing for the proper endowments of their vicars and perpetual curates, but also for aid in supporting those local charities, on which the well-being of the poor of the land, both physically and morally, so much depends.[62]

Such proposals would, he believed, remove to some extent the complaints of the Commissioners and ensure a return to the intentions of their founders. He concluded –

I have before me in the adjoining city well or adequately endowed cures, – flourishing schools for all classes, in close connexion with our Cathedral – I see, as I have seen abroad, not only a crowded choir, but a crowded nave, – I hear eloquent preachers, heavenly music . . . I then easily pass on to the conclusion that if the improvements in the management of our property should not be so productive as we hope they will be, that there are still men who are not so cut off from the hearts and the sympathies of our founders, as not to be willing to help so good a cause, by giving some of their wealth to an institution which will be then proved not to be over-rich, but to be crippled in its powers of usefulness for want of means.[63]

Hamilton's report was enthusiastically received by the Dean and Chapter, who circulated its findings in the form of a letter.[64] Bishop Denison followed through the Commissioners' enquiries in the form of two letters later published in connection with the subject. The first pointed out the desirability of forming a 'Capitular Commission' to promote the necessary proposals, and what its course might attain.[65] The other letter outlined the role of the Bishop and Dean and Chapter in respect to their separate functions and duties in connection with the Cathedral and consequent responsibilities.[66] Hamilton upon his own elevation to the episcopate reissued the letters of 1853 with his own accompanying letter about Cathedral reform.[67] In essence what his letter on reform did was to outline the practical situation at Salisbury which had been truly tried during the preceding decade.

In respect to Cathedral preferment, Hamilton when he became Bishop followed the rule of his predecessor Bishop Denison. Prebendal stalls were singularly diocesan –

> I must add what the late Bishop always said namely that should you leave the diocese I shall expect you to resign the stall, as these appointments have been reserved for the special object of connecting more closely the clergy of the diocese with their Bishop and his Cathedral.[68]

The place of the Bishop also took Hamilton's attention. In his journal Hamilton asks the question, *'what are the rights of the Bishop with respect to the Cathedral Church?'* He notes the following –

1. The Bishop has the right of celebrating the holy communion. This is recognized in entries in our registers where it is ruled that the *Principal Dignitary* shall celebrate when the Bishop and Dean are not there to celebrate.
2. The Bishop at any rate by long custom holds his visitations, confirmations and ordinations in the Cathedral Church.
3. There is a [custom] by which provision is made for sermons for all Sundays and chief festivals, with the exception of Holy Thursday – but no days are set apart for the Bishop – whether this omission implies or negatives any claim of right we know not.
4. The Bishop's court has been ever held in some part of the Cathedral. It is now held and has been so far so for time in memorial in the part of the cloisters which adjoins the Cathedral.
5. Has the Bishop any portion of the common fund of the church or any pension or payment from the Chapter?
   [a] None.
6. Do the Dean and canons assist the Bishop in examinations for holy orders and imposition of hands and in the proceedings of the Bishop's court according to the Canons of AD. 1603?
   [a] They do not assist in the examination or the proceedings of the court but they do assist in the imposition of hands at ordinations.
   The Bishop's examining chaplains are to be one of the residentiaries *(sic)*.[69]

Beyond the Cathedral, Hamilton worked in unison with Bishop Denison. Whilst in some instances it was Denison who conceived the new schemes, it was Hamilton who worked them out in practical terms. One such area of mutual involvement was in the sphere of education.

Bishop Denison in 1838 formed a Diocesan Board of Education, in co-operation with the National Society, to assist in forwarding religious education on sound principles in the Church of England. At a public meeting held in 1839 at Salisbury, under the chairmanship of Lord Shaftesbury, Denison noted –

> the importance of good middle schools, the training of teachers, school inspection and the necessity for local action.[70]

In 1840 a joint initiative for the Winchester and Salisbury dioceses, emanating from a conference convened at Romsey, was the setting up of a training school for masters at Winchester and one for mistresses at Salisbury. These two centres were to benefit both dioceses and were in no way intended to be mutually exclusive, but rather as a means of concentrating resources. In Salisbury the training school had a humble beginning –

> The school began in a small way, with one lady at the head to manage all details and instruct the pupils. It began with one pupil in a small house in the Palace Walk. It was not long before more accommodation was required, and in 1852 the present premises in the close, called the King's House, were taken as a training college. The cost of the buildings, including the value of the fees given by Dean and Chapter, was above £8,000, a sum largely raised by the personal exertions of the Bishop. But the whole cost of the King's House and adjoining buildings and its structural alterations amounted to no less a sum than £15,000. Since that time the college has received great additions, and a chapel has been added to it, where the students attend morning and evening prayer, but come to the Cathedral on Sundays. No less than 2,400 trained students have been sent out from this college to various schools in this and in other dioceses.[71]

Hamilton, for his part, was Secretary to the Board of Education, and assumed to himself the unofficial role of chaplain to the training school. It was he who saw to the smooth running of this body and calmed any difficult situation which might arise. His lectures and sermons did much to raise the intellectual and spiritual standards of those students with whom he came in contact.[72] The education minute of July 25 1850 received a mixed reaction up and down the country. However, Hamilton saw its effect on the training school in Salisbury as being of some positive value, that would ensure a well filled college, well prepared pupils and regular payments.[73]

Hamilton was no less active in the proposals for the foundation of Marlborough College, a public school for boys in the diocese. In 1842 the Revd. Matthew Wilkinson was appointed headmaster. He was succeeded by the Revd. G. E. L. Cotton, who later became Bishop of

Calcutta. The school took its first pupils in 1843, numbering around
200, and this number rose to 500 by 1847, most of whom were boarders.
A large proportion of the boys were the sons of clergymen, whose fees
were reduced – 30 guineas a year compared with 50 guineas for the
sons of laymen. Hamilton assisted in answering any general enquiries
about the school –

> I dare say you will be so kind as to give me a little information about
> the projected school at Marlborough, chiefly as I understand for the
> sons of the clergy. Are not shares £50 each? And does not one share give
> the right to one nomination and so on by fifties, and is not the further
> expense to the friend of the boy to be £30 a year? And what is the extra
> expense supposing the boy nominated is of lay extraction? And when is
> the school likely to open? And where may subscriptions be paid?[74]

Hamilton remained, despite the grandeur of his office and position in
the Cathedral and diocese, very much the pastor, overflowing with love
for ordinary people in whatever walk of life he encountered them. His
experience of St. Peter's, Oxford, and with the Tractarians, equipped
him to live and work with strength and humility – labouring for the
spiritual as well as the material well-being of the people of Salisbury
diocese. He was both popular and respected by clergy and laity inside
and outside the diocese, even by those whose churchmanship was
different from his own.[75] He moved with ease and freedom amongst the
poor of the city, and would, whenever possible, on a Sunday arrange
for six to eight of them to dine with him. When there was a cholera
epidemic at Salisbury during 1849, he worked amongst the sick and
suffering poor, without any regard for his own personal health. His
charitable endeavours in this were curtailed only by his failing health.[76]

Another of his absorbing involvements came with the Wiltshire
Female Penitentiary. This society had commenced in 1831. In 1851
Bishop Denison purchased a house outside the close near St. Martin's
church, previously occupied as a school and chapel by Roman
Catholics. It became known as the Diocesan House of Mercy.

> Bishop Denison had a great part in the foundation of the House of
> Mercy for penitents. It began in a small way in a house just outside the
> close, under the care of some good ladies and a matron. When the
> Roman Catholics gave up some premises near St. Martin's church, the
> Bishop by private letters that he himself wrote, and other
> [instrumentalities] collected a sufficient sum to purchase the building.
> And there the home was established. As long as he lived he gave it his
> thought and care. Since his time the buildings have been increased and
> improved. A chapel has been added in memory of a most excellent
> layman, much interested in the work, the Hon. Christopher Bouverie.
> And it has been placed under the good care of the Clewer Sisters. The

chaplain has furnished me with some figures, which show the amount which has been expended upon it, viz., between £8,000 and £9,000. The number of reclaimed penitents that have gone forth from this home shows that God's blessing has rested upon it.[77]

It was Hamilton who, shortly before his election to the see of Salisbury in April 1854, was principally responsible for the reorganising of the 'the penitents'. He was never timid in taking his opportunity to teach the Catholic faith.[78] The spiritual well-being of his own domestic servants was of some concern to him, about which he wrote –

> I began this morning a course of short Advent lectures to my servants which will I trust be useful to them, and help us all, and as I prepare them and they in listening to them – to keep this coming Xmas in a more truly Christian spirit. My subject this morning was church sermons. How they were helped to that knowledge and those duties which are our daily bread.[79]

The city churches were not without some significance in his life at this time. He was especially active at St. Thomas's church, where he would attend the evening service and preach.[80]

In the light of his not inconsiderable pastoral experience, he felt that there was a definite need for a small *Family Service Book* which he was able to produce in 1842, for his former parish of St. Peter's, Oxford; it was dedicated to Bishop Richard Bagot.[81] In later years Hamilton developed a *Spirituality of Family Prayers* a stage further.[82] The preface notes that the volume is designed to be, 'in harmony with the structure of the Book of Common Prayer'.[83] In alluding to the sources he points out that the selections made are not from the Book of Common Prayer, but (and here he followed the example of William Palmer in his *Origines Liturgicae*) 'very considerable part of it is taken from ancient sources'.[84] Its selection of a daily theme determines the selection of scriptural verses and prayers. The weekly pattern being –

Sunday – Creation of Light: Resurrection of Christ: Descent of Spirit.
Monday – Creation of Heavens: Entry of Our Lord into Jerusalem.
Tuesday – Creation of Sea, Land and Fruits of Earth: Cursing of Fig Tree and cleansing of Temple.
Wednesday – Creation of Sun, Moon and Stars: Judas' agreement to betray Jesus.
Thursday – Creation of Birds and Fishes: Institution of the Eucharist and Ascension.
Friday – Creation of Man, Animals and Reptiles: Passion of Christ.
Saturday – God's rest after Creation: Our Lord in Grave.

The actual structure being: morning/evening prayer, scriptural verses, confession, Lord's prayer, versicles and responses, psalm, apostles' creed, prayers and the grace.

Liturgically, the compilation is excellent. The structure of the services is simple and identical for morning and evening. There is variety: the form of confession differs each time; the mode of recitation is varied – sometimes it is corporate (e.g. the Lord's prayer and creed), sometimes the family repeats after the head of the household, sometimes it is antiphonal. The services are by no means a monologue by the head of the house. Everyone is encouraged to participate actively in that there are sections of versicles and responses after the Lord's prayer, and the prayers often include a short litany. The psalms are well chosen, both for their length and content, and the prayers are not at all prolix or obscure. There are a few indications of Hamilton's Tractarian sympathies. The Sunday morning service includes a prayer to be used before holy communion, and on Thursday evening God is blessed and praised for 'that holy, immaculate and Blessed Virgin Mary . . . and for all the Saints'.[85] Dr. Pusey approved of the book –

> I liked it much and think the increased share given to the family above our ordinary family prayers a great advantage.[86]

John Keble too liked it –

> And will you for yourself receive my thanks for your collection of *Family Prayers,* which I very much like.[87].

The work shows his concern for a living religion. While encouraging prayers at home, he does not discourage people from attending church itself. He likewise envisages people singing the psalms at home as was the case at church. In all, a work not without significance.[88]

In March 1854, Bishop Edward Denison dictated a letter to the Prime Minister, Lord Aberdeen, suggesting Hamilton as his successor. It was this personal intercession on Denison's part rather than Hamilton's family connections that brought him to the fore in this matter of succession –

> From this my death bed and in the sight of God, I wish to be permitted to say to your lordship that from an intimate acquaintance of 30 years I have reason to think that no other person would be as likely to fill my place in the diocese, with the sole view to the highest interest of the Church of Christ, as Walter Kerr Hamilton now precentor.
>
> It is impossible for me almost in the act of dying to express to your lordship the grounds of this conviction, though I am able abundantly – but I feel it an act of duty to God and to your lordship not to withhold information which may possibly aid you in the highest of all your functions.[89]

Soon after Denison died and was buried on March 15 in the cloister of his Cathedral at Salisbury. He was a man of immense ability and enthusiasm and his death was a blow of some magnitude, not only to Hamilton but to churchmen at large.[90] The vacant see was first offered to John James Blunt, the Lady Margaret Professor of Divinity at Cambridge. He was on three subsequent occasions urged to accept the nomination, but refused on the grounds he was, at 57, too old to take on a bishopric. Lord Aberdeen now felt able to comply with Denison's dying wish that Hamilton might succeed him at Salisbury and thereupon decided to offer him the appointment. Accordingly, Aberdeen summoned Hamilton to see him on March 18 to discuss the matter. It was at this meeting that Hamilton learnt for the first time of Denison's letter of request. Hamilton reacted with surprise and amazement. Feeling unworthy he declined the offer. However, he was persuaded by Aberdeen to consider more carefully his decision. This he agreed to do and fixed an appointment for three o'clock the following afternoon to give his final answer. Meanwhile he went to see his old friend William Ewart Gladstone. They talked at some length about the nomination. Gladstone convinced him to accept the bishopric of Salisbury and noted in his diary –

> After breakfast Hamilton came & we entered upon his subject. He finally left me near three, & went to accept the bishopric. A new and auspicious day for the Church of England!... I have been more overcome & overdone by this day than by any day's *labour* for a long time; and I cannot describe the end of it otherwise than as being stunned by God's mercy.[91]

This proved to be one of the most agonising decisions Hamilton had to make in his lifetime.[92]

Hamilton returned to the Prime Minister and accepted the nomination and Aberdeen recommended Hamilton to Queen Victoria for the see of Salisbury. The Queen for her part was less enthusiastic about the appointment –

> The Queen approved but much to her distress started 'to hear from all sides that he [Hamilton] is considered extremely High Church in his views'. It was too late to stop the appointment; from this time forward the Queen was to be more cautious in accepting the recommendations for ecclesiastical appointments even of trusted Prime Ministers like Lord Aberdeen. She probably suspected that Hamilton's friend, Gladstone, a leading minister of Aberdeen's government, had had a hand in the appointment. The appointment of Bishop Hamilton, which Mr. Gladstone jocularly called 'the sin of Sarum', was an important part of the background of the conflict over church appointments during the ministry which the Bishop's son describes in such interesting detail in his diary.[93]

To the Prime Minister's credit, he defended his appointment to the Queen –

Aberdeen told the Queen in answer to her protests that Hamilton was moderate and that it would be unwise and unjust to exclude good men in consequence of a tendency either to High Church or Low Church.[94]

This assessment by Aberdeen is echoed by Dr. M. A. Crowther –

Had an extreme ritualist been appointed to the bench instead of mild ones like Hamilton and Wordsworth, there would probably have been a storm in the church greater than that over Hampden.[95]

Aberdeen's appointment and Gladstone's persuasion were in a shrewd cause.

Hamilton was one of those keen to make the Tractarian movement accessible to members of the Church of England as a whole. He had broadened the Church's liturgical and spiritual life while carefully declining to be drawn into the various *causes célèbres* of the most partisan and combative of the Tractarians. In the heated atmosphere of the 1840s Hamilton had like his cousin, Hook, suggested and followed a positive path. Hook, not surprisingly, was –

quite intoxicated with gratitude and joy of the appointment of Walter Hamilton to the bishopric of Salisbury. I had half expected it. I have wished for it. I have even prayed for it. What an honour it is to Lord Aberdeen to have fixed upon the very man whom the Church if it had been voted in Synod would have selected – the man best calculated to carry out the Bishop's plans – who has been in fact the Prime Minister of the Diocese.[96]

The *Guardian* of the day noted public reaction to Hamilton's appointment to Salisbury –

It is with much gratification that we publish the intelligence we have received of the appointment of the Rev. Walter Kerr Hamilton, precentor and canon of Salisbury to the vacant see of Sarum.   .
Whether as a scholar or a gentleman – a friend or churchman – the new Bishop stands in every way pre-eminent; and we have reason to believe that it would have been the greatest consolation to his predecessor.

The *Times* of the same day states –

He is said to possess considerable powers as a preacher, but is chiefly remarkable for the simplicity of his character and the consistent piety of his life. It may safely be predicted that he will tread worthily in the steps of his lamented friend and predecessor.

The *Morning Post* remarks –

He was distinguished as an earnest, energetic parish priest most assiduous among the poor, and cultivating the most kindly feeling with all classes of his parishioners, by whom he was truly beloved.

However, the *Guardian* also notes how angry the *Daily News* is at the appointment, and in a letter in leader type comments –

It is more than high time for the Liberal party to remonstrate with the government on the disposal of church patronage. Mr. Hamilton was for a series of years well known to the University of Oxford, of which he was member, for his vehement opposition to Liberal government and especially to the plans successively proposed by the government of Lord Melbourne and Lord John Russell for extending and liberalising national education. Mr. Hamilton's subsequent course up to a very recent period had been one of cordial co-operation with the extreme Tractarian party.[97]

At Salisbury the news was favourably received. A rather typical example of the reaction can be gleaned from the following letter –

Who so qualified to act upon his counsels, and to carry on in its efficiency the machinery of the diocese, as the one who participated so largely in those counsels, and to whom so much diocesan labour and responsibility was entrusted? May he, from whom all good counsels proceed, and who is the author and finisher of every good work, establish, strengthen, settle you, that so you may indeed rule this diocese wisely, and be a pillar of the Church![98]

And –

I honestly believe (and I am sure you will find), that no appointment could have given [more] satisfaction to the diocese at large, nor one which is more calculated to diminish the grief which we feel at our recent loss.[99]

In keeping with the custom of the day, Hamilton was given the degree Doctor of Divinity by his University at Oxford.[100] Some of his former pupils gave him his episcopal ring.[101] His mother provided his episcopal habit.[102]

Walter Kerr Hamilton was consecrated Bishop of Salisbury in Lambeth Palace Chapel by the Archbishop of Canterbury, Dr. John B. Sumner, assisted by the Bishops of Winchester, Charles R. Sumner; Chichester, Ashurst T. Gilbert; and Oxford, Samuel Wilberforce. The Bishop of New Zealand, George A. Selwyn, also was amongst those present to this occasion.[103] Remarking on Hamilton's consecration, Gladstone said, 'This was indeed a great occasion'.[104] The new Bishop was presented at Court on May 16 1854 at 3 p.m. His enthronement was at 11 a.m. on May 31 1854 and was an event shared by both the city and Church alike.[105] Hamilton became the 91st Bishop of Salisbury. His diocese covered most of the counties of Wiltshire and Dorset, with some 50 to 60 livings under his patronage. Some short time after his election, Hamilton reviewed his position and the possible implications upon his life –

My principle is that we clergy cannot live too simply and I should wish to do everything as carefully and plainly as possible. I have always as yet striven to do so, and I feel that my altered circumstances only make the duty the more imperative.[106]

So began an episcopate of some substance for Victorian England. Dr. D. Newsome remarks –

that with W. K. Hamilton's appointment to the bishopric of Salisbury a new era of progress in Catholic principles had begun.[107]

Hamilton's episcopate went on to distinguish him as a leading apologist of the post-Tractarian era. His respect for the fundamental principles of the movement exhibited themselves in his zeal for the pastoral care of his diocese, and in his love of the Church as a whole.

NOTES

1. Gladstone's comment to R. Ornsby, R. Ornsby, *Memoir of James Robert Hope-Scott* (1884), 1, p. 256. Gladstone commented further on Hamilton, 'It is true that at an early date Bishop Hamilton had strong "evangelical sympathies". But his change, or development, took place soon and so to speak at once. There was *no* change during the last thirty years of his life.' *Ex inform.* H. C. G. Matthew, editor, *The Gladstone Diaries with Cabinet Minutes and Prime-Ministerial Correspondence.*
2. Hamilton had actually left Oxford without resigning his living of St. Peter-in-the-East. His place was temporarily filled by William Adams (1814 - 1848), Hamilton eventually resigned his living in favour of Adams in December 1841.
3. S(alisbury) D(iocesan) A(rchives), Chapter Minute Book, Vol. XXIV, pp. 86-7.
4. P(usey) H(ouse), O(xford), Moberly Ms., Letter, J. R. Hope to W. K. H., November 3 1842, London.
5. SDA, Chapter Minute Book, Vol XXIV, pp. 118-22. This appointment was made in 1843 and not 1841 as in H. P. Liddon, *Walter Kerr Hamilton: Bishop of Salisbury. A sketch, reprinted, with additions and corrections, from 'The Guardian'* (1869), p. 22.
6. W. K. H. served under three Deans – Pearson, Lear and H. P. Hamilton. During his time as canon he only missed 27 out of 81 Chapter meetings.
7. Liddon, *Life W. K. H.,* p. 25.
8. F. Lear, 'Reminiscences of the Past 80 Years'. A paper read at the Palace, Salisbury, at the "Ordinatorum Conventus", June 7 1910, pp. 1-4.
9. A. E. Bridge, 'Walter Kerr Hamilton: a Tractarian in the making', unpub. M. Litt. thesis, Oxford Univ. 1988, Chapter 2.
10. K. R. Long, *The Music of the English Church* (1971), p. 331.
11. B. Rainbow, *The Choral Revival in the Anglican Church, 1839 - 1872* (1970), p. 262.
12. *Ibid.,* p. 260.
13. Lear, Reminiscences, p. 16. For further details on A. T. Corfe, see *Dictionary of National Biography,* 1, pp. 1141-2.
14. A. T. Corfe, *A Collection of Anthems with a list of Services used in the Cathedral Church of Salisbury* (1852).
15. There are a number of letters in his papers to this effect (Wren Hall, Sarum; Pusey House, Oxford; Bodleian Library, Oxford).
16. S. L. Ollard, *A Short History of the Oxford Movement* (1915), pp. 182-3.
17. SDA, Chapter Minute Book, Vol. XXV, pp. 37-8.
18. *Ibid.,* p. 38.
19. Rainbow, *The Choral Revival,* p. 261.
20. SDA, Chapter Minute Book, Vol. XXIV, pp. 118-19, 162a, 229. These references all indicate his interest and well being and care for the choristers. D. H. Robertson, *Sarum Close. A History of the Life and Education of the Cathedral Choristers for 700 Years* (1938), p. 280.
21. *Ibid.,* p. 284.

22. *Ibid.*, p. 288.
23. W. H. Hutton (ed.) *Robert Gregory, 1819-1911* (1912), p. 162.
24. PHO, Moberly Ms., Letter, W. K. H. to his father, Archdeacon Anthony Hamilton, November 1849, Paris. W. K. H. to his [parents], November 13 1849, Brussels.
25. SDA, Chapter Minute Book, Vol. XXIV, p. 229.
26. *Ibid.*
27. These candlesticks are still to be seen in the Cathedral at Salisbury.
28. SDA, Chapter Minute Book, Vol. XXIV, pp. 87, 118.
29. *Ibid.*, p. 87. He was first appointed in 1841 and held the office all the time he was canon.
30. Lear, Reminiscences, p. 17.
31. G. F. A. Best, *Temporal Pillars* (1964), p. 433.
32. C. F. Garbett, *The Claims of the Church of England* (1947), p. 78.
33. Best, *Temporal Pillars,* pp. 433-4.
34. *A Letter to the Very Rev. the Dean of Salisbury by the Rev. Walter Kerr Hamilton, M.A.* (1853).
35. PHO, Moberly Ms., Note Book, Cathedral, 1848. Hamilton outlines at some length his thoughts on the matter, especially his concern for the clergy.
36. See Bridge, thesis, chapter 2.
37. This concept of Pusey's was in 1861 taken up by Hamilton as Bishop of Salisbury.
38. P. Butler (ed.), *Pusey Rediscovered* (1983), p. 141.
39. See A. E. Bridge, 'The Foundation of Chichester Theological College', unpublished article, Pusey House, Oxford, 1979.
40. Robertson, *Sarum Close,* p. 296.
41. *Letter,* p. 8.
42. *Ibid.*, p. 12.
43. *Ibid.*, p. 13.
44. *Ibid.*, p. 14.
45. *Ibid.*, p. 15.
46. *Ibid.*, p. 16.
47. *Ibid.*
48. *Ibid.*, p. 18.
49. *Ibid.*, p. 20. SDA, Chapter Minute Book, Vol. XXV, pp. 37-8. This gives his movements in this direction at Salisbury in respect to lay vicars.
50. *Letter,* p. 21.
51. *Ibid.*
52. *Ibid.*, pp. 21-2.
53. *Ibid.*, p. 22.
54. *Ibid.*, p. 23.
55. *Ibid.*, p. 24.
56. *Ibid.*
57. *Ibid.*, pp. 24-5. The Bugmore Hospital was a benevolent institution for the needy of Salisbury and surrounding districts.
58. *Ibid.*, pp. 25-6.

59. *Ibid.,* p. 26.
60. *Ibid.,* pp. 27-8.
61. *Ibid.,* p. 28.
62. *Ibid.,* p. 29.
63. *Ibid.,* pp. 35-6.
64. H. P. Hamilton, *Dean of Salisbury, to The Revd. R. Jones, June 1853, The Close, Salisbury. Suggestions: From the Dean and Chapter of Salisbury for the Reform of their Cathedral.*
65. *A Letter from the late Bishop to the Commissioners about the rearrangement of Capitular Estates. E. Sarum to the Revd. R. Jones, 16 August, 1853.*
66. *A Letter from the late Bishop in answer to certain questions addressed to him by the Commissioners. E. Sarum to the Revd. R. Jones, 1 September, 1853.*
67. *W. K. Sarum to all members of the Church in the Diocese of Salisbury, 12 January, 1855.*
68. Letter, W. K. H. to L. Foote, June 17 1854, Sarum. Wiltshire County Archives (1854), Vol. 1, pp. 102-3.
69. W. K. H., Diocesan Journal.
70. Lear, Reminiscences, p. 12.
71. *Ibid.,* p. 13.
72. Training School Lectures and Sermon for 1851, 1852 and 1853 – the Sunday texts feature.
73. PHO, Moberly Ms., Letter, W. K. H. to Bishop Denison, January 2 1853, Salisbury.
74. *Ibid.,* Letter, R. I. Wilson to W. K. H., September 21 1842, Bisley.
75. He was often consulted by evangelical clergy about suitable men to have as curates. *Ibid.,* Letters, E. Holland to W. K. H., October 14 1842, Langley. H. Wilberforce to W. K. H., December 21, 1844, Maidstone.
76. Liddon, *Life,* p. 42.
77. Lear, Reminiscences, pp. 14-15.
78. PHO, Moberly Ms., Lecture notes for 1850 and 1851. Note Book, August 11 1849, pp. 1-2, 10, 13-14, 20, 21, 99-100.
79. *Ibid.,* Letter, W. K. H. to mother, December 1 1851, Salisbury.
80. Liddon, *Life,* p. 35.
81. *Morning and Evening Services for everyday in the week and other prayers, arranged for the use of the families residing in the parish of St. Peter's-in-the-East, Oxford. By their former Pastor, Walter Kerr Hamilton* (1842).
82. *Notes for Lectures at Family Prayers, February 13, 1850.* This took the form of some 20 sections: God, Trinity, God the Father, God the Son, God the Holy Ghost, the Catholic Faith, the Creation, Incarnation, First Adam, Baptism, a member of Christ, the Soul, Heaven, Angels, Temper and Character, Hell, paradise, Baptismal Vow, the three enemies, Satan.
83. *Ibid.,* p. vi.
84. *Ibid.,* W. Palmer, *Origines Liturgicae* (1832), 1, pp. 301-8.
85. *Morning and Evening Services for everyday in the week,* p. 159.
86. PHO, Moberly Ms., Letter, E. B. Pusey to W. K. H., January 16 1843,

Brighton.
87. *Ibid.,* Letter, John Keble to W. K. H., December 7 1842, Hursley.
88. I am indebted to the Revd. P. G. Cobb, Vicar of All Saints, Clifton, Avon, for his liturgical expertise.
89. PHO, Moberly Ms., Letter, E. Denison to Lord Aberdeen, March 4 1854, Salisbury. This letter was dictated at 11.45 p.m.
90. For the best assessment/biography of Edward Denison see *Memoir of Edward, Lord Bishop of Salisbury* (privately printed for the *Annual Register* for 1854-1855) by R. J. Phillimore. Hamilton and Denison had been friends since Oxford. Hamilton was one of Denison's executors and guardian to his children, the other being George Denison. PHO, Moberly Ms., Letter, E. Denison to W. K. H., June 13 1844, Salisbury.
91. M. R. D. Foot (ed.), *The Gladstone Diaries,* 4, 1848-1854 (1974), p. 602.
92. PHO, Moberly Ms., Note Book, Narrative and reflections of W. K. H.'s appointment as Bishop by Lord Aberdeen, dated March 25 1854.
93. D. W. R. Bahlman (ed.), *The Diary of Sir Edward Walter Hamilton, 1880 - 1885* (1972), 1, pp. xiii-xiv. J. P. Parry, *Democracy and Religion: Gladstone and the Liberal Party, 1867-1875* (1986), p. 37. 'It was during the premiership of Aberdeen that the first Tractarian bishop, W. K. Hamilton, was appointed (1854)'.
94. O. Chadwick, *The Victorian Church* 1, (1966), p. 468.
95. M. A. Crowther, *Church Embattled: Religious Controversy in Mid-Victorian England* (1970), p. 144.
96. PHO, Moberly Ms., Letter, W. Hook to R. Hook, March 21 1854, Leeds.
97. *The Guardian,* March 22 1854, p. 242.
98. PHO, Moberly Ms., Letter, F. W. Fowle, to W. K. H., March 22 1854, Amesbury.
99. *Ibid.,* Letter, W. Briscoe to W. K. H., March 20 [1854], Coombe.
100. *Ibid.,* Letter, The Warden of Merton College to W. H. K., April 11 1854, Oxford.
101. *Ibid.,* Letter, W. K. H. to [?] Laurell, May 15 1854, London. This letter lists the names of his pupils. The ring is still in the possession of the diocese of Sarum. It is kept in the safe and can be seen upon request.
102. *Ibid.,* Misc. Lt. Bell. W. K. H. to mother, March 10 1854; March 24 1854, Salisbury.
103. Lambeth Palace, Archbishop's Act Book 1850 - 1859, Vol. XVII, p. 223. Also W. H. Jones, *Fasti Ecclesiae Sarisberiensis* (1879), 1, p. 122.
104. M. R. D. Foot (ed.), *The Gladstone Diaries,* 4, 1838-1854 (1974), p. 619.
105. SDA, Chapter Minute Book, Vol. XXV, p. 56. *Guardian,* May 31 1854, p. 437.
106. PHO, Moberly Ms., W. K. H. to mother, May 18 1854, Salisbury. Misc. Lt. Bell.
107. D. Newsome, *The Parting of Friends* (1966), p. 381.

From Close To Open: a future for the past[1]

J. H. Churchill and Alan Webster

1. A growing consciousness of mission

Cathedrals are in no sense places of retirement, either for the clergy or for the members of their staff – musical, administrative or maintenance – or for the growing numbers who constitute their congregations. As the rest of this chapter will indicate, they have complex and occasionally controversial roles as centres of liturgical reform and tradition, educational centres for the young and for adults, diocesan and county centres, as well as places which must be visited by the tourists in any city.

Cathedrals are seen as places of growth. The collection of essays *Grow or Die*, edited by Alexander Wedderspoon, contains a list of fresh and inspiring activities sponsored by or taking place within Cathedrals –

> During the last twenty years...the staff, the worshippers – everyone concerned with Cathedrals – has been increasingly committed to the interpretation of the Christian faith. There used to be a time when Cathedrals seemed almost not to be part of the Church, let alone aware of the need to make the Christian faith intelligible, to let the gospel speak to our contemporary society, particularly in the centre of cities. 'Go away, we are going to have a service' is the caricature of some attitudes in the past. Now I suppose the most common remark is 'Welcome to your Cathedral. How can we help you?' No doubt the question is often 'Tell me the way to the crypt...or the toilets...or the Whispering Gallery?' But these questions, if they can be answered and the conversation continued, will lead to companionship on the pilgrimage. What so many come seeking in Cathedrals is experience – worship or music or a conversation which speaks to them. Cathedrals are growing because this experience is a reality...they are centres of the spirit for the community.[2]

The Archbishop of Canterbury preached in St. Paul's in 1987 on the role of the Cathedral in the city. His theme was taken from the psalm

'I will lift up mine eyes unto the hills; from whence cometh my help'. He saw the role of a Cathedral as a place of worship and prayer where our minds are lifted – a place of friendship and affection and warmth – a place where there is real care for those who work and carry responsibility in a city. It is also a place of prophecy where the will of God is proclaimed for the Monday to Friday world. He pointed to these roles in contrast to the Barchester past –

> It has not always been an uplifting experience to preach at St. Paul's. In 1833 Sydney Smith said 'To go to St. Paul's is certain death, the thermometer is several degrees below zero. My sentences are frozen as they come out of my mouth...' but today St. Paul's is warm...it's a kind of temple set on a hill – and I cannot doubt that time and time again as you have seen the cross above the dome set not only above the Cathedral, that even today, above much of this great city your heart has been uplifted with positive affection for those who live and work and carry heavy responsibility in the city.[3]

An acute Dutch theological observer, Albert van den Heuvel, then on the staff of the World Council of Churches, analysed the functions of Cathedrals under fourteen headings.[4] (1) A sign of pro-existence, i.e. a centre for the gospel for the world and for the world's structures; (2) A symbol of diversity in unity; a church must be pluriform; (3) A Pentecostal laboratory: a place where we can speak in our own tongues about God and the meaning of life; (4) The theatre of basic drama; (5) A temple of dialogue; (6) A centre of creativity; (7 & 8) An academy for committed information, and a clinic for public exorcism; (9) An international exchange; (10) A broadcasting station for the voice of the poor; (11) A tower of reconciliation; (12) A motel for pilgrims; (13) The house of vicarious feasts; (14) The hut of the shepherd.

Cathedrals have actualised these titles. Coventry itself has in its John Kennedy House, a motel for pilgrims; all Cathedrals have made themselves much more the hut or base of the bishop than was customary in the nineteenth century. As for basic drama, Norwich staged a Lent Passion on the death by self-burning of Jan Palak in St. Wenceslas Square, Prague, which involved hundreds of participants, many of whom said afterwards that they had understood the passion of Christ for the first time. From Carlisle to Truro, Cathedrals have called together representatives of the community and so become signs of pro-existence, though they would not have used that word. Checking Albert van den Heuvels's list against the replies to the survey carried out for this chapter reveals that in the last twenty years every one of his roles of mission has been carried out in some English Cathedral or other.

His check list for Cathedrals in the second half of the twentieth century has been much studied since it was first delivered in 1966, at the annual conference of Deans and Provosts. This valuable annual residential occasion gathers those in charge of all Cathedrals in England, greater or smaller, older and newer, with some visitors from over the various borders, and occasionally from overseas. The value, and the seriousness of concern, for the mission of Cathedrals generated has resulted in a number of conferences, mostly annual, for other Cathedral personnel, treasurers, precentors and organists, architects, librarians, Cathedral shop managers. These form valuable means of exchanging ideas and information. The possibility of such consultation has done much to move Cathedrals from being 'private chapels of the Dean and Chapter'. In the last few years the wider Pilgrims Association has served both Cathedrals and the greater parish churches, with an annual conference and useful information and contact with the tourist industry up and down the country. This has been particularly helpful for Cathedral visitors' officers, education officers, voluntary guides, and secretaries of Cathedral Friends. However far the discussion and the concern may seem to spread at times, its purport comes back to the Cathedral, and in a sense must enter through its doors, and look again at its sweeping vista, to find ways through it to help the visitor become a pilgrim and catch a glimpse of the glory of God.

2. A focus for worship in continuity and revision.
One of the simplest figures for a Cathedral is that of the blackbird under the piecrust. It is a suitably decorative blackbird, but serves a nourishing purpose. It lifts up the whole crust allowing the fruit to give off its goodness. So a Cathedral lifts up a whole area, diocese, and county, to God in prayer, allowing all its peoples to expand themselves in praise.

This is a remarkably persistent theme. You can see it in the very structures of the great Medieval constructions, both in the massive Norman crossings, and in the soaring Gothic clerestories; you can see it also in the historic structures of church life, both in the chapters and choirs which served some Cathedrals and in the religious communities which served others. Perhaps surprisingly, the combination of Chapters, choirs, and buildings proved strong enough, in this country, to bring Cathedrals through a Reformation which suppressed religious communities, and weakened the sense of worship. But it brought two important matters back to the agenda, the need to involve the worship of the whole people of God, laity as well as clergy, and the whole man, understanding as well as body and feelings. For a time Cathedrals receded into distant shrines, saved only by their architecture and the daily round of worship. But revival in music and preaching, and improving transport, created links with dioceses, counties and visitors.

A high standard of musical offering is an important element, in conjunction with the architecture, which generally assists the sound, in the offering of an expression of transcendence. It has a high priority, but there is a sliding scale of fulfilment, as other claims are met. Still over half the Cathedrals maintain a daily sung evensong, with one day off, as well as the Sunday sung Eucharist. But not so many maintain their own schools; others use existing schools, both independent and local authority. This calls on the co-operation of parents, and, in the process draws them into the work, and often the worship of the Cathedral. All this has helped to make the daily round again an offering of the whole people, not just of Chapter and choir.

This has become true of all the worship. Though larger Cathedrals attract hundreds of visitors each Sunday, so that they form the major part of the congregation, the regular flock plays an important part with Chapter and choir and building, in creating the experience of worship for them. It is interesting to note a broad consensus across Cathedrals, and between Chapters and congregations, of worshipping at the Eucharist to the *Alternative Service Book,* and at evensong to the Prayer Book. The *A.S.B.* itself provided rubrics for the combination of using old texts to fit new settings. The use of the alternative rites has opened other avenues to greater movement in services, and participation in the use of lay members of the congregation for readings and offertory processions. This takes on a wider significance when members of parish parties visiting are used.

Both by their ability to host parish congregations, and their position in a diocese, Cathedrals are in a position to give a liturgical lead. It is interesting to note that even a Cathedral with big national and international responsibilities, such as Canterbury, took up the task of introducing the alternative services to its diocese. It was fitting that the other metropolitan Cathedral, York, received as its Dean in 1975 Dr. Ronald Jasper, then chairman of the Liturgical Commission and the chief architect of the revised services; he used an altar in the spacious nave of York, wisely raised on a movable platform of several steps, for the very effective Sunday Eucharists there. More recently many

Cathedrals have provided both the space and the personnel to give demonstrations of the new services for Ash Wednesday, Holy Week, and Easter. Wide use is made of the variety of spaces a Cathedral offers to provide for services for different occasions and different groups, with a celebration in the round here, a space cleared for drama there.

Another combination of response can be seen on many a week's service list. Though much is standard, there will be one or more special services. Cathedrals often appear to be more used by their counties than their dioceses, who, of course have other churches to use. A great number of county organisations will want to use their Cathedral for an occasion of celebration, thanksgiving or renewal, making considerable demands on creative time and skill; in turn the Cathedral will seek to draw on the folk to provide material for prayers, and participants for readings, and intercessions. On larger civic and national occasions this calls for the creation of whole sections of liturgy which require the weaving together of scripture, music and literature. Coventry Cathedral has produced particularly interesting examples of this.

Young people and schools are most likely to make use of the space and the ambience to make their own worship. This may be just the annual schools' carol service, when it is all too often the adults' service, and then the advisers' rather than the teachers'. At other times a school may realise that a spacious transept can give a fine resonance for the school brass, and for its actors and poets, and with some forethought a natural occasion of worship can be offered. So it can by a primary group with room to sing and dance freely. These happen frequently enough nowadays for some groups to arrive without warning and to trust that they can be given houseroom. That may be easier to provide than time. The time becomes one of the attractions that has encouraged all-night vigils by diocesan youth groups in Cathedrals over the last twenty years. The buildings have much to offer at night in their beauty, their large spaces, and their smaller ones for groups. There is the stirring thought of sharing with the Medieval monks in their night prayers, and present excitement of sharing in a dawn Eucharist, and in breakfast in a convenient refectory in the Cathedral grounds.

So the round of worship comes full circle, round the centuries, round the span of human age and expression, and round the clock. In all these fields Cathedrals today provide the opportunity for the needed combination we have already noted. There is the combination of the traditional and the contemporary in worship, the involvement of young and older in congregations, choirs, and servers of both sexes now, the mixture of set services and *ad hoc* creations for particular occasions, which may have quite different words and music. In all this any Cathedral Chapter would say that it tries to hold before itself, and before those who use the building, the aim of doing this as well as possible to fit the building, and that the building itself helps to do this; in fact the more spacious it is the easier it is. And the regular round of daily worship, of communion celebrated in the early morning, probably also later on some days, and evensong sung in the early evening, provides the encouragement and an open invitation, round the day, to savour the expectant surroundings, or to drop into prayer.

3. A centre for a diocese and for a county

The very name Cathedral describes the church with the seat or *cathedra* of the bishop. Though an Augustine could preside over his Cathedral and his diocese in Hippo and find time to write his many books, before the Middle Ages Cathedrals had their own clergy and life, and bishops had theirs. Though at times the separation has been stressed from either side, the relationship remains of the Cathedral providing the worship base for the bishop and the diocese. How this is used varies with circumstances of the diocese's shape, and the position of the bishop's house, and other responsibilities, such as a college of the University in Oxford, and the national responsibilities at St. Paul's.

In a number of places the bishop's house forms part of the close, or is adjacent to it. There the bishop is able to attend a weekday service, or celebrate in the Cathedral during the week, as his diary allows. In other dioceses he lives at a distance, though he may drop in occasionally. His principal visits will be to preside at ordinations, probably twice a year nowadays, and one or two particular confirmations for adults or for Cathedral candidates, and to celebrate or preach at Easter and Christmas, and some other special occasions. Though these may not add up to more than ten in a year, they are sufficent for the bishop to be a familiar figure at his Cathedral. It is more difficult for him to keep his Cathedral in mind in his reckoning about his diocese. The Dean and Chapter have to do more about that, but fortunately, the Dean is a member of the bishop's staff meeting in most dioceses.

Most Cathedrals provide the venue for the services for some diocesan organisations in the year. These will often want to go the rounds, and gather in another part of the diocese another year. The diocese may want to spread occasions in this way when it itself gathers for purposes such as stewardship or celebrates something of its continuing history that its Cathedral is its worship base, and often was closely involved in the original spread of the Christian mission in the area. Furthermore some of these diocesan and organisational occasions benefit from supporting displays and exhibitions, and a Cathedral offers facilities for these. Lichfield mounted a notable occasion with the missionary societies in connection with the 1978 Lambeth Conference.

The relationship is by no means one way. Cathedrals go out to their dioceses with a variety of invitations. From some it is simply to parishes to come and join in Cathedral worship as a body for a Sunday outing. In a large scattered diocese this can be a happy day out, with a good deal to look at, and a chance for picnic lunch after sharing in the Lord's table in the Mother Church. In other places, parishes come together as a deanery to sing a 6.30 evensong in the Cathedral, with massed choirs. Other invitations will be for short courses of addresses or lectures. Some of these will be at a short evening service followed by an opportunity for questions and discussion; others will be straight talks with similar provision. These will be particularly useful to those from small parishes, or who otherwise want a changed and wider stimulus both from speaker and from fellow discussers.

The further strand of relationship is through the persons of the residentiary and greater Chapters, the successors of some of the turbulent prebendaries of the past. The Church Commissioners provide the stipends of two residentiaries to be principally engaged on the work of the Cathedral. This has left bishops free to appoint two canons in many cases to do diocesan jobs, such as clergy or lay training, education, social responsibility. This ought to work well, bringing useful people to both diocese and Cathedral, and making good links between them. But there is continual need to make sure that the diocese does not encroach on the canons principally for the Cathedral, and leaves its two appointments with sufficient time to do their part in the Cathedral round. Honorary canons, mostly senior parish clergy, are another link, but it is rather up to them to make it by their interest. Preaching in the parishes by Cathedral clergy is a more useful link, it is generally felt, than honoraries preaching in Cathedrals.

In many cases the greatest interest comes from the county, its statutory and voluntary bodies, those in positions of responsibility, and many ordinary folk. They value greatly the Cathedral as a focus and centre of the county, especially when it has a long history. Some Cathedrals also have a very strong place in their city, though they will always have to share that with the parish churches to a certain extent. But only the Cathedral can minister as a focus to the county. There may be complications when a Cathedral serves parts of two counties, or less than a whole; for most, there is a clear responsibility, and it is mutual, so that the county turns to the Cathedral. Through the county, the Cathedral is in touch with the major agencies of society, education, health, social services. Many of us were kept busy providing occasions for all these to mark the great reorganisation of counties in 1974, and we have been glad to continue to relate concerns since.

This relationship stretches further. National concerns press on the local authorities, and they will bring some of these to the Cathedral, often in conjunction with local groups, as is the case of ecological concern. At the same time, the Cathedral is very much part of the wider Church, and the wider world, and will want to bring to local notice the needs of the world, for the hungry, the political prisoner, and more. Coventry has built up strong international contacts from its rebuilding and uses one canon to specialise in this field. Cathedrals can provide an occasion for prophetic preaching and prayer, and the space for display, perhaps itself incorporating a vigil. It is, of course, not only outside things to be noted, but it may be needs in its own city or area. Bradford did a notable work in providing buildings and organisation for workshops for the unemployed.

Alongside this increasing involvement with the work and responsibilities of the wider community, Cathedrals have continued, and increased a long-standing participation in the artistic expression, in the widest sense, of society. This is indeed built-in to buildings of major architectural and historical interest, and we must look at this more closely later. But further, since the seventeenth century, Cathedrals have been heirs to a tradition, of universal significance, of English church music. From this has grown the use of Cathedrals as centres of music and drama in a variety of ways. Besides broadcasting choral evensong the B.B.C. uses Cathedrals for a number of concerts, as do many orchestras, chamber groups, and choirs. Cathedrals have played a major part in promoting festivals over the centuries, from the Three Choirs of Gloucester, Hereford and Worcester, to a new arts festival at Lichfield. Chichester has fostered its city's festival of music and drama. Manchester provided the venue for the Royal Exchange theatre at its beginning.

This day by day relationship in work and recreation gives a Cathedral and its clergy an intimate view of a county and many of its leaders. It reveals their problems, but also their aspirations and potential. These are the stuff of God's redeeming work, if only they can be brought to awareness between people. Cathedrals try to assist this by arranging discussions and conferences for various groups. Cathedrals as far apart as Carlisle and Truro have arranged consultations for their whole county, gathering ones and twos from statutory and voluntary, work and leisure, institutions and groups. They have been able to do this more easily in their thinly spread areas, where people stand out as individuals, and Cathedrals, too, as natural centres.

4. An educational resource for adults and children

Features of life have an extraordinary way of appearing in different guises in successive generations. There is the great output of learning of Augustine during his episcopate at Hippo, and then the remarkable centres of study at the Irish bishops' settlements, as the remains at Glendalough testify. With the pacification brought by the Normans came the beginnings of Cathedral schools, some of which have continuing institutions to this day, as at York, Canterbury, and Lincoln. Though the growth of learning and speculation found it needed a freer field, and grew into Universities, the teaching mission of Cathedrals remained strong enough to produce reformed schools at the Reformation, and theological colleges in the nineteenth century.

Now, in this last quarter of the twentieth century, Cathedrals offer their educational resources in a mixture of ways, to adults and children, by structures and arrangments, in the religious field, and across the range of life. In the course of its round of worship, the congregations of regulars, droppers-in, and visitors from a distance, and the perspective of the Cathedral looking out over the wider community and the world, rather than over a parish, sermons must carry as much teaching as exhortation, and must look to the needs of the world as much as to those of the hearers. From this perspective of preaching arises the arrangement of courses, either at the regular round of services, at special short services, either by the Cathedral clergy or by distinguished visitors. Cathedrals generally have the premises to provide the opportunity for the questions and discussion which are so much needed, as is the coffee, for educational digestion. They also have the position in the local communities of the cities and counties to draw a mixed gathering to make a fruitful discussion.

We have already seen how these facilities of Cathedrals have lent themselves naturally to the mounting of conferences and consultations. It is interesting to note that Cathedrals still retain an image of openness, and availability to the dropper-in, to encourage a hope of genuine education rather than any thought of indoctrination. As a result Cathedrals have been able to play their part in assisting the expansion of Universities. Though in the nineteenth century it was a matter of political and economic expediency to divert the wealth of Durham into the foundation of its University, now the way is both more modest and more open. Coventry Cathedral has built up its own programme of adult education and conferences to such a level that it is now planning to develop a conference centre in the University of Warwick. Guildford runs joint conferences with its neighbour, the University of Surrey. Chelmsford Cathedral has done much in adult education itself, but now the energy of the Provost has been able to work with Anglican chaplains to the University of Essex, to provide open lectures on theology and its applications for the first time in that University.

Cathedrals have provided natural centres for receiving the offerings of University extra-mural lectures in theology and its applications. These have been well used in connection with both lay adult education, and the programme of non-residential ordination training. These two are run together, in some cases, at least for some years of a course. In other cases lay courses may prepare for University external examinations, or for a local bishop's certificate. In the latter field Cathedrals have played a considerable part in nurturing what is now an important element in ordination training in the country. The first non-stipendiary course, that of Southwark, has its base in the Southwark chapter house. The Salisbury and Canterbury courses grew around their Cathedrals; others have drawn on Cathedral clergy as their principals. There is more to be explored in the near future here in the use of joint lectures, occasions, and facilities for lay and ordination training, as further thought is given to interweaving residential and non-residential periods in ordination training.

Two other items of Christian education are carried on by most Cathedrals, one well noted, the other often unnoticed. Cathedrals are, before all, houses of prayer. They are expected to be places where people can turn into readily to pray, and they normally have sufficient space for the needy soul to drop on their knees with freedom. With the increase of visitors and activity, most Cathedrals have taken steps to ensure that at any rate one chapel is kept free and quiet for private prayer. Many Cathedrals will have a place and paper available for people to leave names and causes for which they would be glad to have prayers offered at the Cathedral altar. Others have a pricket stand available for people to light candles as their act of intercession. Such actions invite further thought about prayer, so many Cathedrals provide group occasions for intercession and contemplative prayer. Further help is offered in the provision of quiet days, which a Cathedral can often house either in a chapel in the Cathedral, or more likely in an ancillary building. A Cathedral is able to offer personal help from a group of experienced priests for prayer, for counsel, and for absolution.

The unnoticed piece of education which has developed in recent years is that of Cathedral congregations. The general recovery across the churches of the active share of the laity in the Christian mission has affected Cathedrals in a very practical way. Their size and economic complication require professional staff. Not so long ago it covered everything, with vergers taking all the collections. Now Cathedrals raise strong bands of sidesmen, and stewards for larger occasions, use lay people's voluntary expertise in financial management: Wakefield has a volunteer chapter clerk. Women of Cathedral congregations work hard providing coffee and welcome after numerous Cathedral occasions, and men and women from congregations and further afield make up the guides and welcomers who provide the vital service to thousands of visitors. But all this is not just to build up and enhance 'our church'; it is to enable our Cathedral to fulfil its service to God and to the world around, to be a church for others, not just for ourselves. So Cathedral congregations have to learn and accept what Archbishop Habgood called in his address at the installation of Dean Southgate of York 'the self-denying vocation of Cathedral congregations'. This is, of course, the real vocation of all Christian congregations; it is to be hoped that awareness in Cathedrals may be spread, by writing, talking, and watching.

One piece of awareness has been the need to welcome and provide for small children at Cathedrals, both on regular occasions, and special ones. This is a further demand on the vocation of the congregation to staff creches and Sunday schools, for which the Cathedral is normally blessed with room. But this is a small corner of a Cathedral's work with children. Its guides must soon learn to make special arrangements for them, both as they come with family parties and in school or other groups. A major tool in this has been the production by most Cathedrals of specific children's guide booklets, and quizzes planned for different age groups. These prove great boons to family parties, especially on wet holiday days. For school parties, most Cathedrals have built up from this a whole pack of information which schools can obtain in advance to prepare for a class visit, so that children are motivated to look for things when they come, and then are anxious to express this in answering a quiz, or free writing or drawing. To provide for this most Cathedrals have space at least in pews or a hall. York pioneered the provision of a special room for them to use, and provided a former teacher, a Whitby Sister, as a children's officer to assist them. Others have since followed suit.

Children's officers have the advantage of time to assist schools both in planning and preparing for visits, and in following them up and reflecting upon them. There is a great need and opportunity to help teachers explore the educational riches of a Cathedral. What had looked like an esoteric building for elaborate worship turns out to be, in many cases, the cradle of that part of the country. Here, too, men and women's thoughts about life and death have been formed, and reformed. Here both architecture and music, and often the decorative arts, have developed over the centuries. Here today comes a great cross-section of local life, and all of it, and all of us, young and old, are challenged by the great building, its beauty and its history, to look at life in the perspective of God Almighty and his revelation in Jesus Christ. 'Out of the mouths of babes and sucklings thou hast brought perfect praise', Jesus quoted from Psalm 8 on Palm Sunday, according to Matthew 21.16. The words and thoughts stirred in children can do much to start teachers and parents opening their eyes and minds to the questions raised by a Cathedral. Its resources are considerable for both young and old.

5. A centre for theological and social outreach

Jesus Christ was described in the New Testament as a prophet. It is natural that major Christian sanctuaries should be places of prophetic utterance, where preaching is taken seriously. In the past twenty years Cathedrals have drawn great congregations for the preaching of those who are regarded as twentieth century prophets, Martin Luther King and Desmond Tutu. In Cathedrals the theologians who stand on the frontier between the Church and the world, Hans Kung, Jurgen Moltmann, and in earlier days, William Temple, have caught the attention of crowds. In the setting of a crowded Cathedral service, the utterance of an Archbishop can cause major controversy. In 1982 at the ending of the South Atlantic war, the sermon of the Archbishop of Canterbury calling for reconciliation and mourning for the Argentine, as well as the British dead, was extremely outspoken. The Word from Cathedral pulpits can still stir hearts and minds.

Many of those on the staffs of the Cathedrals are committed to social action. At one time in the 1970s the Deans of Liverpool and Manchester and the Provost of Birmingham were all chairmen of local race relations bodies. The Dean of Bristol has been a practical champion of Corymeela, a centre of reconciliation in Ulster. Many Cathedrals gave a lead in the Faith in the City movement, St. Paul's organising special meetings for business, finance and social work leaders in the basement of the *Financial Times*, with one meeting at the Bank of England itself. A British Council of Churches service in London for black-led churches gathered representatives from many parts of England.

Cathedrals continue to encourage writers and thinkers: Peter Baelz of Durham, David Edwards of Southwark, Tom Baker of Worcester, Trevor Beeson of Winchester, as well as many canons at Cathedrals, have made notable contributions to scholarship. Edward Patey, when canon of Coventry and afterwards Dean of Liverpool, not only published popular apologetics but decided to donate more than half his working day to the needs of the community.

The survey carried out for this chapter reveals much (though certainly not enough) effort by Cathedrals to give a practical lead in the community. A full list would be too long. Typical Cathedral activities include the founding of a night shelter, the provision of an almoner for those caught in the poverty trap, housing for Ugandan Asian refugees, exhibitions of the work of caring agencies, regular financial support from admission to a Cathedral Treasury for Christian Aid, Cathedral staff serving directly on committees dealing with housing and unemployment, close association with the Samaritans, with A.I.D.S. counselling and much else.

It must be admitted that Cathedrals concerned with theological and social outreach must surmount difficulties, the busyness and bittiness of the institution constantly interrupting the work of the staff for outside causes. Large churches, occasionally with spacious closes, can create an us-and-them atmosphere. It was of Cathedral clergy (though others can sin in this way) that Bishop Leslie Hunter remarked, 'Those who stand on their dignity will be left standing.' Parish church Cathedrals may be short of cash and staff, but they can often achieve more than the grander establishments by being less weighed down with dignified traditions and complicated customs. Certainly few Cathedrals can match the outgoing work of Coventry or Derby.[5]

The prophetic calling of the church is nowhere more obvious than at the thronged tomb in his Cathedral of Archbishop Oscar Romero who was shot during the Eucharist while appealing for an end to the death squads in his country of El Salvador. Such courage to stand against the stream is needed – true, less dramatically – in English Cathedrals in their prophetic protest against secular consumerism and the overwhelming power of the market. The dogged faithfulness and sometimes sheer cussedness of the builders and guardians of Cathedrals, whether they are recent creations or have lasted down the centuries, has enabled them to stand in the middle of cities. This gives their prophetic concern for truth and justice a privileged position in our world.

6. Architecture and art for all

A few years back, a Dean received a letter inviting the Friends of his Cathedral to become corporate members of the Association of Friends of Museums. He dictated a rapid reply pointing out that though his Cathedral contained various treasures from the past, they were all part of a complex for the present witness to, and worship of, the living God, not a funeral parlour but a lighthouse. A few days later he received another letter, telling him of the new area museums service, which had recently been set up by statute, and offered conservation service at reasonable cost. In particular, the agency understood that the Cathedral had two Medieval copes in its possession, and offered to come to give free advice, on possibilities for their conservation. This offer was gladly accepted, and led on to the Chapter's learning from other Cathedrals' experience the value of collecting together various loose treasures to make them all available to visitors in a small museum. A room in one of the remaining monastic buildings was brought back into use for this, and the tour of interest to visitors thereby extended.

In such practical steps the lesson of conservation for use and availability is learned. It is no isolated or detached appreciation of art. Yes, we can sit under soaring arches from the Middle Ages at Salisbury, or from the twentieth century at Coventry, but the structure and crowning spire of the former must be saved at a cost of millions, and the wear and tear of just a quarter of a century met at the latter. So the worth and care of architecture for the glory of God, and the salvation of mankind, are learned in the hard school of repair and appeals.

A major project of conservation has recently been completed at Wells in the rehabilitation of the West front. This is decorated with rows of Medieval figures of saints, kings and worthies, which had worn badly in the weather, and, to some, gave the appearance of a slightly fussy extra to the building. But expert opinion confirmed that this was indeed the finest collection of Medieval sculpture in Europe, a mighty reredos or backcloth to quicken imagination and devotion. To save it meant, at the time in the late 1970s, raising the first appeal to run into several millions. But by able presentation, using the fruit of the expert advisers, many were drawn to contribute and the money raised. The figures were restored to recognisability; the obliterated crowning figure of Christ was replaced by a sculpture commissioned from David Wynne. The Medieval builders had wisely left a splendid green vacant in front of the Cathedral; this was filled with thousands for a great open air Eucharist of thanksgiving for the completion and revealing of, the work in 1986, with the great West front forming an imposing backdrop. Since then it continues to whet the imagination of visitors as they come to the Cathedral.

Few have such opportunities for constructive repair, let alone for new building. Coventry had the one call in England for total rebuilding after wartime bombing, and this was completed in 1962. It was skilfully done, with many interesting features. The skill could be measured by the amount of new thinking it generated about the mission of Cathedrals. This was helped by the wise provision of good ancillary accommodation including a small hostel. They were fortunate to be able to use John Piper to design some of their windows, and Graham Sutherland for the great tapestry behind the high altar. Chichester also has been able to use a Sutherland tapestry behind its Medieval high altar, and a Chagall window in Medieval tracery.

Liverpool has bravely completed the great building designed and begun in years of Edwardian expansiveness. In spite of thoughts that the building was large enough already, the completion of the Western bays and entrance has given a fine sense of completeness to the lines of the building, both externally and internally. The completed Western nave provides a wonderful place for music and drama and for more adventurous non-liturgical worship. Now the Cathedral has built a close of houses for the Chapter on the waste ground around the Cathedral, enhancing the battered landscape of that part of Liverpool, and greatly reducing what had become a serious security problem.

Closes have been a major contribution to city centres in the see towns. Some such as Canterbury preserve a number of Medieval houses, others, such as the large closes at Norwich and Salisbury have fine Georgian houses. These are considerable responsibilities, but Chapters and their surveyors have worked hard to maintain and improve the property, and so enhance the approach to, and surroundings of Cathedrals. In spacious closes there will be houses to let to produce much-needed income. In others there will be just enough to house the Chapter and perhaps some other staff, and provide offices and meeting places. With the increase of activities and visitors there is a general need to provide some form of both meeting and eating places around the Cathedral. All sorts of places have been found or created. For both St. Albans and Southwark this has meant building a new chapter house, and St. Edmundsbury hopes to complete a new cloister to meet its needs.

The task of repair continues to be the major tool to enable the great structures of Cathedrals to open eyes to the vision of God. Perhaps nothing does this quite so obviously as the windows. There was a splendid by-product of the wartime precaution of removing the great quantity of stained glass from York Minster. After the war a workshop was set up to clean and repair the glass before it was returned, a process which took many years. But it left a skilled workshop which is now able to do work for other Cathedrals and churches, as well as its own. The restoration of its own great rose window after the 1984 South transept fire is well known, but the electrifying effect of cleaned, repaired and protected Medieval glass can be seen in many quarters. Many of the larger Cathedrals maintain their own team of masons, and do a major job in providing training and thereby help to keep this craft alive. For other skills Cathedrals are glad to draw on the resources available, and in the process provide a good deal of employment for art and fabric restorers. There are some opportunities for new commissions, for windows, furniture, vestments, and other objects in use, and occasionally in statuary. Others have found a more immediate way to keep the creative work of the artist linked with a great shrine of the creative God, by organising the funding of an artist-in-residence at Durham, and a composer-in-residence at Wakefield, and the commissioning of drama at Chelmsford, and an opera at Ripon.

7. Tourists and Pilgrims

As most Cathedrals do not charge, there are no accurate admission figures. St. Paul's, Canterbury and York top the list with over two million visitors each year. Probably 30 million people visit Cathedrals annually, and most Cathedrals report a continual increase in these numbers, though some, such as Salisbury, have experienced no increase or even a slight decline in 1988. The figures from Cathedrals who have co-operated with this report, are as follows –

> Bristol 15,000; Canterbury 2,250,000; Carlisle 100,000; Chelmsford 60,000; Chester 635,000; Chichester 250,000; Coventry 389,000; Derby 20,000; Durham 500,000; Ely 200,000; Exeter 300,000; Gloucester 250,000; Guildford 80,000; Leicester 20,000; Lichfield 200,000; Lincoln 250,000; Liverpool 300,000; Manchester 20,000; Newcastle 20,000; Norwich 500,000; Portsmouth 20,000; Ripon 150,000; Rochester 250,000; St. Albans 200,000; St. Edmundsbury 70,000; St. Paul's 3,000,000; Salisbury 400,000; Sheffield 10,000; Southwark 250,000; Southwell 75,000; Truro 250,000; Wakefield 50,000; Wells 300,000; York 2,250,000. Figures were also obtained for Christmas worshippers who include many who come to Cathedrals only at Christmas in order to worship as twentieth century pilgrims. Some of these numbers are very great. Canterbury welcomes 35,000, Lincoln 15,000, Norwich 10,000, St. Albans 10,000, St. Paul's 10,000, Worcester 15,000, York 12,000.

The startling rise in the number of tourists and pilgrims has led Cathedrals to respond, as rapidly as funds and administrative energy permits. Only ten Cathedrals do not have a Visitors' Centre/Refectory and several more are being built. The training of staff is taken seriously. At Derby, vergers are sent on counselling courses. Interpretive exhibitions are designed to explain the history of the building. Perhaps more significant are those exhibitions designed to enable visitors from a secular environment to understand how the faith is alive and how the challenge of Darwin, Marx and Freud may be met. Those Cathedrals which take seriously the philosophical challenge to religion in a scientific secular culture serve their visitors better than those which confine themselves to archaeological and historical exhibitions; spectators may become pilgrims. 'Not for the likes of us' is an attitude which still keeps some tourists standing outside or mentally hostile when inside. Tourists may also become pilgrims if they are welcomed by sensitive and warm-hearted guides, if there are spaces for silence and prayer, and if they feel at ease in the Cathedral they are visiting. Hints that the church is alive and helpful stimulants – music being practised, exhibitions that suggest that the community, of which this is the church, is a caring community: for example, the travelling exhibition

of paintings by people in prison, problems of poverty, race, ecology —
seem to encourage pause then prayer.

Some more adventurous schemes are in the pipeline. Lichfield is
planning a Conference House, Norwich is re-opening its Centre in the
Close, Winchester looks forward to several developments...the list is
long. Tourism and pilgrimage are being taken more seriously than ever
before. The ministry of Cathedrals is now fully shared with volunteers,
and the organising staff of visitors' officers, education officers and
young people's officers now include women as well as men. Tourism
and pilgrimage have been powerful levers, not only helping the
Cathedral finances but opening the life of the Cathedral to the outside
world.

8. Statutes and finance

The statutes of most Cathedrals were revised in 1963 under the
chairmanship of the then Bishop of Leicester before the major changes
outlined in this chapter began. The revision of the statutes was
conservative, and few take account of the need to create a team to head
such complex, continual and costly activities as those now
characteristic of the English Cathedrals. Some Cathedrals, such as
Coventry and Liverpool, have revised their statutes. There is need for
a general revision in view of the interest in Cathedrals and the extent
of their use, which are now greater than at any other time in their
history. Many Cathedrals have statutes which make the taking of
decisions, the day-to-day life, and even the repair of the fabric
extraordinarily difficult.

The difficulties start with the appointment of the staff. In Cathedrals
these are appointed by various authorities. All Deans, and many
canons, are appointed by the Crown. In practice this involves the Prime
Minister's patronage secretary carrying out various consultations,
always including the diocesan bishop, other canons and local worthies,
but the appointment is actually made by No. 10. There is no
appointments committee, yet, with representatives working together
and carrying corporate responsibility, analogous to the Crown
Appointments Commission for Bishops, or the committees which make
University or school appointments. The General Synod is considering
this, but there may be political resistance to any change. Provosts are
usually appointed through various forms of local patronage, and this
in practice has considerable advantages.

Political influence in Church appointments has been criticised. In a
leading article entitled 'Dean and Downing Street', the appointment to

St. Paul's in 1988 was analysed in detail in the first leading article in
The Times –
> It will be said in the Church that there has been political bias in the
> appointment...that may be the case. It is not necessarily grounds for
> criticising Mrs. Thatcher. She is a politician; the office she holds is a
> political office; the powers of patronage attached to it are surely there
> to be used...Nonetheless, the continuance of the patronage system in
> those cases where it still applies is an anomaly. If it was right to put the
> nomination of archbishops and diocesan bishops largely into the
> Church's own hands when the Crown Appointments Commission
> system started in 1977, it can hardly be wrong to go at least as far as that
> in the case of lesser dignitaries. Mrs. Thatcher would find it difficult to
> resist a demand for such reform.

A working party is now being set up in the Synod.

Oliver Fiennes, in his farewell lecture to the Greater Chapter of
Lincoln Cathedral after twenty years as Dean ('Bad Dreams and Bright
Visions'), delivered on St Hugh's Day, 1988, described the Chapter as –
> A fellowship held together with enormous effort against all the
> odds...they stem primarily from the method of appointment and the
> freehold of the Dean, the canons residentiary, and the canons non-
> residentiary...It is an exciting time for Cathedrals, but the organisational
> structure as set up by the statutes and by custom, is almost unworkable.
> It is deadening. It leads inevitably to stress and overwork...I plead for
> escape from the confines of irresponsible and unplanned appointments
> to senior positions and from life-long freedom of tenure for those who
> have achieved such positions.

Dean Fiennes' plea and process is so powerful that special attention
will be paid to this well considered assessment in the reforms which lie
ahead. The failure experienced at Lincoln and at other Cathedrals to
create a group who will work together is extremely damaging. The
Dean of a Cathedral is not only, as the Dean of Winchester has said
in half-humour, a curate with four vicars, but placed in a position
where 'major disagreements are inevitable'. No modern enterprise
dealing with such intense activities, so large a staff, and such
considerable finances, could succeed with such an adversarial system
enshrined in statutes.

Changes are essential. In the view of the Dean of Lincoln, the
freehold for residentiary canons must be abandoned; an appointment
board for all Cathedral clergy should be set up; the leading lay staff,
women and men, should attend some of the Chapter meetings.
Cathedrals are now so important in the life of the Church and the
nation, employing a staff (in the case of Lincoln of 145, and in the case
of some other Cathedrals of between 200 and 300) that the wholly

inadequate system of appointment with freehold must be reviewed. At the same time the need for the integration of the lay staff, both paid and voluntary, needs to be carried further. The position under most statutes that absolute authority for decision lies in the hands of four or five clergy – the Administrative Chapter – has some advantages but also many snags in view of the present-day Cathedral complexities and responsibilities. Consultation on all aspects of the Cathedral life is needed.

A survey of the finances of many Cathedral appeals reveals a surprising variety of approach. It needs to be realised that Cathedrals are not funded by the state, nor wholly by the Church Commissioners or their dioceses. As the 43 Cathedrals are self-governing, there is no one source for surveying Cathedral finances. It is not that all Cathedrals are secretive about finance (though some are); it is the absence of an effective office which can collect, analyse and advise. However, the survey carried out for this chapter paints a reasonably accurate picture of initiative, goodwill and hard work.

Taking examples at random. Wells raised and spent £2,300,000 between 1975 and 1986 to restore the West front and the high vaults of the nave. Bristol created a trust for long term development. Canterbury's major appeal in 1979, along with endowments, has maintained its very elaborate structure in good condition. Carlisle has recently raised £900,000. Chichester has a successful development trust with a strong claim on the loyalty of the county of Sussex. Coventry has just raised £600,000. Durham is well endowed and has had no appeals but raises considerable sums from fees for climbing the tower. Ely has raised £4,000,000 for a major restoration. Exeter raised £1,000,000 to endow the music and another million to carry out restoration work, each under an independent and different body of trustees. Gloucester is appealing for £4,000,000 for major restoration. Lichfield has raised £1,250,000 by a low-key appeal to public authorities and industry, and has recently received a grant of £1,000,000 from European funds in recognition of its work for tourism and education.

Lincoln has a permanent appeal for its fabric fund 'to prevent panic appeals'. St. Paul's has raised £1,000,000 from the city as endowment, and in addition has endowed much of its music. Manchester is financed mainly from endowments but is considering a major appeal. Newcastle has raised £500,000 by appeal and sold its Tintoretto in 1986 for £765,000. Norwich relies on property, endowments and a continuous fabric appeal, a shop, a visitors' centre and its 4,000 Friends. Christ

Church, Oxford, is part of the foundation of Henry VIII and it is independent financially. Portsmouth, which has no endowments, is starting to appeal for £3,000,000. Ripon is appealing for £1,500,000. Salisbury is appealing for £6,500,000 for the spire, tower and West front. Southwark has raised £900,000 for a new chapter house. Truro has a Fabric Endowment Fund. Wakefield launched an appeal in 1987 but it was not a success. However, a Bishop Treacy Memorial Hall has been built. Worcester is appealing for £4,000,000. York has an on-going appeal and has raised and spent very large sums in the past 25 years over major restorations and reconstruction after the fire.

Unlike continental Cathedrals which are either maintained by the state, as in France, or supported by a Church Tax as in Germany, English Cathedrals are responsible for their own finances, hence the appeals which have just been listed. Most Cathedrals receive some help from the Church Commissioners, and almost all, with the exception of a few Northern Cathedrals off the tourist route, are dependent upon the offerings and the takings at shops. Sometimes (as at St. Paul's), large sums come from the tourist gift trade. A few Cathedrals charge for admission. Some, like St. Paul's, have an arrangement with commercial tourist companies to receive fees from conducted parties. All receive legacies, sometimes substantial. Most have Friends whose support is valuable, especially as voluntary workers. One Cathedral quantifies the value of voluntary service from its Friends as £60,000 a year. A number of appeals has been assisted by local authority rates. In total (though there is no fully reliable figure) it seems that the 43 Cathedrals are appealing for £50,000,000, all with reasonable hope of success. Despite escalating costs, especially of salaries, the fabric inside and out of English Cathedrals is as expertly conserved as that of any Cathedrals in the world.

To the sympathetic this determined financial ingenuity is admirable. A more critical view would condemn the time, energy and occasionally openness to patronage which the continual task of raising money inflicts upon the staff. Encouragement rather than cash comes from several recent initiatives. Cathedral Camps, a youth movement created and led by Robert Aagaard, arranges each year for 500 students to spend part of their summer holidays at their own expense under expert guidance repairing fabric and maintaining grounds. This fusion of Barchester and Outward Bound is helping a number of the younger generation to realise the privilege and responsibility of Cathedrals.

9. Into the future

The Roman Catholic historian, Professor Adrian Hastings, has discussed the link between a well-established church and the millions of people who have no regular connection and little clear belief. Nevertheless they have some personal sense of religious meaning. Here the Cathedrals are of special importance – 'Probably the Church of England's most valuable surviving public asset'.[6] Certainly the use of Cathedrals on television emphasises their role. National and royal occasions at Westminster Abbey and St. Paul's, or the annual Royal Maundy at Cathedrals round the country, make them so well known that they are a natural focus for visitors. Then they may become a place of prayer, a momentary monastery.

The contrast between contemporary Cathedrals and their role in 1800 could hardly be sharper. In that year St. Paul's had less than a dozen communicants on Christmas Day. Now, like all English Cathedrals, worshippers at Christmas are counted in their thousands. The atmosphere of every Cathedral has been totally changed. When George Eliot visited Exeter Cathedral she found it barred, dark and forbidding. Even when Barchester was benign, Cathedrals were not serving their Church and the community as they are today. A critical and sympathetic visitor, however, might well contrast the vitality of the crowded streets of English cities with the atmosphere, friendly but detached and perhaps rather rarified, which is often encountered. The contrast between the vitality, courage and integration with the people found in a Cathedral in Poland or parts of rural Africa, or Hispanic America, is still too great. Perhaps much lies in the hands of the musicians who must not only preserve an incomparable tradition, but find styles of music appreciated and valued by the thronging visitors. To reflect the mystery of the divine will continue to tax all those concerned with the witness, way of life and worship of English Cathedrals.

The independence of Cathedrals in a media-dominated consumerist world, where political and financial leaders have growing influence, is precious. Lay advisers, high stewards' committees are needed to give advice and encouragement for this aspect of Cathedral work. The Church, thanks to world tourism, can use its independent information network more thoroughly, not as in the days of Christendom to control, but to persuade and alert. The Conference of European churches at Sigtuna in Sweden in 1988, with representatives from Lisbon to Leningrad, saw this role as crucial in the pursuit of theological truth and social justice and responsibility. This task for Cathedrals will be even more vital in the next century.[7]

NOTES

1. Much of the information for this paper was gathered in a special survey of the 43 English Cathedrals undertaken by the authors in 1988/89 and supported by the University of Nottingham Department of Adult Education.
2. A. B. Webster, 'Cathedrals and Growth', in A. Wedderspoon (ed.), *Grow or Die* (1981), pp. 58-70.
3. Unpublished sermon by Archbishop Robert Runcie, November 30 1987.
4. Coventry Cathedral, April 22-25 1966.
5. See. G. Hewitt (ed.), *Strategist for the Spirit* (1985), pp. 99-100.
6. A. Hastings, *History of English Christianity, 1920-1985* (1986), p. 666.
7. A new era will open in 1991 when the Care of Cathedrals Measure is accepted by Parliament. A Fabric Commission will ensure accountability and prevent attempts at asset-stripping such as the proposed sale of the *Mappa Mundi*. State aid will be one more source of finance but it will not replace the need for wise and enthusiastic support from all those who value the role of Cathedrals today. See A. B. Webster, 'The Accountability of Cathedrals', a paper available from the Church Commissioners.

BIBLIOGRAPHY

The Bibliography comprises books, articles and pamphlets referred to in the footnotes of the papers. It does not purport to be a comprehensive Bibliography of English Cathedrals during the period under review. Calendars have not been listed.

The Acts of the Dean and Chapter of the Cathedral Church of Chichester, 1545-1642, ed. W. D. Peckham, Sussex Record Society, 58 (1959).
Admissions to Trinity College, Cambridge, ed. W. W. R. Ball and J. A. Venn (1913).
Alumni Cantabrigienses, ed. J. Venn (1922-7).
Alumni Oxonienses, ed. J. Foster (1891-4).
A. R. Ashwell and R. G. Wilberforce, *Life of the Right Reverend Samuel Wilberforce* (1883).
G. E. Aylmer and R. Cant (eds.), *A History of York Minster* (1977).
D. W. R. Bahlman (ed.), *The Diary of Sir Edward Walter Hamilton, 1880-1885* (1972).
W. W. R. Ball, *Cambridge Papers* (1918).
P. L. S. Barrett, 'Philip Williams - the acceptable face of pluralism', *Winchester Cathedral Record*, 57 (1988).
G. Baskerville, 'The Dispossessed Religious of Gloucestershire', *Transactions of the Bristol and Gloucester Archaeological Society*, 49 (1927).
G. Benson, *York from the Reformation to the year 1925* (1925).
I. D. Bent, 'The Early History of the English Chapel Royal, *ca* 1066-1327', Cambridge Ph.D. thesis, 1968.
G. F. A. Best, *Temporal Pillars* (1964).
A Biographical Register of the University of Oxford, A.D. 1501-1540, ed. A. B. Emden (1974).
F. Blomefield, *An Essay towards a Topographical History of the County of Norfolk* (1806).
G. H. Blore, *Thomas Rennell, Dean of Winchester, 1805-1840* (1952).
A. E. Bridge, 'Walter Kerr Hamilton: a Tractarian in the making', Oxford M.Litt. thesis, 1988.
A. E. Bridge, 'The Foundation of Chichester Theological College',

unpublished article, Pusey House, Oxford, 1979.

J. Browne, *The History of the Metropolitan Church of St. Peter, York* (1847).

R. V. H. Burne, *Chester Cathedral, from its founding by Henry VIII to the accession of Queen Victoria* (1958).

F. Bussby, 'Winchester Cathedral, 1789-1840', *Winchester Cathedral Record,* 44 (1975).

F. Bussby, 'The Great Screen - part II, *Winchester Cathedral Record,* 48 (1979).

F. Bussby, *Winchester Cathedral, 1079-1979* (1979).

Canterbury College, Oxford, ed. W. A. Pantin, Oxford Historical Society, New Series, 8 (1950).

P. Butler (ed.), *Pusey Rediscovered* (1983).

W. O. Chadwick, *The Victorian Church* (1966-70).

M. P. Chappell, *Dr. S. S. Wesley* (1976)

Chapter Acts of the Cathedral Church of St. Mary of Lincoln, 1547-59, R. E. G. Cole, Lincoln Record Society, 15 (1920).

I. J. Churchill, *Canterbury Administration* (1934).

V. A. Clanchy, *Jane Austen and Winchester* (1973).

V. A. Clanchy, 'Jane Austen and the Williams family', *Hampshire* (December, 1976).

P. Clark, *English Provincial Society from the Reformation to the Revolution* (1977).

P. Clark, 'The Ramoth-Gilead of the Good: urban change and political radicalism in Gloucester, 1540-1640', in P. Clark, A. G. R. Smith and N. Tyacke (eds.), *The English Commonwealth, 1547-1640* (1979).

C. Clay, '"The Greed of Whig Bishops?": Church Landlords and their Lessees, 1660-1760', *Past and Present,* 87 (1980).

A. B. Cobban, *The King's Hall within the University of Cambridge in the later Middle Ages* (1969).

W. Cobbett, *Rural Rides,* ed. G. Woodcock (1967).

H. Cole, *King Henry the Eighth's Scheme of Bishopricks* (1838).

C. S. Collingwood, *Memoirs of Bernard Gilpin* (1884).

P. Collinson, *Archbishop Grindal, 1519-1583* (1979).

J. B. Colson, *The Reparation of the Nave Roof [of Winchester Cathedral]* (1898).

J. Coombs, *George and Mary Sumner* (1965).

C. H. Cooper, *Annals of Cambridge* (1842-1908).

A. T. Corfe, *A Collection of Anthems with a list of Services used in the Cathedral Church of Salisbury* (1852).

The Correspondence of John Cosin, ed. G. Ornsby, Surtees Society, 52 (1869).

Cranmer's Miscellaneous Writings, ed. J. E. Cox, Parker Society (1846).

J. Crook, *A History of the Pilgrims' School [Winchester]* (1981).

J. Crook, 'Half-a-century of choral indiscipline: George Chard and his choir, 1802-1849', *Southern Cathedrals Festival Programme* (1981).

J. Crook, 'Winchester Cathedral, 1079-1905: a brief history' in I. T. Henderson and J. Crook, *The Winchester Diver* (1984).

J. Crook, 'Fifty years of choral misrule: George Chard and the choristers of Winchester Cathedral', *Winchester Cathedral Record*, 56 (1987).

C. Cross, 'Achieving the Millenium: the Church in York during the Commonwealth', in G. J. Cuming (ed.), *Studies in Church History*, 4 (1967).

C. Cross, 'Dens of Loitering Lubbers: Protestant protest against Cathedral foundations, 1540-1640', in D. Baker (ed.), *Studies in Church History*, 10 (1972).

M. A. Crowther, *Church Embattled: religious Controversy in Mid-Victorian England* (1970).

The Diary of Samuel Pepys, ed. R. C. Latham and W. Matthews (1970-83).

A. G. Dickens, *The English Reformation* (1964).

Documents Illustrating the History of St. Paul's Cathedral, ed. W. S. S. Simpson, Camden Society, New Series, 26 (1880).

Documents relating to the Foundation of the Chapter of Winchester, ed. G. W. Kitchin and F. T. Madge, Hampshire Record Society, 1 (1889).

Documents illustrating early education in Worcestershire, 685-1700, ed. A. F. Leach, Worcestershire Historical Society, 31 (1913).

Durham School Register, ed. T. H. Burbidge (1940).

A. D. Dyer, *The City of Worcester in the sixteenth century* (1973).

G. Dyer, *The Privileges of the University of Cambridge* (1824).

D. L. Edwards, *A History of King's School, Canterbury* (1957).

K. Edwards, *The English Secular Cathedrals in the Middle Ages* (1949. 2nd edn 1967).

Elizabethan Peterborough. The Dean and Chapter as Lords of the City, ed. W. T. Mellows and D. H. Gifford, Northamptonshire Record Society, 18 (1956).

G. R. Elton, *Reform and Renewal* (1973).

J. T. Evans, *Seventeenth Century Norwich* (1979).

S. J. A. Evans, 'Cathedral Life at Gloucester in the Early Seventeenth Century', *Bristol and Gloucestershire Archaeological Transactions*, 80 (1961).

Extracts from the earliest minute books of the Dean and Chapter of Norwich, 1566-1649, ed. J. F. Williams and B. Cozens-Hardy, Norfolk Record Society, 24 (1954) .

The Fabric Rolls of York Minster, ed. J. Raine, Surtees Society, 35 (1859).

W. A. Fearon, *The Passing of Old Winchester* (1924).

E. H. Fellowes, *English Cathedral Music from Edward VI to Edward VII* (1941).

First Report of Her Majesty's Commissioners appointed to inquire into the state of the Cathedral Churches of England and Wales (1854).

A. Fletcher, *A County Community in Peace and War: Sussex, 1600-1660* (1975).

A. Fletcher, 'Factionalism in town and countryside: the significance of Puritanism and Arminianism', in D. Baker (ed.), *Studies in Church History*, 16 (1979).

A. Foster, 'The Function of a Bishop: the career of Richard Neile, 1562-1640', in R. O'Day and F. Heal (eds.), *Continuity and Change: personnel and administration in the Church in England, 1500-1642* (1976).

The Foundation of Peterborough Cathedral, ed. W. T. Mellows, Northamptonshire Record Society, 13 (1941).

C. F. Garbett, *The Claims of the Church of England* (1947).

W. J. Gatens, *Victorian Cathedral Music in Theory and Practice* (1986).

H. Gee, *The Elizabethan Clergy and the Settlement of Religion, 1558-1564* (1898).

The Gladstone Diaries with Cabinet Minutes and Prime-Ministerial Correspondence, ed. M. R. D. Foot and H. C. G. Matthew (1968-   ).

R. A. Godfrey, 'Cathedral Virgers through the centuries', *Winchester Cathedral Record,* 24 (1978).

A. W. Goodman and W. H. Hutton, *The Statutes governing the Cathedral Church of Winchester* (1925).

Grace Book [Gamma], ed. W. G. Searle (1908).

S. Gunton, *The History of the Church of Peterburgh* (1686).

H. P. Hamilton, *Dean of Salisbury, to The Revd. R. Jones, June 1853, The Close, Salisbury. Suggestions: From the Dean and Chapter of Salisbury for the Reform of their Cathedral.*

W. Harrison, *The Description of England,* ed. G. Edelen, Folger Shakespeare Library (1968).

B. F. Harvey, 'The Monks of Westminster and the University of Oxford', in *The Reign of Richard II,* ed. F. R. H. Du Boulay and C. M. Barron (1971).

A. Hastings, *History of English Christianity, 1920-1985* (1986).

G. Hewitt (ed.), *Strategist for the Spirit* (1985).

D. I. Hill, *The Six Preachers of Canterbury Cathedral, 1541-1982* (1982).

J. W. F. Hill, *Georgian Lincoln* (1966).

History of the University of Oxford, 3, The Collegiate University, ed. J. K. McConica (1986).

A History of St. Paul's Cathedral and the men associated with it, ed. W. R. Matthews and W. M. Atkins (1957).

J. M. Horn (ed.), *Le Neve, Fasti Ecclesiae Anglicanae, 1541-1857, 3* (1974).

W. H. Hutton (ed.), *Robert Gregory, 1819-1911* (1912).

M. James, *Family, Lineage and Civil Society* (1974).

G. W. and L. A. Johnson, *Josephine Butler - an autobiographical memoir* (1928).

W. H. Jones, *Fasti Ecclesiae Sarisberiensis* (1879).

D. N. King, 'Winchester Cathedral under Deans Rennell and Garnier', *Winchester Cathedral Chronicle* (1972).

The King's School, Ely, ed. D. M. Owen and D. Thurley, Cambridge Antiquarian Record Society, 5 (1982).

G. W. Kitchin, *Edward Harold Browne* (1985).

G. W. Kitchin, *The Great Screen of Winchester Cathedral* (1899).

C. S. Knighton, 'Collegiate Foundations, 1540-1570, with special reference to St. Peter in Westminster', Cambridge Ph.D. thesis, 1975.

C. S. Knighton, 'Canterbury Cathedral's University Studentships under Henry VIII', *The Cantuarian,* 49 (April 1985) .

M. D. Knowles, *The Religious Orders in England* (1948-59).

W. D. Larrett, *A History of the King's School, Peterborough* (1966).

The Last Days of Peterborough Monastery, ed. W. T. Mellows, Northamptonshire Record Society, 12 (1947).

W. Laud, *Works,* Library of Anglo-Catholic Theology (1853).

A. F. Leach, 'The Origin of Westminster School', *Journal of Education,* New Series, 27 (1905).

A. F. Leach, *Educational Charters and Documents, 598-1909* (1911).

F. Lear, *Reminiscences of the Past 80 Years* (1910).

The Letter Book of John Parkhurst, ed. R. A. Houlbrooke, Norfolk Record Society, 43 (1974-5).

A Letter to the Very Rev. the Dean of Salisbury by the Rev. Walter Kerr Hamilton, M.A. (1853).

A Letter from the late Bishop to the Commissioners about the rearrangement of Capitular Estates. E. Sarum to The Revd. R. Jones, 16 August, 1853.

A Letter from the Late Bishop in answer to certain questions addressed to him by the Commissioners. E. Sarum to the Revd. R. Jones, 1 September, 1853.

Letters of Humphrey Prideaux sometime Dean of Norwich to John Ellis sometime Under-Secretary of State, 1674-1722, ed. E. M. Thompson, Camden Society, New Series, 15 (1875).

The Life of the Reverend Humphrey Prideaux, D. D. Dean of Norwich (1748).

H. P. Liddon, *Walter Kerr Hamilton: Bishop of Salisbury. A sketch, reprinted, with additions and corrections from 'The Guardian'* (1869).

N. Linnell, 'A unique copy of Richard Crakanthorp's *Logic', The Library,* VI, 4 (1982).

F. D. Logan, 'The Origins of the so-called Regius Professorships: an aspect of the Renaissance in Oxford and Cambridge', in D. Baker (ed.), *Renaissance and Renewal in Christian History* (1977).

K. R. Long, *The Music of the English Church* (1971).

W. T. MacCaffrey, *Exeter, 1540-1640* (1958).

R. A. Marchant, *The Puritans and the Church Courts in the Diocese of York, 1560-1642* (1960).

D. Marcombe, 'The Dean and Chapter of Durham, 1558-1603', Durham Ph.D. thesis, 1973.

D. Marcombe, 'The Durham Dean and Chapter: old abbey writ large?' in R. O'Day and F. Heal (eds.), *Continuity and Change: personnel and administration of the Church in England, 1500-1642* (1976).

D. Marcombe, 'Church leaseholders: the decline and fall of a rural élite', in R. O'Day and F. Heal (eds.), *Princes and Paupers in the English Church, 1500-1800* (1981).

D. Marcombe, 'A Rude and Heady People: the local community and the Rebellion of the Northern Earls', in D. Marcombe (ed.), *The Last Principality: politics, religion and society in the Bishopric of Durham, 1494-1660* (1987).

A. G. Matthews, *Walker Revised* (1948).

B. Matthews, *The Music of Winchester Cathedral* (1975).

B. Matthews, *The Organs and Organists of Winchester Cathedral* (n.d.).

S. Meacham, *Lord Bishop: the life of Samuel Wilberforce, 1805-1873* (1970).

Memoir of Edward, Lord Bishop of Salisbury (privately printed for the

Annual Register for 1854-1855).

A. C. Miller, 'Herbert Astley, Dean of Norwich', *Norfolk Archaelogy,* 38, 2 (1982).

Miscellaneous Writings and Letters of Thomas Cranmer, Archbishop of Canterbury, Martyr, ed. J. E. Cox, Parker Society (1846).

P. C. Moore, 'The Development and organisation of Cathedral Worship in England, with special reference to choral services, from the Reformation to the 19th century', Oxford D.Phil. thesis, 1954.

M. Morgan, 'The Suppression of the Alien Priories', *History,* New Series, 16 (1941).

Morning and Evening Services for everyday in the week and other prayers, arranged for the use of the families residing in the parish of St. Peter's-in-the-East, Oxford. By their former Pastor, Walter Kerr Hamilton (1842).

C. Moxley, *Cathedral, College and Hospital* (1986).

T. Newcombe, *Life of John Sharpe, D. D.* (1825).

D. Newsome, *The Parting of Friends* (1966).

Notes for Lectures at Family Prayers, February 13, 1850.

S. L. Ollard, *A Short History of the Oxford Movement* (1915).

N. Orme, *English Schools in the Middle Ages* (1973).

R. Ornsby, *Memoir of James Robert Hope-Scott* (1884).

D. M. Owen, 'Synods in the diocese of Ely', in G. J. Cuming (ed.), *Studies in Church History,* 3 (1966).

D. M. Owen, *The Library and Muniments of Ely Cathedral* (1973).

W. Palmer, *Origines Liturgicae* (1832).

J. P. Parry, *Democracy and Religion: Gladstone and the Liberal party, 1867-1875,* (1986).

E. H. Pearce, *The Monks of Westminster* (1916).

Peterborough Local Administration, ed. W. T. Mellows, Northamptonshire Record Society, 9 (1939).

E. Pine, *The Westminster Abbey Singers* (1953).

A. F. Pollard, *Wolsey* (1929).

B. Rainbow, *The Choral Revival in the Anglican Church, 1839-1872* (1970).

The Record of Old Westminsters, ed. G. F. R. Barker *et. al.* (1928-63).

Register of the University of Oxford, 1, ed. C. W. Boase, Oxford Historical Society, 1 (1885).

Registrum Matthei Parker, ed. E. H. Thompson and W. H. Frere, Canterbury and York Society, 35, 36, 39, (1928-33).

Remarks and Collections of Thomas Hearne, 10, ed. H. E. Salter, Oxford Historical Society, 67 (1915).

Reports of Cases in the Courts of Star Chamber and High Commission, ed. S. R. Gardiner, Camden Society, New Series, 39 (1886).

D. H. Robertson, *Sarum Close. A History of the Life and Education of the Cathedral Choristers for 700 Years* (1938).

The Roll of the Freemen of the City of Canterbury from A.D. 1392 to 1800, ed. J. M. Cooper (1903).

Sacrist Rolls of Ely, ed. F. R. Chapman (1907).

J. Sargeaunt, *Annals of Westminster School* (1898).

W. K. *Sarum to all members of the Church in the Diocese of Salisbury, 12 January, 1855.*

J. J. Scarisbrick, *Henry VIII* (1968).

P. A. Scholes, *The Puritans and Music in England and New England* (1934).

J. Simon, *Education and Society in Tudor England* (1966).

P. Slack, 'Religious Protest and Urban Authority: the Case of Henry Sherfield, iconoclast, 1633', in D. Baker (ed.), *Studies in Church History,* 9 (1972).

P. Smart, *A Sermon Preached in the Cathedral Church of Durham, July 7 1628.*

The Statutes of the Cathedral Church of Carlisle, ed. J. E. Prescott (1903).

The Statutes of the Cathedral Church of Durham, ed. A. H. Thompson, Surtees Society, 143 (1929).

C. J. Stranks, *This Sumptuous Church: the story of Durham Cathedral* (1973).

J. Strype, *Ecclesiastical Memorials* (1822).

R. Surtees, *History of Durham* (1816-40).

L. E. Tanner, *Westminster School: its buildings and their associations* (1924).

L. E. Tanner, *Westminster School* (1934).

N. P. Tanner, *The Church in late Medieval Norwich, 1370-1532* (1984).

A. H. Thompson, *The Cathedral Churches of England* (1928).

A. H. Thompson, *The English Clergy and their organisation in the later Middle Ages* (1947).

M. Tillbrook, 'Arminianism and Society in County Durham, 1617-42', in D. Marcombe (ed.), *The Last Principality: politics, religion and society in the Bishopric of Durham, 1494-1660* (1987).

Vetus Liber Archidiaconi Eliensis, ed. C. L. Feltoe and E. H. Minns, Cambridge Antiquarian Society, Octavo Series, 48 (1917).

Visitation Articles and Injunctions, ed. W. H. Frere, Alcuin Club, 14, 15, 16 (1910).

J. Walker, *An attempt towards recovering an account of the numbers and sufferings of the clergy of the Church of England etc.* (1714).

R. B. Walker, 'Lincoln Cathedral in the reign of Queen Elizabeth', *Journal of Ecclesiastical History,* 11 (1960).

C. Webb, 'York Minster, 1625-77: a prosopographical study', York M.A. thesis, 1988.

A. B. Webster, 'Cathedrals and Growth', in A. Wedderspoon (ed.), *Grow or Die* (1981).

A. B. Webster, 'The Accountability of Cathedrals', Church Commissioners (1990).

S. S. Wesley, *Reply to the Inquiries of the Cathedral Commissioners relative to the improvement in the Music of Divine Worship in Cathedrals* (1854).

H. F. Westlake, *Westminster Abbey* (1923).

C. E. Woodruff and H. J. Cape, *Schola Regia Cantuariensis: a History of Canterbury School, commonly called the King's School* (1908).

J. Youings, *The Dissolution of the Monasteries* (1971).

INDEX